Bible Nurture and Reader Series

From a child thou hast known
The HOLY SCRIPTURES
which are able to make
thee wise unto salvation.

Bible Nurture and Reader Series

We Learn More About God

Teacher's Manual

Grade 1

Units 2, 3

Rod and Staff Publishers, Inc.
Crockett, Kentucky 41413
Telephone (606)522 4348

BIBLE NURTURE AND READER SERIES

"If you train your children carefully until they are seven years old, they are already three-quarters educated." This quote recognizes the importance of the critical early years in molding a child's life. The influences of childhood become powerful, lasting impressions.

The type of schoolbooks used certainly affects the developing appetites of our children for reading material. We will not instill in them appreciation for godly values by feeding them frivolous nonsense. We hold the Bible to be the highest guide for life and the best source of training for our children. The Bible reveals God and His will. Proverbs 9:10 says, "The fear of the Lord is the beginning of wisdom: and the knowledge of the holy is understanding." It is important that our children are exposed to truth from the beginning of their learning experience.

For the student to be exposed to the truth of God's Word only in textbooks is not sufficient to give him the very best. It is necessary for the tutor, be he parent or other teacher, to be firmly rooted in the Word of God and have the power of God's presence in his life. The Bible must be treasured as God's message to mankind. On that conviction this series is built, with the Scriptures as its very substance.

This book is designed as part of a series and will be most useful if so used. The grade one material includes the following books.

Pupil's Reader Unit 1	Worksheets Unit 1
Pupil's Reader Units 2, 3	Worksheets Units 2-4
Pupil's Reader Units 4, 5	Worksheets Unit 5
Phonics Workbook Unit 1	Printing Practice Unit 1
Phonics Workbook Units 2, 3	Printing Practice Units 2, 3
Phonics Workbook Units 4, 5	Printing Practice Units 4, 5
Reading Workbook Unit 1	Teacher's Manual Unit 1
Reading Workbook Units 2, 3	Teacher's Manual Units 2, 3
Reading Workbook Units 4, 5	Teacher's Manual Units 4, 5

Copyright, 1986

First edition, copyright 1964; revisions 1970, 1985

By

Rod and Staff Publishers, Inc.
Crockett, Kentucky 41413

Printed in U.S.A.

ISBN 0-7399-0366-7

Catalog no. 11192.3

11   12   13   14   —   15   14   13   12   11   10   09   08   07

Table of Contents

A Word of Appreciation

It is with thanksgiving to God that we present these textbooks to those who are concerned about the spiritual welfare of their children. We believe that children are a heritage of the Lord and a sacred trust and that we dare not fail them in any area of their lives.

The *Bible Nurture and Reader Series* is possible only because of the work and leading of God in the lives of many faithful servants of His. We think first of all of our parents, ministers, and teachers who had a concern for us and faithfully taught and nurtured us in the Word of God. We appreciate those who have had a vision of the need for textbooks based on the Bible and have given their encouragement and help in the writing and publishing of these books.

We appreciate the work of the author, Sister Lela Birky, who has a deep burden for Bible-based school texts to nurture children in the fear of God.

We want to give recognition to the fact that we have used ideas from many textbooks, workbooks, reference books, and other sources. Sister Amy Herr was the writer for the present revision of the workbooks and teacher's manuals. Acknowledgement is also given to Sisters Marla Martin and Pauline Witmer and many other teachers who have developed and shared helps for teaching this series. Much effort was again devoted to artwork for the new books.

The Lord has provided strength in weakness, grace in trails, wisdom because we have none, joy in service, victory in opposition, financial help, and faithful laborers in this work. May His Name receive honor and praise, and may we rejoice that we can be laborers together with Him.

Teaching Aids

Alphabet-picture Cards

The set of alphabet-picture cards used with unit 1 includes cards for the consonant digraphs, *sh, th, th, wh,* and *ch.* If you do not have them, it is recommended that you make wall cards showing these digraphs and pictures of objects beginning with the sound (sheep, thimble and thread, the word *the,* whale, and chick). It is valuable to have these basic sounds posted for reference and review. (Note that *th* is the symbol which corresponds with this course, not *th* as found in the set of cards.)

Flash Cards

Flash cards provide quick, easy review and drill. Keep the packs current according to the directions given in the lesson plans. There are many variations of procedure which help to keep flash card drill effective. Use one method until it is routine before you explain the procedure for another. Introduce a new method when you want a variation to boost interest.

1. Hold the pack in your hand so the class can see the first card. Let the first child say that sound or word. Remove the front card and add it to the back of the pack, and let the next child say what is on the exposed card. Was he right? If your cards are labeled on one corner of the back, you can tell by moving the front card far enough to let you see the corner. Occasionally sliding the used card into the middle of the pack will vary the order of answers.

2. Let the class give response in unison. This is a good warmup exercise but should not constitute a large part of flash card practice. This helps to develop working with the group, but individual recitation is important to develop individual responsibility.

3. With small groups, see who can be first to say what is on the card. Have the group standing, and let the one with the first correct response sit down and refrain from giving the next answers until all have been seated. Then start over or have the children stand as they give correct answers.

4. Hand the card to the child who first responds correctly. The children will be eager to see how many cards they can claim. Frequent use of this method may feed the competitive spirit and could also bring undue attention and frustration to the slower student in an unbalanced class.

5. With word or phrase cards, hold the pack with the front card facing you. Turn it to give the class or individual a brief view of the card, then turn it back to you. Can the students recognize and say what was on the card? With practice you should be able to shorten the viewing time to a quick flash.

6. Almost recess time? Flash two or three cards in rapid succession to one student. Excuse him to get his wraps and stand in line for dismissal while you flash a few cards to the next child, and the next, and the next . . .

7. Play travel. Let a student from the front of the class stand beside

the desk of the child behind him. Flash a card for those two to say. The one who first gives the correct response steps back to the next desk in the row, and the loser sits in the seat. Should one child win every match the whole way around the class, have him sit down and let the loser take the floor.

8. Have the class stand. Flash a card for the first child and give him a timed opportunity to say it. (Count to three or four or five silently.) Say your last number aloud if the student has not responded, and have him take his seat. Flash a card for the next child. As the children are eliminated, shorten the timed interval until all are down except the winner.

9. Teamwork. Have the children stand in two columns facing you. Flash a card for the heads of the lines. The one who says it first gains a point for his team and they both go to the end of the lines.

10. Lay a number of cards on a table, or prop them on the chalk tray. Say the sound or word, or give a clue to the word and let someone point to the correct card and say what is on it. You may want to have the child pick up the card so you can replace it with another one.

11. Lay phrase cards on the floor in an aisle to represent the rungs of a ladder a foot or so apart. Let someone climb the ladder by saying each phrase before he steps over it. If the aisle is wide enough, lay a second column facing the other way for him to read as he steps down. Otherwise have him walk from the top to his seat or to the end of the line. Change a phrase or two between each climber.

Variation of the ladder for limited space: Lay the cards around the edge of a desk or table and have the child walk around the table as he says them.

12. Allow students with spare time to flash cards to each other. Direct their procedure and keep an eye on the activity so that it does not become an unprofitable playtime.

13. Have the students give words that begin with the sound on the card.

The flash cards mentioned in this course are available from the publisher.

Charts

Make charts for the combinations that you will teach. Post them where the children will see them often and be reminded of the sounds they have studied. Use these charts for convenient review.

Unit 2

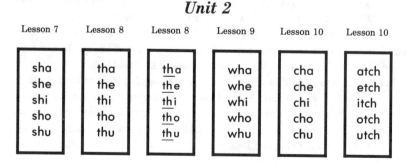

Lesson 7	Lesson 8	Lesson 8	Lesson 9	Lesson 10	Lesson 10
sha	tha	th̲a	wha	cha	atch
she	the	th̲e	whe	che	etch
shi	thi	th̲i	whi	chi	itch
sho	tho	th̲o	who	cho	otch
shu	thu	th̲u	whu	chu	utch

Lesson 13	Lesson 13	Lesson 13	Lesson 14	Lesson 14	Lesson 14	Lesson 14
sca	sma	sta	sna	spa	sla	swa
ske	sme	ste	sne	spe	sle	swe
ski	smi	sti	sni	spi	sli	swi
sco	smo	sto	sno	spo	slo	swo
scu	smu	stu	snu	spu	slu	swu

Lesson 16	Lesson 16	Lesson 16	Lesson 16	Lesson 17	Lesson 17	Lesson 17
bla	bra	cla	cra	fla	fra	gla
ble	bre	cle	cre	fle	fre	gle
bli	bri	cli	cri	fli	fri	gli
blo	bro	clo	cro	flo	fro	glo
blu	bru	clu	cru	flu	fru	glu

Lesson 17	Lesson 18	Lesson 18	Lesson 18	Lesson 18	Lesson 20	Lesson 20
gra	pla	pra	twa	tra	dra	scra
gre	ple	pre	twe	tre	dre	scre
gri	pli	pri	twi	tri	dri	scri
gro	plo	pro	two	tro	dro	scro
gru	plu	pru	twu	tru	dru	scru

Lesson 20	Lesson 20	Lesson 21	Lesson 21	Lesson 21	Lesson 21	Lesson 23
stra	spra	spla	squa	shra	thra	alt
stre	spre	sple	sque	shre	thre	elt
stri	spri	spli	squi	shri	thri	ilt
stro	spro	splo	squo	shro	thro	olt
stru	spru	splu		shru	thru	ult

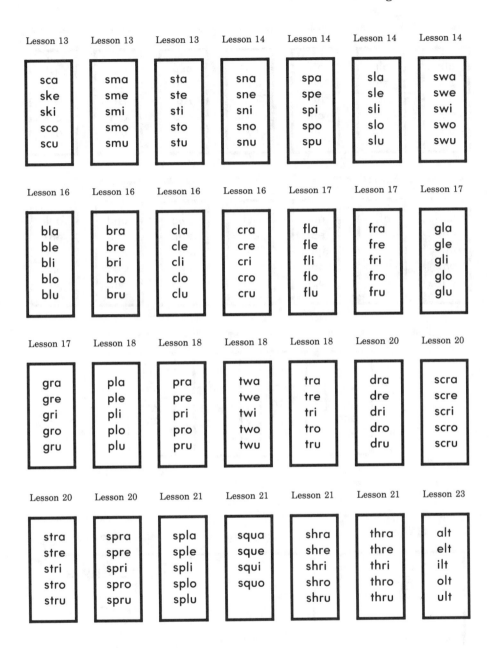

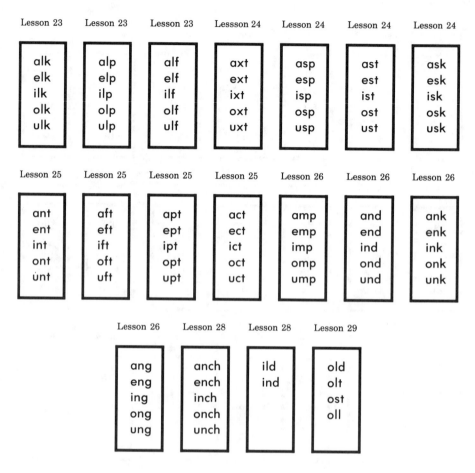

Lesson 23	Lesson 23	Lesson 23	Lessson 24	Lesson 24	Lesson 24	Lesson 24
alk	alp	alf	axt	asp	ast	ask
elk	elp	elf	ext	esp	est	esk
ilk	ilp	ilf	ixt	isp	ist	isk
olk	olp	olf	oxt	osp	ost	osk
ulk	ulp	ulf	uxt	usp	ust	usk

Lesson 25	Lesson 25	Lesson 25	Lesson 25	Lesson 26	Lesson 26	Lesson 26
ant	aft	apt	act	amp	and	ank
ent	eft	ept	ect	emp	end	enk
int	ift	ipt	ict	imp	ind	ink
ont	oft	opt	oct	omp	ond	onk
unt	uft	upt	uct	ump	und	unk

Lesson 26	Lesson 28	Lesson 28	Lesson 29
ang	anch	ild	old
eng	ench	ind	olt
ing	inch		ost
ong	onch		oll
ung	unch		

Unit 3

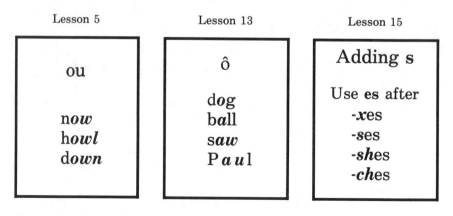

Lesson 5	Lesson 13	Lesson 15
ou	ô	Adding s
now	dog	Use **es** after
howl	ball	-*x*es
down	saw	-*s*es
	P*au*l	-*sh*es
		-*ch*es

Suggestion: Use a different color for the letters shown in italics.

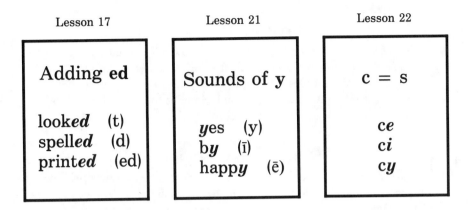

Lesson 17

Adding ed

look*ed*   (t)
spell*ed*   (d)
print*ed*   (ed)

Lesson 21

Sounds of **y**

*y*es   (y)
b*y*   (ī)
happ*y*   (ē)

Lesson 22

c = s

c*e*
c*i*
c*y*

Lesson 23

g = j

g*e*
g*i*
g*y*

Printing Practice

The *Bible Nurture and Reader Series* includes Printing Practice workbooks to accompany these units. The printing lessons in unit 2 correspond with the phonics lessons, using the sounds in words and sentences.

Unit 3 teaches capital letter forms and relates to the reader for that unit.

Checking and Grading

Since it is beneficial for the children to correct their own mistakes, you may wish to have the class go over the lesson each day after everyone is finished. Have them say the answers in their books and correct the ones they had wrong. To prevent temptation for the children to claim a corrected answer as their original, you could give them colored pencils for the review and require that the regular pencils stay in their desks.

Perhaps time will not allow for such a review session immediately following the working period. Instead, you may wish to do it at the beginning of class the next day.

Know your students and keep close tabs on their progress. If you circulate and observe their work and corrections, this class review will suffice for grading much of the time.

Periodically you may have the students hand in their workbooks for you to check and take a closer look at their work. Let them take their books to your desk or a table as they finish the lesson and stack them with the pages open for your convenience.

If you are recording percentage grades, do so from the lessons that you correct. Lessons which are more suitable for recording grades are marked in the teacher's manual with *Gradebook* and the number of points in the exercise.

Phonetic Symbols

/ā/ as in *pay*
/ē/ as in *see*
/ī/ as in *by*
/ō/ as in *go*
/ū/ as in *cube*
/o͞o/ as in *food*

/ou/ as in *out*
/oi/ as in *boy*
/ô/ as in *saw*

sh/ as in *she*
/ch/ as in *chop*
/wh/ as in *when*
/th/ as in *thin*
/t̲h̲/ as in *that*
/ng/ as in *sing*
/zh/ as in *measure*

/a/ as in *hat*
/e/ as in *yes*
/i/ as in *sit*
/o/ as in *top*
/u/ as in *bug*
/oo/ as in *foot*

/är/ as in *park*
/èr/ as in *her, fir, bur,*
    earn, and worm
/ôr/ as in *corn*
    (allowing /ōr/)
/ãr/ as in *square* and *chair*
    (allowing /er/ or /ar/)
/ēr/ as in *dear* and *deer*
    (allowing /ir/)

Phonics
Unit 2

(See page 211 for Reading.)

GENERAL PLAN

By the completion of unit 1 all the letters of the alphabet have been studied. Arrange the alphabet-picture cards in alphabetical order and continue to drill them.

Drill, drill, drill! Continue to review the vowel sounds and the new combinations that will be taught in unit 2. For a scheduled review, follow the suggestions given at the beginning of each lesson in the teacher's manual. Do not try to cover these drills in one session, but aim to use them all throughout the day.

Strive for efficiency in the routine reading of the edge lists, which can otherwise be a great time-consumer. If older students are available, have the first graders read the new list to them, then come to you for the timed test from the previous lesson. Listen to one child read the words standing to your right while the next child waits to your left. There will be a minimum of time wasted as you give the stop signal to the first child, note his number, and turn to the one waiting on the left for his go signal. The child who is finished should be able to mark his own word-reading chart and the next one ready for timing may replace him at your right. If anyone reaches a higher number than the reading chart provides, you could have them color the whole column and paste a star at the top.

Phonics Lessons   Unit 2

LESSON 1

Long *A* Spellings: a-e, ai, ay

Be prepared

Separate the flash cards into three packs: alphabet from set 1, consonants, and vowels. Remove the alphabet pack for later use. (Mention the distinction as you practice briefly with the pack of consonant sounds, and then change to the vowel pack.)

A. Introducing the spellings

Part 1

Have the children find page 6. "What sound do you see at the top of the page? How do you know it is /ā/ and not /a/? When does that letter say /ā/ in a word?" The children should be able to give the rule of silent *e*. "The words for the pictures in the first row have the /ā/ sound because there is an *e* at the end of the word. See the letters at the beginning of the row. You may say, '*A, blank, e,*' when you see letters like that. There is an *a* in the word, then there is a consonant, and then an *e* at the end. We will use a blank to stand for the consonant because there are many different consonants that may be used in such words." Let someone tell you the name of the first picture and have one child or several go to the board and print the sounds they hear in the word. Practice the other words as well, without doing the work in the books. Then erase the board and let the children print the words in their books.

Part 2

"Sometimes we have the /ā/ sound in a word when it does not have an *e* on the end. Look at the next group of letters at the side of the page. Do you see *a, i, blank?* When you see *ai* together in a word, the word has the /ā/ sound. The blank is there because there is always a consonant after these letters, and it may be one of many different consonants." Print some *ai* words on the board for the children to sound, and make it clear that the *i* makes no sound at all, it is there only as a signal to say /ā/. Let someone print the words on the board for the pictures in the second row. Erase the board again and let the children do that part in their workbooks.

Part 3

"Look at the letters at the edge of the page in the bottom part. What do you see? You are used to thinking of *y* as a consonant. When we use the *y* like this though, it is a vowel. In these words, the *y* helps to make the long *a* sound. You do not see a blank with these letters. That is because there will be no consonant sound after the /ā/ sound. We use *ay* to write words like this. [Print *bay, hay, may, pay, way* on the board.] When you hear /ā/ at the end of a word, it is spelled with *ay*. When you hear /ā/ in the middle of a word, it is spelled with *ai* or else there is an *e* on the end." Let some of the children show how to print the words for the bottom of the page then have the class print the words in their books.

Seatwork workbook, page 6

Have the children sound the row of words in each section of the page and circle the word that fits best with the picture for that row.

B. Using the spellings

Review the rule that *ay* is used at the end of a word while *ai* or *a-e* are used for medial /ā/. Print *w__k__* on the board. "What vowels would we use to make this word have the /ā/ sound?" Let someone fill in the correct vowels and say the finished word. Print *p __ __ d* and have someone print the correct letters in those blanks to say /ā/. "Why should we use *ai*?" The two blanks together tell us it cannot be *a-e,* and since there is a consonant on the end, it cannot be *ay.* Then print *h __ __* and let someone finish the word and discuss the reason for the letters used. Continue practice as long as you think it is needed for the children to understand the principle.

Seatwork workbook, page 7

Have the children print the correct letters to make each word have the /ā/ sound.

C. Reading

Have the children sound the words they have completed and read them orally to you or an older student. The word reading chart at the back of the workbook does not provide space for a timed score for lesson 1.

D. Spelling

Tell the children that you will refer to *a-e* as rule one, and *ai-* as rule two. Pronounce /ā/ words and /a/ words for them to spell, saying *rule one* or *rule two* for those words with medial /ā/.

Extra activity

"Find all the words on page 7 that begin with capital letters and copy them on a piece of paper. They are written with a capital letter because they are people's names. Draw a picture of a boy or a girl for each name."

Lesson 1   Unit 2

ā

1

a-e

Circle the correct word.

gaze   safe   pale   (rake)   came

2

ai-

Circle the correct word.

rain   (sail)   maid   jail   wait

3

ay

Circle the correct word.

may   day   lay   gay   (pay)

6

Finish the words.

1. bake
2. ray
3. quail
4. Jay
5. name
6. maid
7. nail
8. bay

9. Gail
10. wave
11. Fay
12. base
13. pave
14. Kay
15. gay
16. hail

17. cain
18. jail
19. fame
20. raid
21. vain
22. say
23. hay
24. daze

LESSON 2
Long *E* Spellings: ee, ea, -e

Be prepared
Daily drill
  Consonant flash cards

Lesson 2   Unit 2

ē

1
ee

week   beet   peet

Circle the correct word.

(weed)   weep   peep   deep   seed

2
ea

leak   bead   peak

Circle the correct word.

beak   veal   weak   heat   (bean)

3
-e

me   we   ye

Circle the correct word.

be   (he)   me   we   ye

Vowel flash cards—Add *ai* and *ay* from set 5. (Ask the children, "Is *y* a consonant or a vowel?")

A. Introducing the spellings

Part 1

"Turn to the phonics workbook, page 8. What is the sound for the symbol at the top of the page? When does a word have that sound?" The children

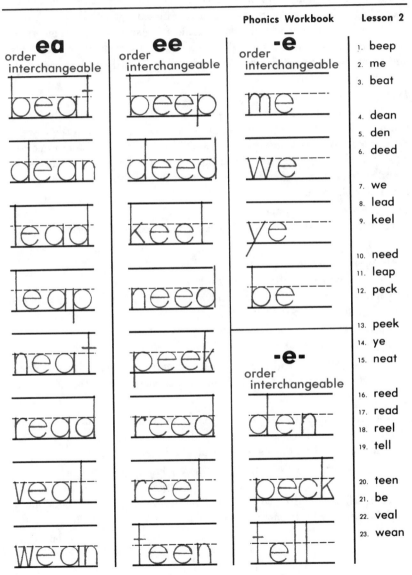

Phonics Workbook   **Lesson 2**

order **ea** interchangeable	order **ee** interchangeable	order **-ē** interchangeable	
beat	beep	me	1. beep
			2. me
			3. beat
dean	deed	we	4. dean
			5. den
			6. deed
lead	keel	ye	7. we
			8. lead
			9. keel
leap	need	be	10. need
			11. leap
			12. peck
neat	peek	**-e-** order interchangeable	13. peek
			14. ye
			15. neat
read	reed	den	16. reed
			17. read
			18. reel
			19. tell
veal	reel	peck	20. teen
			21. be
			22. veal
wean	teen	tell	23. wean

9

have learned to use the /ē/ sound for two *e*'s together. Let someone show how to write the words for the pictures in the first row. Erase the board and have the class print the words in their books.

Part 2

"Sometimes a word has the /ē/ sound because it has these two vowels together." Print *ea* on the board. Practice some words with that spelling and let someone print the words for the second row of pictures, using that digraph. Explain that there is no blank to indicate whether these letters should be at the end of a word or in the middle, because they may sometimes be used at the end or in the middle. Demonstrate by printing *see, seed, tea,* and *team* on the board. Erase the words on the board and have the class print in their books.

Part 3

"We have another way to write the /ē/ sound, and that is only for the end of a word that does not have any other vowels. What are the vowels? What other letter is sometimes a vowel?" Print *we* on the board and ask what vowels the children can see in the word. "The only vowel it has is the *e,* and the *e* is at the end of the word. It says /ē/. What is the word?" Practice as for the other sections.

Seatwork   workbook, page 8

Tell the children to follow the directions for each of the rows of words on the page.

B. Using the spellings

Review the three different spellings of /ē/.

On page 9, have the children tell what sound the *e* makes in each of the four sections of the page. They are to copy the words from the edge list into the correct column according to the vowel spelling.

C. Reading

Let the children read the edge list to someone, then give each one a 30-second timed test on the words in the exercise on page 7.

D. Spelling

Tell the children to use the *ea* spelling for words with medial /ē/ and *e* alone for words with the final /ē/ sound. Pronounce these words for them to spell with spelling blocks or print on the board or paper:

read	beat	he	lead
we	heap	peak	be

Then tell the children to use *ee* instead for the medial /ē/ sound and *e* alone for /e/ words. Pronounce these words for them to spell:

deep	get	jeep	heed
wet	feel	vex	beg

LESSON 3
Long *I* Spellings: i-e, ie, -y

Be prepared

Daily drill

    Consonant flash cards

    Vowel flash cards—Include *ee* and *ea* from set 5 and *-e* from set 9.

A. Introducing the spellings

Part 1

Discuss the long *i* symbol at the top of page 10 in the workbook and the *i-e* spelling at the edge of the page. Let someone show how to print the words for the pictures in the first row and have the class print the words in their books.

Part 2

"Sometimes you will see *ie* together in a word and that says /ī/, too. Sometimes it will be at the end of a word and sometimes it will be in the middle." Print the words for those pictures.

Part 3

Ask again to have the vowels recited, including the consonant that is sometimes a vowel. Print *dry* on the board and ask the children to find a vowel. "There is no vowel except *y* in that word, so *y* will need to be a vowel this time, too, because every word needs to have a vowel." The children have not been sounding out blends, so you may need to say the word for them. Show them that you can hear the sound of both the *d* and the *r* very close together. They will have a few words with blends in the last part of the page.

Seatwork   workbook, page 10

The children are to circle the correct word for each picture as usual in parts 1 and 2, and match a word to each picture at the bottom of the page.

B. Using the spellings

Review the three spellings of /ī/. Print words on the board with blanks for the children to fill in the correct vowels. A long blank calls for the two letters *ie*, two short blanks separated by a consonant call for *i-e*, and one short blank at the end of a word will be *y*.

Seatwork   workbook, page 11

Have the children complete the words with the correct vowel to give them the /ī/ sound.

See if the children can read and understand the direction for the bottom of the page. Have someone read the four vowel sounds in the list at the right edge of the first box. Then ask for the word beside number one. "Which of those four vowel sounds do you hear in that word? Draw a line from the word to the vowel sound."

C. Reading
Proceed with the edge list as usual.

Lesson 3   Unit 2

ī

1
i-e

fire   kite   nine

9

Circle the correct word.

wipe   size   quite   (ride)   bite

2
ie

lie   pie   fie

Circle the correct word.

lie   (die)   tie   vie   fie

Match the words and pictures.

3
-y

by   fry   sky   cry   my

D. Spelling

Tell the children that you are referring to *i-e* as rule one, and *ie* as rule two, and *-y* as rule three. Pronounce words from the edge list for them to spell and give a rule number for each word.

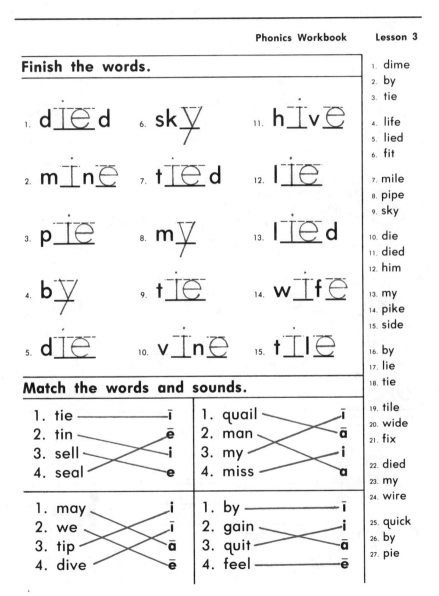

Phonics Workbook   Lesson 3

Finish the words.

1. d͟i͟e͟d   6. sk͟y͟   11. h͟i͟v͟e

2. m͟i͟n͟e   7. t͟i͟e͟d   12. l͟i͟e

3. p͟i͟e   8. m͟y͟   13. l͟i͟e͟d

4. b͟y͟   9. t͟i͟e   14. w͟i͟f͟e

5. d͟i͟e   10. v͟i͟n͟e   15. t͟i͟l͟e

Match the words and sounds.

1. tie	ī	1. quail	ī
2. tin	ē	2. man	ā
3. sell	i	3. my	i
4. seal	e	4. miss	a

1. may	i	1. by	ī
2. we	ī	2. gain	i
3. tip	ā	3. quit	ā
4. dive	ē	4. feel	ē

1. dime
2. by
3. tie
4. life
5. lied
6. fit
7. mile
8. pipe
9. sky
10. die
11. died
12. him
13. my
14. pike
15. side
16. by
17. lie
18. tie
19. tile
20. wide
21. fix
22. died
23. my
24. wire
25. quick
26. by
27. pie

11

LESSON 4
Long *O* Spellings: o-e, oa, oe, ow, -o

Be prepared
Daily drill
   Consonant flash cards

Lesson 4   Unit 2

ō

1
o-e

cone   rope   yoke

Circle the correct word.

home   sole   (bone)   hole   rode

2
oa-

coat   boat   toad

Circle the correct word.

moan   coax   road   (soap)   goat

3
oe

hoe   foe   doe

Circle the correct word.

doe   foe   roe   woe   (Joe)

Vowel flash cards—Include *ie* from set 5 and *-y* from set 9.

A. Introducing the spellings
Part 1

Discuss the long *o* symbol at the top of page 12 and the *o-e* spelling at the edge of the page. Let the children print the word for the first row of

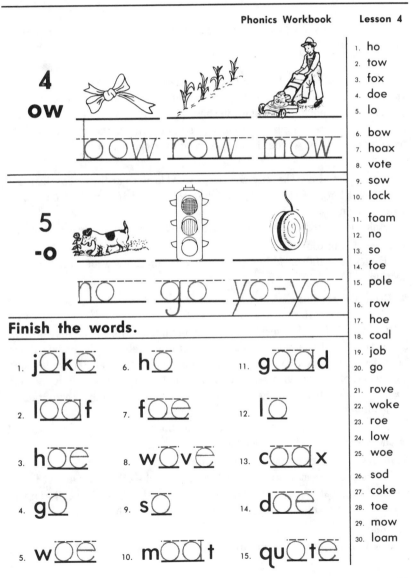

Phonics Workbook   Lesson 4

4
ow

bow row mow

5
-o

no go yo-yo

Finish the words.

1. jo̅ke̅
2. lo̅o̅f
3. ho̅e̅
4. go̅
5. wo̅e̅
6. ho̅
7. fo̅e̅
8. wo̅ve̅
9. so̅
10. mo̅o̅t
11. go̅o̅d
12. lo̅
13. co̅o̅x
14. do̅e̅
15. quo̅te̅

1. ho
2. tow
3. fox
4. doe
5. lo
6. bow
7. hoax
8. vote
9. sow
10. lock
11. foam
12. no
13. so
14. foe
15. pole
16. row
17. hoe
18. coal
19. job
20. go
21. rove
22. woke
23. roe
24. low
25. woe
26. sod
27. coke
28. toe
29. mow
30. loam

13

pictures.

Part 2

"Who can tell me another way to spell the long *o* sound?" The children should find the *oa* in the next part of the page and recognize what it means. "What does the blank after the *a* mean? When you use these letters to spell /ō/ in a word, there will be a consonant after the /ō/ sound. Print these words."

Part 3

"What is the next spelling for /ō/? This one will always be at the end of a word. Print these words."

Part 4

"Look at the top of the next page. There are still more ways to write the /ō/ sound. What letters do you see before the row of pictures? Is *w* a vowel or a consonant? *W* is like *y* in these words. We do not hear the *w* sound at all. It is there to help make the /ō/ sound. This is also a spelling to be used at the end of words. Print the words for these pictures."

Part 5

"And sometimes the only vowel in a word is one *o* at the end of the word. Then it is a long *o*, just like the *e* or the *y* at the end of a word with no other vowels. Print these words."

Ask the children to tell you which spellings are used at the end of words.

Seatwork workbook, page 12

Have the children follow the directions for the row of words in each section.

B. Using the spellings

Review the different spellings of /ō/.

On page 13 of the workbook, tell the children to lightly cross out the *ow* at the top of the page. Print the remaining spellings on the board and point to them as you mention the use for each one. Use *-o* for a single blank at the end of a word with no other vowel, *oe* for a double blank at the end, *oa* for a double blank in the middle, and *o-e* for the blanks interrupted by a consonant.

Print some samples of each kind on the board and have the children fill in the blanks with the correct letters.

Seatwork workbook, page 13 (bottom)

Print the correct vowels in the blanks to make the words have the /ō/ sound. Long *o* at the end of a word can be spelled *oe* or *o*. The children will need to decide which spelling to use by the size of the blank.

C. Reading

Include the words the children have completed with the edge list if you desire.

D. Spelling

Tell the children to use *o-e* for any words with /ō/ in the middle, and *ow* for any words that end with /ō/. Pronounce the following words for the children to spell with spelling blocks or print on the board or on paper.

mow	vote	zone	tow
hole	sow	row	quote

Then tell them to use *oa* for medial /ō/ and *oe* for final /ō/.

moan	loaf	woe	toe
foe	coal	coax	hoe

LESSON 5
Long *U* Spellings; u-e, ew

Be prepared
Daily drill
  Vowel flash cards—Include *oa, ow, oe* from set 5 and *-o* from set 9.

Lesson 5   Unit 2

Ū

1
u-e

cube   mule   tube

Circle the correct word.

tune   yule   fume   (cute)   duke

2
ew

few   mew   pew

Circle the correct word.

hew   dew   (new)   yew   few

Circle all the vowels.

1. fail
2. mew
3. keep
4. way
5. tow
6. by
7. wait
8. nay
9. room
10. my
11. yoke
12. sky
13. bite
14. be
15. row
16. seat
17. low
18. gay
19. new
20. died
21. pay
22. me
23. pew
24. bean
25. beef

14

Alphabet flash cards from set 1 (Practice to keep the image of the capitals familiar. Have the children raise their hands every time they see a vowel, including *y* and *w*. Then call on someone to say the two sounds of that vowel, or in the case of *y* or *w* to tell when it is a vowel.)

Phonics Workbook   **Lesson 5**

Mark the long vowels.

1. hāze	fōal	hēal	dāy	tīde
2. cūbe	nāil	fēe	bāle	dōe
3. lēaf	bē	vīe	mīte	yē
4. sāy	sōw	māze	lōan	pāin
5. wōe	hēap	dūke	lāy	hōle
6. rāil	fūme	dīe	hōax	fēet
7. tīne	bēe	gō	gāin	nō
8. mōw	mūle	tēam	tōte	wē

Match the words and sounds.

1. he: — ā
2. cave: — ē
3. dew: — ī
4. goal — ō
5. bike — ū

1. sail — ā
2. few: — ē
3. lo: — ī
4. by: — ō
5. heat — ū

1. rove — ā
2. pew: — ē
3. my: — ī
4. bail — ō
5. reef — ū

1. seek — ā
2. wife: — ē
3. boat — ī
4. dune: — ō
5. ray: — ū

1. way: — ā
2. cube: — ē
3. tied — ī
4. row: — ō
5. we: — ū

1. Joe: — ā
2. hew: — ē
3. Jane: — ī
4. meal — ō
5. pie: — ū

1. cute
2. new
3. dune
4. fume
5. hew
6. cut
7. tuck
8. cube
9. jug
10. few
11. dew
12. cure
13. huff
14. duck
15. mew
16. cute
17. bug
18. pew
19. duke
20. tune
21. rub
22. mute
23. new
24. pure
25. bus

15

A. Introducing the spellings

Part 1

Discuss the long *u* symbol and the *u-e* spellings on page 14. Make sure the children see the pattern as used for all the vowels except one. Let them tell you which one was not taught that way. The pattern *e-e* is sometimes used in words to spell the /ē/ sound, but not very often. (Examples are *breve, scene, mete, Eve.)*

Part 2

"What sound do you think the two letters in the next part spell? Yes, it is the /ū/ sound even if the word does not have the letter *u* in it. Is *w* a consonant or a vowel? When it is used to help make the /ū/ sound, it is a vowel. Print the words.''

Seatwork workbook, page 14

The rows of words in parts 1 and 2 should be done as usual.

Explain the directions for the bottom of the page. Caution the children to circle the *y*'s and *w*'s only when they are vowels. They appear as consonants in some of the words.

B. Using the spellings

Print a selection of long vowel words on the board. "What is the first word? What long vowel sound do you hear in the word? Find the vowel that makes the long sound and put a macron over it. If there are any other vowels in the word, they do not sound. Do not mark them. Be careful not to get your macron over the silent vowel when it is right beside the long vowel." Have all your samples pronounced and marked.

Seatwork workbook, page 15

See if the children can read the directions for the page and assign the exercises.

C. Reading

Proceed with the edge list as usual.

D. Spelling

Pronounce some/ū/ and /u/ words for the children to spell. Let them decide which /ū/ spelling to use by observing whether the sound is in the middle of the word or at the end.

Extra activity

Circle all the vowels in the matching exercise of page 15 or in edge lists that have already been used for timed tests.

LESSON 6
Review of Long Vowels

Be prepared

1. Daily drill

   Consonant flash cards

   Vowel flash cards—Include *ew* from set 5.

2. Make a chart of the three vowel rules, page 16 of the workbook.

A. Long vowel rules

Read the vowel sounds at the top of page 16.

Help the children to read the rule in box number 1. "When we see an *e* at the end of a word, it tells us the vowel in the word will have the long sound." They will probably need more help to read rules 2 and 3, but they should be able to read enough to recall the rule when asked for it. Print some sample words on the board for the children to pronounce and analyze. "Which rule tells you to say the long vowel sound in this word?"

Seatwork workbook, page 16

Have the children put the number of the rule that applies in the blank before each word.

B. Changing the vowel sound

Print *ran* on the board. "Say this word. Does it have a long or short vowel sound? I want someone to print the word with an *i* in it at the right place to change the vowel sound of the word from short *a* to long *a*. Now what is the word?" Summarize by printing *ran + i = rain*. Help the children to understand the equation. Let them finish this equation: *lid + e = _____.* Have them put the *e* inside the word to make a digraph.

> net + a = _____
>
> sop + a = _____

Seatwork workbook, page 17

Have the children do as you have been practicing in class.

After the words are printed, tell them to read down the list of short vowel words, then down the list of long vowel words that they made.

C. Reading

Proceed with the edge list as usual.

D. Spelling

Post the vowel rule chart and tell the children they can use it to help them spell their words correctly. Ask them to give the spellings for /ā/ and print *a-e, ai,* and *ay* on the board. Pronounce the word *pain* (or *pane*) and ask the children if they would know which spelling to use. Tell them that in such cases you will say *rule 1* or *rule 2* to let them know which one to use. Let someone go to the board and print the word using rule 1. Then let someone print it using rule 2 and surprise the class by telling them that they are both words spelled correctly. Explain the meanings of the two words if you wish.

Pronounce the word *pay* and ask if they know the correct spelling for that word. Remind them that /ā/ at the end of a word is always *ay*, so you will not need to tell them a rule number although the word would fit under

---

Lesson 6   Unit 2

ā   ē   ī   ō   ū

> ## 1. We see an *e* at the end.

> ## 2. We see 2 vowels together.

> ## 3. We see 1 vowel. It is at the end.

Print the correct number.

3 sö	3 my	1 vīne
2 töad	1 wāke	2 pëak
1 bäse	2 few	2 fäin
1 nöte	2 wöe	1 jöke
2 lïed	1 sïze	3 wë
3 gö	2 jëep	2 röw
2 new	1 püre	3 sky

rule 2.
Pronounce the following words for the children to spell.

peg	quail (rule 2)	yell	jail (rule 2)
name (rule 1)	wax	sip	say
rock	lay	fuss	haze (rule 1)

Phonics Workbook **Lesson 6**

Print the new word.

1. van + i = vain

2. mad + i = maid

3. fed + e = feed

4. men + a = mean

5. bed + a = bead

6. did + e = died

7. cot + a = coat

8. rod + a = road

1. can
2. job
3. lay
4. mine
5. dew
6. jug
7. nap
8. we
9. seem
10. leg
11. late
12. foe
13. will
14. die
15. hope
16. tax
17. buzz
18. bow
19. leaf
20. tune
21. jet
22. by
23. ho
24. sin
25. cob
26. wait
27. goat

17

Extra activities

1. Mark the long vowels in the exercise on page 16.

2. Head three columns on a writing paper with *1, 2,* and *3* to represent the three rules and look in the reader or other books for words to copy in the correct columns.

3. Label words in old edge lists with *1, 2,* or *3* to show which long vowel rule applies.

LESSON 7
Consonant Digraph: sh

Be prepared
1. Daily drill
   Alphabet flash cards (Have the children raise their hands for the vowels and let someone say the two sounds for the vowel or tell when it is used as a vowel.)
   Vowel flash cards—Remove the short vowels and the cards marked with a macron. (Have the children say the long vowel sound and *rule 1, rule 2,* or *rule 3.* You quote the rule after the children have identified it.)
2. Locate the *sh* alphabet-picture card and the *sh* flash card from set 5.
3. Make a wall chart for the combination of vowels with *sh.*

A. Introducing the sound
   "We have studied all the letters of the alphabet, but there are still some sounds that we have not studied. What sound do you make when you want someone to be quiet? /sh/ Can you think of some words that begin with that sound?"

she	should	shield	shack
shove	share	shin	ship
shine	shed	sheep	shell
sharp	shake	shaggy	shovel
shoe	shook	shame	shoulder

   "How can we write that sound if there are no more letters? We use two letters together to spell the /sh/ sound. [Show the alphabet-picture card for *sh.*] When you see *sh* together, the sound is /sh/. We do not hear the /s/ sound, and we do not hear the /h/ sound.

   "*S* and *h* are consonants. When two letters make one sound, we call it a digraph. /Sh/ is a consonant digraph." Show the *sh* flash card and add it to the pack of consonant sounds.

   Practice blending the sound with short vowels and with long vowels. Build some words on the board for the children to read.

sha	*she*	*shi*	*sho*	*shu*
shack	shed	ship	shock	shun
sham	shell	shin	shot	shut
shā	*shē*	*shī*	*shō*	*shū*
shake	sheep	shine	shone	
shame	sheet	shy	shoal	

Seatwork   workbook, page 18
   "What letters do you see at the top of the page? What sound do those two letters make? You are to print *sh* in the space at the beginning of each

word. Then sound the word you made and draw a line from the word to the correct picture."

B. Using the Sound

Using words built in part A, print pairs of words on the board to compare /sh/ with /s/.

Lesson 7   Unit 2

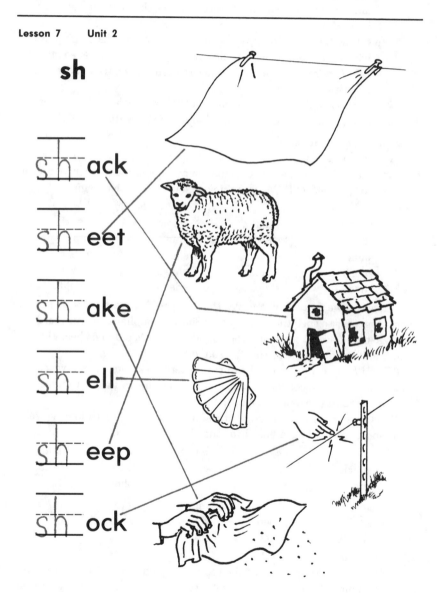

sh

sh_ack

sh_eet

sh_ake

sh_ell

sh_eep

sh_ock

shack-sack   sham-Sam   shell-sell, etc.

Let the children read the words slowly and carefully.

Practice using the new sound at the end of words as you print the following combinations on the board.

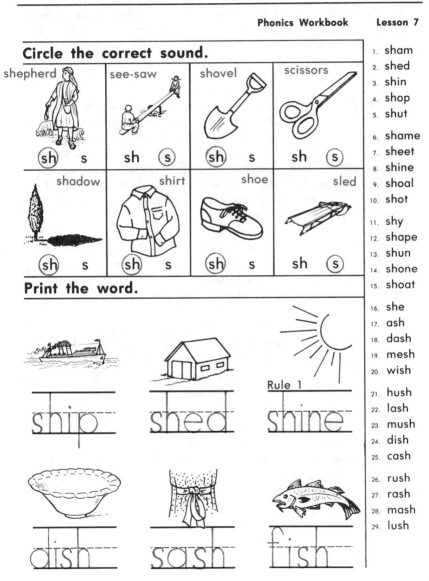

Phonics Workbook   Lesson 7

Circle the correct sound.

shepherd	see-saw	shovel	scissors
(sh) s	sh (s)	(sh) s	sh (s)

shadow	shirt	shoe	sled
(sh) s	(sh) s	(sh) s	sh (s)

Print the word.

ship   shed   Rule 1 shine

dish   sash   fish

1. sham
2. shed
3. shin
4. shop
5. shut

6. shame
7. sheet
8. shine
9. shoal
10. shot

11. shy
12. shape
13. shun
14. shone
15. shoat

16. she
17. ash
18. dash
19. mesh
20. wish

21. hush
22. lash
23. mush
24. dish
25. cash

26. rush
27. rash
28. mash
29. lush

19

ash	esh	ish	osh	ush
cash	mesh	dish		hush
dash		fish		lush
lash		wish		mush
mash				rush
rash				

Seatwork workbook, page 19 (top)

The children are to distinguish between the /sh/ sound and the /s/ sound and circle the correct beginning sound for each picture.

C. Reading

Proceed with the edge list as usual.

D. Spelling

Ask for the long *e* spellings and print *ee, ea,* and *-e* on the board.

Pronounce *be* (or *bee*) and ask the children if they know which spelling to use. Have someone print the word according to rule 3. Then print *bee* and tell them that is also a word. "The long *e* spellings for rule 2 are sometimes used at the end of a word, so you will not know whether to use one vowel or two vowels unless I tell you. I will say *rule 2* when the /ē/ sound at the end of the word has two vowels. I will say *rule 3* when the /ē/ sound at the end of the word has just one letter."

Pronounce *see* (or *sea*) and have someone print the word according to rule 2. Print the other form as well after the student has printed his choice. "Both of these words are spelled correctly, and you cannot tell which way to spell such words by just hearing the word. But today I will not give you any words to be spelled with *ea,* so every time I say *rule 2* spell your word with *ee.*

"I will not need to say a rule number when the /ē/ sound is in the middle of the word. What will the spelling be for words with /ē/ in the middle?" (ee)

Pronounce the following words for the children to spell.

sheep	see (rule 2)	shell
fish	she (rule 3)	shake (rule 1)
shade (rule 1)	shack	sheet
rush	cash	lash

Seatwork workbook, page 19 (bottom)

The children are to print the whole word for each picture. The little *1* above the lines for the third picture is to tell them to spell the long *i* sound according to rule 1.

LESSON 8
Consonant Digraph: th, <u>th</u>

Be prepared

1. Daily drill

   Consonant flash cards—Include *sh.*

   Vowel flash cards, without short vowels or macrons (Have the children say the vowel sound, identify the rule number, and quote the rule if they are able.)

2. Find the alphabet-picture cards and flash cards for /th/ and /<u>th</u>/. The alphabet-picture card for /th/ shows the symbol as t̶h̶. You may want to change it to <u>th</u> with white correction fluid and black marker.

3. Make wall charts for the combinations of /th/ and /<u>th</u>/ with vowels.

A. Introducing the sounds

"Today we will study another digraph. It is a new sound that we write with two letters. You are using this digraph in some of your reading words." Print *them, that,* and *the* on the board and have someone pronounce them. Underline the <u>th</u> in each word and see if someone can tell you what the sound is for those two letters. Have all the children make the sound. Explain how to produce the sound if anyone has trouble. "Put your tongue on your teeth and make a buzzing sound in your throat." Compare the sound to that of a buzzing fly.

"Now look at this word." Print *things* on the board. "What sound do you say at the beginning of this word? Everyone may say the sound." Explain that the tongue is put on the teeth in the same way as for /<u>th</u>/, but the only sound is that of blowing air out between the tongue and teeth. "We use the same letters to spell both sounds. You will know which sound to make when you know the word. We have another way to show the difference between the sounds. When you see a line under the <u>th</u>, it means you are to make the buzzing sound." Print the digraph on the board twice and underline the one. Point to one, then to the other as the children make the corresponding sound for you. Then have the children open their workbooks to page 20 and point to the correct digraph as you pronounce these words for them.

thing	this	theme	thy
thine	thud	that	than
them	thick	thin	then
thorns	the	thus	thistle
throne	thumb	thought	though

Practice combining /th/ and /<u>th</u>/ with vowels and build some words for the children to read.

tha	*the*	*thi*	*tho*	*thu*
		thick		thug
		things		thud
		thin		

th $\bar{a}$ th $\bar{e}$ th $\bar{\imath}$ th $\bar{o}$ th $\bar{u}$

theme

(Note the final *e* spelling which works for
/ē/ just like it does for the other vowels.)

Lesson 8   **Unit 2**

th

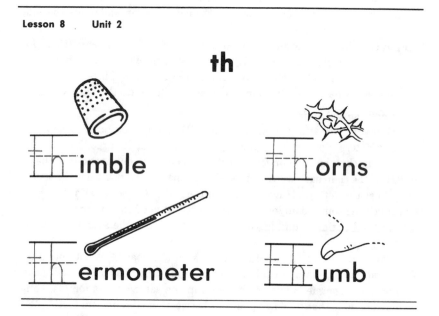

imble   orns

ermometer   umb

th

fa er

mo er

bro er

fea er

<u>tha</u>	<u>the</u>	<u>thi</u>	<u>tho</u>	<u>thu</u>
that	then	this		thus
than	them			

<u>thā</u>	<u>thē</u>	<u>thī</u>	<u>thō</u>	<u>thū</u>
	thee	thine		
		thy		

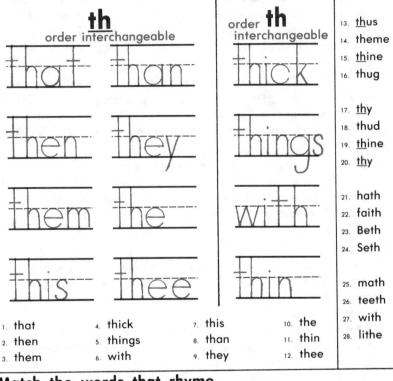

13. <u>th</u>us
14. theme
15. <u>th</u>ine
16. thug
17. <u>th</u>y
18. thud
19. <u>th</u>ine
20. <u>th</u>y
21. hath
22. faith
23. Beth
24. Seth
25. math
26. teeth
27. with
28. lithe

1. that 4. thick 7. this 10. the
2. then 5. things 8. than 11. thin
3. them 6. with 9. they 12. thee

Match the words that rhyme.

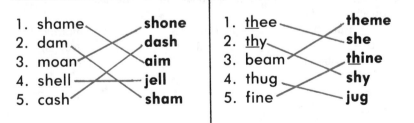

1. shame — sham
2. dam — dash
3. moan — aim
4. shell — jell
5. cash — shone

1. <u>th</u>ee — thine
2. <u>th</u>y — she
3. beam — theme
4. thug — shy
5. fine — jug

21

Seatwork workbook, page 20

"Print *th* in each blank in the words on the page. Do not underline any of the letters, but think of the sound shown by the digraph in that part of the page. Then try to read the words."

B. Using the sounds

Practice combining the *th* sounds after vowels and build words. (See the lists on page 21 of the workbook for words the children can read or sound.)

Seatwork workbook, page 21 (top)

"What are the two sounds of *th*? You can see them at the top of the page. Under each sound there are blank spaces for you to print words. Find the list of words below the blanks. What is the first word? Do you hear /th/ or /th/ in that word? Print the word in the correct part of the page."

C. Reading

Print *rain* and *cane* on the board and have someone say the two words. "Do the words rhyme? Do they look alike? Now that we know different ways of writing the long vowel sounds, you cannot tell rhyming words only by the way they look. Two words can have the same sound but have different letters."

Seatwork workbook, page 21 (bottom and edge)

"The directions at the bottom of the page say, *Match the words that rhyme.* Be sure to sound the words carefully as you match them."

Include the words the children have printed in the lists as part of the edge list for this lesson.

D. Spelling

Print *tide* and *tied* on the board. Ask someone to show you which word is spelled according to rule 1. "Which word is spelled according to rule 2? When you hear /ī/ in the middle of the word, I will have to tell you whether to use rule 1 or rule 2."

Print *by* and *die* and ask which word is spelled according to rule 2. "Which word is spelled according to rule 3? When you hear /ī/ at the end of a word I will have to tell you whether to use rule 2 or rule 3."

Tell the children to use *ea* today for the /ē/ words that are spelled according to rule 2. Print *ea* on the board for a reminder.

Spelling words:

thy (rule 3)	lie (rule 2)	main (rule 2)
this	tea (rule 2)	he (rule 3)
shine (rule 1)	shy (rule 3)	thick
bean	with	that
thin	them	tied (rule 2)

LESSON 9

Consonant Digraph: wh

Be prepared

1. Daily drill

    Consonant flash cards—Include *th* and <u>*th*</u>.

    Vowel flash cards (Review the long vowel rules as in lesson 8.)
2. Find the alphabet-picture card and flash card for *wh*.
3. Make a wall chart for combining *wh* with vowels.

A. Introducing the sound

Print *wail* on the board and have someone say the word. Let someone give a definition for the word. "What sound does the word begin with? Get your mouth ready to say the /w/ sound, and then blow as you say /w/. That is the new sound for today. Say *wail* with a blowing *w*. Now we have this word." Print *whale* on the board and discuss its meaning. Practice saying the two words and hearing the distinction between /w/ and /wh/. Circle the *wh* in *whale*. "We use these two letters to spell the /wh/ sound."

Demonstrate the difference between *wine* and *whine* in the same way. Practice combining /wh/ with short and long vowels, and build a few words.

wha	*whe*	*whi*	*who*	*whu*
	when	whip		

wh/ā/	*wh/ē/*	*wh/ī/*	*wh/ō/*	*wh/ū/*
whale	wheel	while		
	wheat	white		
		whine		

Seatwork   workbook, page 22

"Print *wh* in the blank at the beginning of each word. Then sound out the word and draw a line from the word to the correct picture."

B. Using the sound

Have the children practice saying the names of the pictures at the top of page 23. If they do not make a distinction between /w/ and /wh/ in their speech, say the words for them and have them circle the sound that they hear.

Seatwork   workbook, page 23 (top)

"Circle the correct sound for each picture."

C. Reading

See if the children can figure out what the directions say for the middle of the page.

In working with this edge list, do not let the children read so fast that they do not say the sounds carefully.

Seatwork   workbook, page 23 (middle and edge)

D. Spelling

Ask for the /ō/ spellings and print *o-e, oa, oe, ow,* and *-o* on the board. Ask someone to spell *rode* (or *road*) on the board. See if someone thinks it could be spelled another way. "Both words are right. I will need to tell you whether to use rule 1 or rule 2 when you have a word with /ō/ in the middle.

Lesson 9   Unit 2

wh

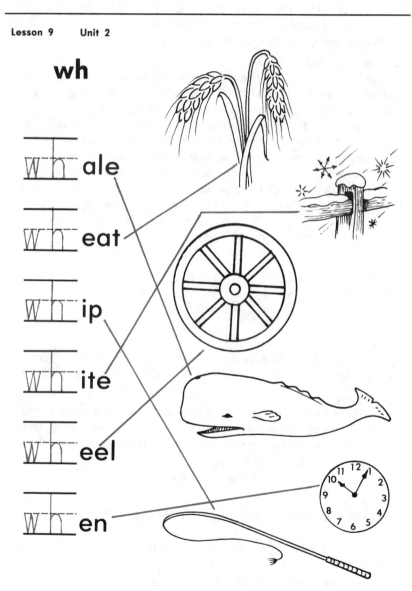

Wh ale

Wh eat

Wh ip

Wh ite

Wh eel

Wh en

"What are the spellings for the end of a word? If I say *rule 3*, which one will you use? [-o] If I say *rule 2*, you will use *oe* or *ow*. Use *ow* today when I say *rule 2* for a word with /ō/ at the end." Print *ow* on the board for a reminder.

"Use *ea* today when you hear /ē/ in the middle of a word, or if I say *rule 2*

Phonics Workbook   **Lesson 9**

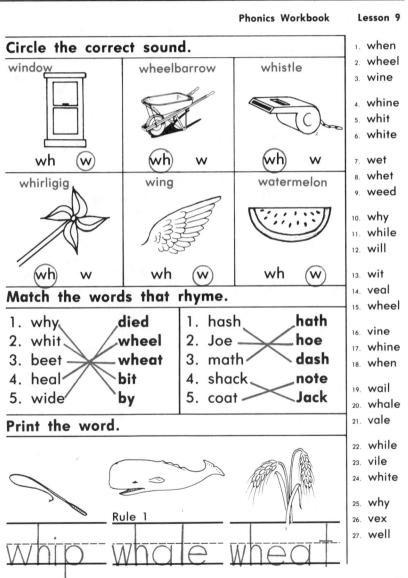

Circle the correct sound.

window	wheelbarrow	whistle
wh (w)	(wh) w	(wh) w
whirligig	wing	watermelon
(wh) w	wh (w)	wh (w)

Match the words that rhyme.

1. why — by
2. whit — bit
3. beet — wheat
4. heal — wheel
5. wide — died

1. hash — hath
2. Joe — hoe
3. math — dash
4. shack — Jack
5. coat — note

Print the word.

Rule 1

whip   whale   wheat

1. when
2. wheel
3. wine
4. whine
5. whit
6. white
7. wet
8. whet
9. weed
10. why
11. while
12. will
13. wit
14. veal
15. wheel
16. vine
17. whine
18. when
19. wail
20. whale
21. vale
22. while
23. vile
24. white
25. why
26. vex
27. well

for a word with /ē/ at the end." Print *ea* on the board as well.
    Spelling words:

white (rule 1)	show (rule 2)	sea (rule 2)
wait (rule 2)	wet	when
no (rule 3)	wheat	be (rule 2)
vote (rule 1)	why (rule 3)	loaf (rule 2)
wax	doze (rule 1)	so (rule 3)

Seatwork   workbook, page 23 (bottom)

Print the words for the pictures, using rule 1 for the blank marked with
1 and using *ea* for the /ē/ word.

LESSON 10

Consonant Digraph: ch, tch

Be prepared

1. Daily drill
   Consonant flash cards—Include *wh*.
   Vowel flash cards (Review long vowel rules.)
2. Find the *ch* alphabet-picture card. Find the *ch* flash card in set 5, and the *tch* card in set 10.
3. Make the wall charts of combinations.

A. Introducing the sound

"What goes ch-ch-ch-ch? Sometimes it is called a choo-choo train. Most trains today do not sound like that, but the old ones did and people still think of that sound for trains. We use two consonants for the /ch/ sound." Show the alphabet-picture card for *ch* and let the children name the letters used in the digraph.

Practice combining *ch* with short vowels and long vowels.

cha	*che*	*chi*	*cho*	*chu*
chap	check	chick	chock	chub
chaff	chess	chill	chop	chuck
chat		chip		chum
		chin		

chā	*chē*	*chī*	*chō*	*chū*
chain	cheek	chide	chode	chew
chafe	cheap	chime	choke	
	cheat	chive		

Seatwork   workbook, page 24

"Print *ch* in the blank at the beginning of each word, then sound the word and draw a line to the correct picture."

B. Using the sound

Name the pictures at the top of page 25 and let the children tell you what sound they hear at the beginning of the words.

Seatwork   workbook, page 25 (top)

Have the children circle the digraph that they hear at the beginning of the word for each picture.

C. Reading

Practice sounding *ch* after vowels. Show the *tch* flash card and tell the children that words that end with /ch/ usually have *tch* after the vowel. The *t* does not make any sound. The three letters sound just like /ch/.

Build words ending with /ch/ for the children to sound.

Seatwork   workbook, page 25 (middle and edge)

D. Spelling

Ask for the /ū/ spellings and print *u-e, ew* on the board. Ask which would be used for /ū/ at the end of a word.

Tell the children to use *ee* for /ē/ words and *oe* for /ō/ at the end of a word when you say rule 2. Print *ee* and *oe* on the board for a reminder.

Lesson 10   Unit 2

Lesson 10: Gradebook: 31 points

ch

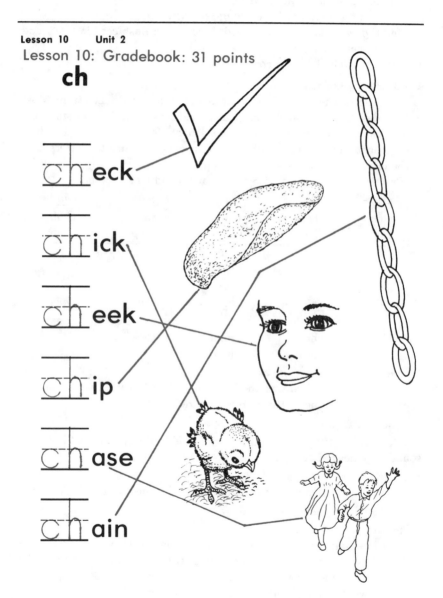

ch eck

ch ick

ch eek

ch ip

ch ase

ch ain

Spelling words:	cheek	chime (rule 1)	cute
	chug	few	chin
	hoe (rule 2)	choke (rule 1)	chain (rule 2)
	joke (rule 1)	chew	chop
	no (rule 3)	chat	chase (rule 1)
	thee	whip	shut

Phonics Workbook   **Lesson 10**

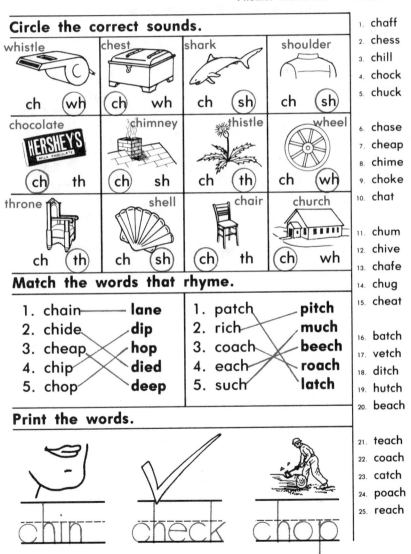

Circle the correct sounds.

whistle	chest	shark	shoulder
ch (wh)	(ch) wh	ch (sh)	ch (sh)
chocolate	chimney	thistle	wheel
(ch) th	(ch) sh	ch (th)	ch (wh)
throne	shell	chair	church
ch (th)	ch (sh)	(ch) th	(ch) wh

Match the words that rhyme.

1. chain —— lane
2. chide — dip
3. cheap — hop
4. chip — died
5. chop — deep

1. patch — pitch
2. rich — much
3. coach — beech
4. each — roach
5. such — latch

Print the words.

chin   check   chop

1. chaff
2. chess
3. chill
4. chock
5. chuck
6. chase
7. cheap
8. chime
9. choke
10. chat
11. chum
12. chive
13. chafe
14. chug
15. cheat
16. batch
17. vetch
18. ditch
19. hutch
20. beach
21. teach
22. coach
23. catch
24. poach
25. reach

25

Seatwork   workbook, page 25 (bottom)

Have the children print the words for the pictures at the bottom of the page.

Extra activity   Home run game

Print the following diagram on the board. Let the children bat one at a time, and run the bases by saying a word beginning with each of the sounds around the base line. If they can say a word for each sound, they score a home run. If they cannot think of a word or say a wrong one, they are out. Point to the sounds in the order they are to be used.

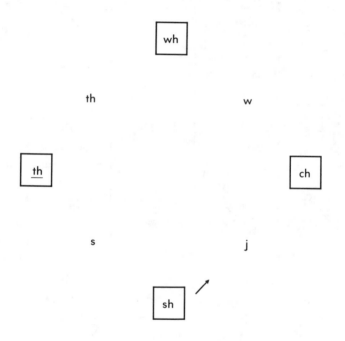

LESSON 11

Double Consonant Endings: ss, ll, ff, zz, ck

Be prepared

Daily drill

Alphabet flash cards (Have the children raise their hands when they see a vowel and tell the two sounds or tell when it is a vowel.)

Consonant flash cards—Separate the digraphs and add *ch* and *tch*. This pack will be referred to as *consonant digraphs* and the rest will be called *consonant sounds*. (Drill the consonant digraphs and ask if they are consonant or vowel digraphs.)

A. Introducing the rule

The children have encountered the double consonant endings in words they have been reading. "There are certain letters that are usually written two times when they come at the end of a word with a short vowel. Can you think of any that are used that way?" Print on the board the double letters the children may be able to supply. Add the remaining ones, and list a few sample words for each double letter. (Samples may be found in the edge list.) You may point out that though *ck* is not a double letter, it is two letters that make the same sound and functions as the other double letters.

Seatwork workbook, page 26

Pronounce the following words to the children and have them print the endings they hear in the words. Caution them that some words will need a double consonant, and some words need only one. Each time the ending sound is one of the sounds at the top of the page, it should have a double letter.

1. bass	9. whiff	17. thick	25. toss
2. wick	10. vat	18. quack	26. dull
3. wag	11. chess	19. mock	27. puff
4. quill	12. pan	20. tax	28. map
5. cuff	13. fuzz	21. yell	29. neck
6. rib	14. chaff	22. hiss	30. fix
7. doll	15. mud	23. buck	31. hem
8. fuss	16. buzz	24. fig	32. whizz

B. Long vowel review

Review the long vowel rules by printing some long vowel words on the board and identifying the rule that applies. Let the children mark with a macron the vowel that has a long sound in each word.

Seatwork workbook, page 27 (top)

"Can anyone read the directions at the top of page 27? Read each word and find the vowel that is making the long sound. Put a macron over the long vowel. Be careful to have it over the long vowel only, and not over some other letters too. When you come to a word that does not have a long vowel, cross out that word."

C. Reading

Proceed with the edge list as usual.

Lesson 11   Unit 2

ss   ll   ff   zz   ck

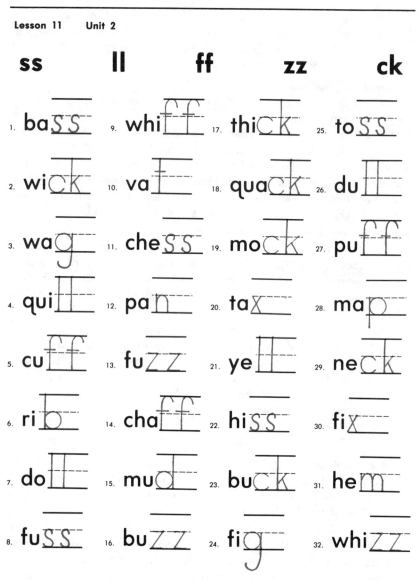

1. ba _ss_
2. wi _ck_
3. wa _g_
4. qui _ll_
5. cu _ff_
6. ri _b_
7. do _ll_
8. fu _ss_

9. whi _ff_
10. va _t_
11. che _ss_
12. pa _n_
13. fu _zz_
14. cha _ff_
15. mu _d_
16. bu _zz_

17. thi _ck_
18. qua _ck_
19. mo _ck_
20. ta _x_
21. ye _ll_
22. hi _ss_
23. bu _ck_
24. fi _g_

25. to _ss_
26. du _ll_
27. pu _ff_
28. ma _p_
29. ne _ck_
30. fi _x_
31. he _m_
32. whi _zz_

D. Spelling

Pronounce any words from the edge list for the children to spell. You may include long vowel words as well, giving any rule numbers needed with them.

| Phonics Workbook | Lesson 11 |

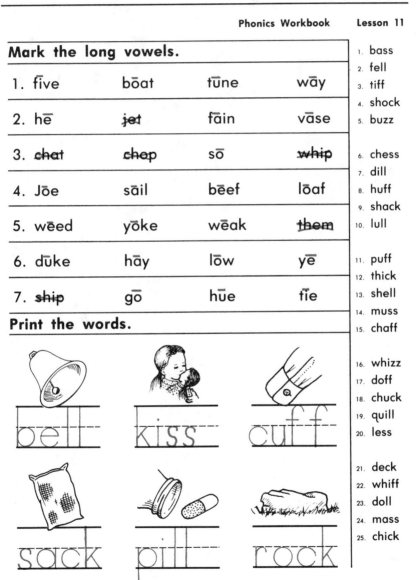

Mark the long vowels.

1. fīve   bōat   tūne   wāy

2. hē   j̶e̶t̶   fāin   vāse

3. c̶h̶a̶t̶   c̶h̶o̶p̶   sō   w̶h̶i̶p̶

4. Jōe   sāil   bēef   lōaf

5. wēed   yōke   wēak   t̶h̶e̶m̶

6. dūke   hāy   lōw   yē

7. s̶h̶i̶p̶   gō   hūe   tīe

Print the words.

bell   kiss   cuff

sack   pill   rock

1. bass
2. fell
3. tiff
4. shock
5. buzz
6. chess
7. dill
8. huff
9. shack
10. lull
11. puff
12. thick
13. shell
14. muss
15. chaff
16. whizz
17. doff
18. chuck
19. quill
20. less
21. deck
22. whiff
23. doll
24. mass
25. chick

27

Seatwork workbook, page 27 (bottom)

"Print the word for each picture."

Extra activity

Have the children take the word beginnings from the first column on page 26 of the workbook and print on a paper as many words as they can make for each one, using single consonants as well as the double consonant endings.

LESSON 12

Review

Be prepared

Daily drill

Consonant digraph flash cards—Include the *ck* card from set 5.

Vowel flash cards—Include short vowels and macrons again.

A. Double consonants and long vowels

Ask for the children to tell the consonants that should be doubled at the end of a short vowel word. Print the following words on the board and have the children note the double letters.

     fell   bass   whiff   buzz   sock

"What kind of vowel sound do you hear in these words? Now we are going to write some words that have the long vowel sound. [Under *fell*, print *feel*.] How do you know this word has a long vowel sound? What happened to the double *l*? [Under *bass*, print *base*.] How do you know this word has a long vowel sound? What happened to the double *s*?" Print *wife, daze,* and *soak,* and make the same observations. State the rule that the double endings are only for words with the short vowel sound.

Print the word *like* on the board and ask, "What would we have to do so that this word would not have a long vowel sound? [We would remove the *e*.] I want someone to print the word with a short vowel and the correct ending." Practice with *dole, teal,* and *cheek* as well.

Seatwork   workbook, page 28

"Turn to page 28 in your phonics book. Does word number one have a long or short vowel sound? Beside the word is the vowel sound we want the word to have. What will you do with the double *s*? You will print the word in the space on your page.

"See the line across your page halfway down. The words for the last part have the long vowel sound. Beside each word is the vowel sound you are to write in the new word. What is the sound beside *file*? What must you remember when you write a short vowel word that ends with *l*?"

Have the children alter the words according to the directions.

B. Final consonant digraphs   workbook, page 29 (top)

"Say the words and circle the sound that you hear at the end of the word."

C. Reading

Proceed with the edge list as usual.

D. Spelling

Print $\bar{a}$ on the board and ask the children to give all the spellings they can for that sound. List them under the long vowel symbol. Print $\bar{e}$ and list all the spellings they can give for that sound. Do the same for $\bar{\imath}, \bar{o},$ and $\bar{u}.$

Pronounce any words from the edge list for the children to spell, giving any needed rule numbers.

Seatwork   workbook, page 29 (middle and bottom)

"Can you read the directions for the middle of the page? Draw a line from

---

Lesson 12   Unit 2

Take this word	Change the vowel	Make a new word.
1. bass	a-e	base
2. sell	ea	seal
3. mull	u-e	mule
4. sock	oa	soak
5. file	i	fill
6. rake	a	rack
7. poke	o	pock
8. deal	e	dell

each set of letters in the row below to one of the long vowels in the row above." Erase the vowels on the board and have them do the matching.

Have them print the word for each picture at the bottom. One of them is a sentence with a blank instead of a picture.

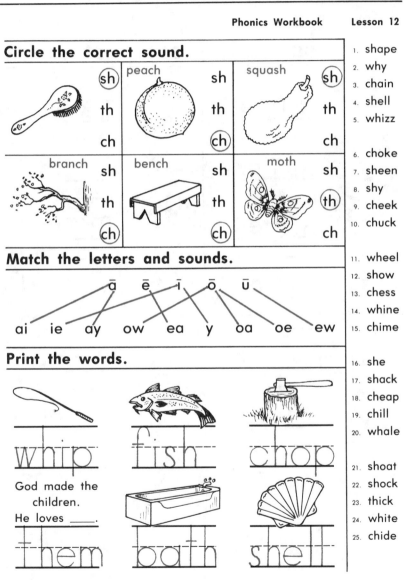

Phonics Workbook   Lesson 12

Circle the correct sound.

	peach		squash	
(sh)	sh	(sh)		
th	th	th		
ch	(ch)	ch		

branch	bench	moth
sh	sh	sh
th	th	(th)
(ch)	(ch)	ch

Match the letters and sounds.

ā   ē   ī   ō   ū

ai   ie   ay   ow   ea   y   oa   oe   ew

Print the words.

whip

fish

chop

God made the children.
He loves ____.

them

bath

shell

1. shape
2. why
3. chain
4. shell
5. whizz

6. choke
7. sheen
8. shy
9. cheek
10. chuck

11. wheel
12. show
13. chess
14. whine
15. chime

16. she
17. shack
18. cheap
19. chill
20. whale

21. shoat
22. shock
23. thick
24. white
25. chide

29

LESSON 13
Consonant Blends: sk, sc, sm, st

Be prepared
1. Daily drill
   Vowel flash cards

Lesson 13   Unit 2

sc	sk	sm	st

sm ile

sm oke

sm ell

sm ash

sk y

sk ip

sk in

sk etch

st ove

st iff

st one

st op

sc ab

sc otch

sc one

sc ale

30

Consonant flash cards
Consonant digraph flash cards
2. Make wall charts for combining these blends with vowels.

A. Introducing the blends
   Print ____ep on the board and let someone sound it. Let the children

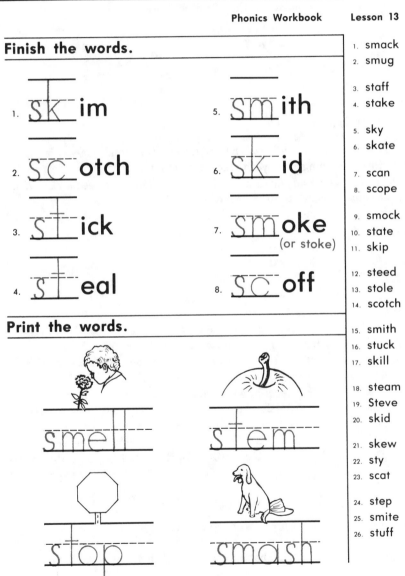

Phonics Workbook | Lesson 13

Finish the words.

1. sk im
2. sc otch
3. st ick
4. st eal
5. sm ith
6. sk id
7. sm oke (or stoke)
8. sc off

Print the words.

smell   stem
stop   smash

1. smack
2. smug
3. staff
4. stake
5. sky
6. skate
7. scan
8. scope
9. smock
10. state
11. skip
12. steed
13. stole
14. scotch
15. smith
16. stuck
17. skill
18. steam
19. Steve
20. skid
21. skew
22. sty
23. scat
24. step
25. smite
26. stuff

31

suggest different words using various initial consonants and print those words under your word fragment. Then ask them to listen to the word you say, and see if they can tell with what sound you begin. Pronounce the word *step* slowly and clearly. Can they identify the two sounds? Print *st* in the blank and explain that this is not a digraph. The two letters do not make a new sound. We still hear the two consonant sounds but they are sounded very close together. We call these two letters a blend.

Have the children sound the blend, and practice combinations.

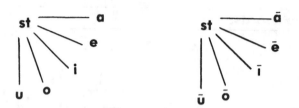

Print ____*ash* and have the children identify the sounds you say in *smash.* Practice combining /sm/ with short and long vowels.

Print ____*im,* and say *skim.* "Which letter should we use for /k/? What letter comes next to the /k/ sound?"

Print ____*uff,* and pronounce *scuff.* "Which letter should we use for /k/ this time?" Practice:

sca	scā
ske	skē
ski	skī
sco	scō
scu	scū

Seatwork   workbook, page 30

"You see the four new blends at the top of the page. One blend belongs with each part of the page. Do you know what the picture is in the first part of the page? The first word will fit to the picture when you have the correct blend printed in the blank. Sound the first word with the *sc* or *sk* blend. (They sound alike.) Sound the word with the *sm* blend. Sound it with *st*. Which one makes a word? Print that blend in the blank. Try that blend in the next blank. Does that make a word? Does it make a word in the next one? And the next one? The same blend belongs in every blank for this section.

"Can you tell what the blend will be in the next box? Does that blend make a word when you try it with each of the endings? Print the same blend in each blank in the box.

"Do the same for all the boxes."

B. Using the blends   workbook, page 31 (top)

"Look at the first word-ending on the page. Try each of the blends from page 30 until you find one that makes a word. Print your blend in the blank. Find a blend for each of the words."

C. Reading

Proceed with the edge list as usual.

D. Spelling

Pronounce words from the edge list for the children to spell.

Seatwork   workbook, page 31 (bottom)

"Print the word for each picture."

LESSON 14
Consonant Blends: sn, sp, sl, sw

Be prepared
1. Daily drill
   Vowel flash cards—Remove the short vowels and macrons again.

---

sn   sp   sl   sw

sp in

sp an

sp ell

sp ine

sn ake

sn ail

sn eak

sn ow

sw eep

sw im

sw ell

sw eet

sl ed

sl y

sl eep

sl ate

(Have the children identify the rule number and quote it for each
long vowel spelling.)

Consonant digraph flash cards (Refer to them as *digraphs.*)

Blends from the wall charts (Say the long or short vowel sounds.)

2. Make wall charts for combinations with the new blends.

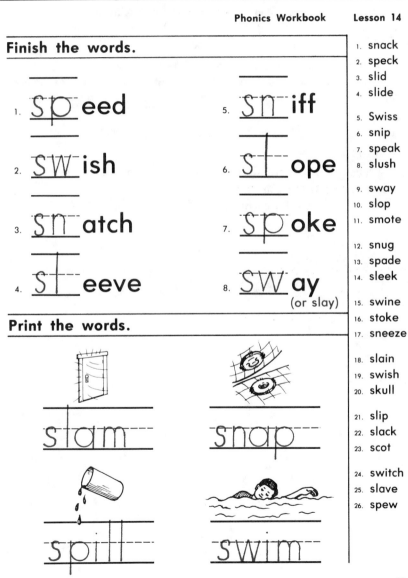

Phonics Workbook   **Lesson 14**

Finish the words.

1. Sp eed
2. Sw ish
3. Sn atch
4. Sl eeve
5. Sn iff
6. Sl ope
7. Sp oke
8. Sw ay (or slay)

Print the words.

slam   snap

spill   swim

1. snack
2. speck
3. slid
4. slide
5. Swiss
6. snip
7. speak
8. slush
9. sway
10. slop
11. smote
12. snug
13. spade
14. sleek
15. swine
16. stoke
17. sneeze
18. slain
19. swish
20. skull
21. slip
22. slack
23. scot
24. switch
25. slave
26. spew

33

A. Introducing the blends

Print ____*ip* on the board and let the children identify the sounds in *snip*. Then have them identify the sounds in *slip*. Practice those blends with short vowels and long vowels.

Introduce *sp* with ____*oke*, and *sw* with ____*eet*. Practice *sp* and *sw* with short and long vowels.

Seatwork   workbook, page 32

"Find the correct blend for each box by looking at the picture and sounding the first word in the box. Try your blend with each of the other words in the box, too. Print the blend in each blank."

B. Using the blends   workbook, page 33 (top)

"Try each of the blends from page 32 until you find one that makes a word for each of these endings. Print the blends in the blanks."

C. Reading

Proceed with the edge list as usual.

D. Spelling

Pronounce words from the edge list for the children to spell.

Seatwork   workbook, page 33 (bottom)

"Print the word for each picture."

LESSON 15
Review

Be prepared

Daily drill

    Consonant flash cards

    Consonant digraph flash cards

    Vowel flash cards (Review long vowel rules.)

    Blends from the combination charts (Say the long or short sound for the vowels.)

    Alphabet-picture cards—If the children have known the letters of the alphabet as sounds only, begin now to use the names of the letters. Say the alphabet daily with the class, using a pointer to follow along the row of alphabet-picture cards.

A. Consonant blends

Print the blends on the board and let the children point to the one they hear in words you say. You may use the last few edge lists for a source of words.

Seatwork   workbook, page 34 (top)

Have the children circle the blend they hear at the beginning of the word for each picture.

B. Rhyming words   workbook, page 34 (bottom)

"Match the words that rhyme. Draw lines as usual. After the matching is done, look at the letter before the word in the second column. Print that letter in the blank before the word to which it is matched."

C. Reading

Part of the edge list is in the word box. You may include all the words in the box if you wish.

D. Spelling

Pronounce words for the children to spell.

Seatwork   workbook, page 35

"There are many vowel sounds on your page. With each sound, there is space for you to print two words that have that vowel sound. You will use the words in the **Word box** in the bottom corner of the page. Say the first word in the box. What vowel sound do you hear? Print the word under that vowel sound on the page. After the word is printed, you may put a check mark beside it in the list."

Extra activity

Have the children find and print pairs of rhyming words from the edge list. Or have them take words from the edge list and think of their own rhymes to print.

Lesson 15 Unit 2	Gradebook: 21 points for this page

Circle the correct blends.

sn (sk) sp	skates	sl sn (sp)	spear	sm sc (sl)	slide
sn sl (sw)	swing	sw (st) sp	stack	sk sp (sm)	smoke
sc (st) sm	stick	(sn) st sl	snowflake	(sp) sw sk	spider
sm (sc) st	scarecrow	(sk) sm st	skunk	sw sc (sl)	sleigh
(sc) sw sn	scarf	(sw) sl st	sweater	sp (sm) sk	smile

Match the words that rhyme. Print the letter.

d 1. sleet   **a.** tie
a 2. spy   **b.** sway
b 3. stay   **c.** smoke
e 4. smock   **d.** heat
c 5. spoke   **e.** shock
f 6. scale   **f.** snail

order interchangeable between pairs

Phonics Workbook   **Lesson 15**

1. snipe
2. spot
3. slay
4. snuff
5. swum
6. swipe
7. slug
8. scan
9. skew
10. steep
11. smack
12. stove
13. stew
14. slow
15. speech
16. switch
17. wax
18. she
19. chop
20. us
21. coat
22. bed
23. few
24. fix
25. slow
26. much

Word box

slot
hay
thy
pie
bag
wish
yes
chain
wheat
mute

35

LESSON 16
Consonant Blends: bl, br, cl, cr

Be prepared

1. Daily drill

Vowel flash cards (Review long vowel rules.)

Lesson 16   Unit 2

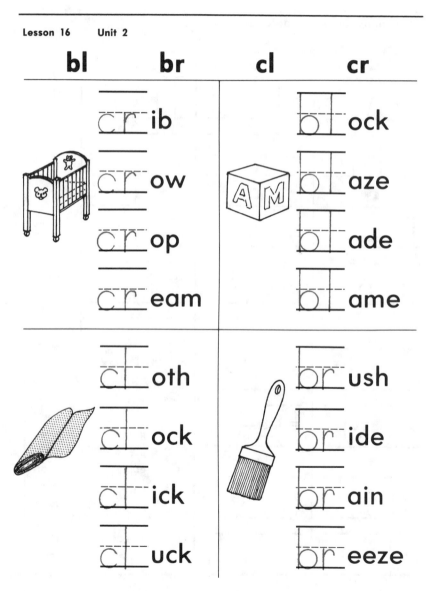

bl	**br**	**cl**	**cr**
	cr ib		bl ock
	cr ow		bl aze
	cr op		bl ade
	cr eam		bl ame
	cl oth		br ush
	cl ock		br ide
	cl ick		br ain
	cl uck		br eeze

36

Consonant digraph flash cards
Consonant blend flash cards—Find all the blends covered to this point
  in set 6. (Have the children say a word beginning with the blend
  shown on each card.)
Alphabet recitation
2. Make wall charts for the new blends with vowels.

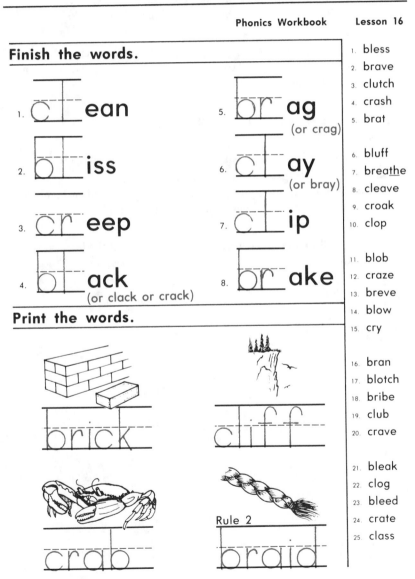

Phonics Workbook   **Lesson 16**

Finish the words.

1. c ean

2. b iss

3. cr eep

4. b ack
(or clack or crack)

5. br ag
(or crag)

6. c ay
(or bray)

7. c ip

8. br ake

Print the words.

brick

cliff

crab

Rule 2   braid

1. bless
2. brave
3. clutch
4. crash
5. brat

6. bluff
7. breathe
8. cleave
9. croak
10. clop

11. blob
12. craze
13. breve
14. blow
15. cry

16. bran
17. blotch
18. bribe
19. club
20. crave

21. bleak
22. clog
23. bleed
24. crate
25. class

37

A. Introducing the blends

Print ____*ack* on the board, and have the children identify the blend when you say *black*. "How many other words can you think of that begin like *black*?" *Brim, click,* and *crash* may be used in the same way to introduce the other blends. Practice the blends with vowels.

Seatwork workbook, page 36

"Look at the picture and sound the words in each box to decide which blend to use. Print the same blend in each blank of the block."

B. Using the blends workbook, page 37 (top)

"Look at the blends at the top of page 36. Print one of these blends in each blank on the top of page 37 to make words. Be sure to read your words after you have finished them."

C. Reading

Proceed with the edge list as usual.

D. Spelling

Pronounce words from the edge list for the children to spell.

Seatwork workbook, page 37 (bottom)

"Print the word for each picture. The little *2* above the last blank is to tell you to use rule 2 for the vowel sound in that word."

Extra activity

Have the children take the word endings from one of the boxes on page 36 and make all the words they can with different beginnings.

LESSON 17

Consonant Blends: fl, fr, gl, gr

Be prepared

1. Daily drill

    Vowel flash cards (Review long vowel rules.)

    Consonant digraph flash cards

    Alphabet flash cards (Identify vowels when you come to them.)

    Alphabet recitation

2. Make wall charts for the new blends with vowels.

A. Introducing the blends

How many words can the children make with the ending _____*op*? Let them identify your blend in *flop.* You may use *free, glad,* and *gray* to introduce *fr, gl,* and *gr.* Practice the blends with vowels.

Seatwork   workbook, page 38

B. Using the blends   workbook, page 39 (top)

C. Reading   workbook, page 39 (edge list)

D. Spelling

Pronounce words for the children to spell.

Seatwork   workbook, page 39 (bottom)

The little *1* above some of the blanks indicates that rule one is to be used in the long vowel spelling.

Lesson 17   **Unit 2**   Gradebook: 28 points

fl	fr	gl	gr

fr og

fr esh

fr oze

fr ied

gr ain

gr ave

gr ass

gr oan

gl ass

gl ad

gl aze

gl ide

fl ag

fl ock

fl esh

fl eet

38

Phonics Workbook   **Lesson 17**

Finish the words.

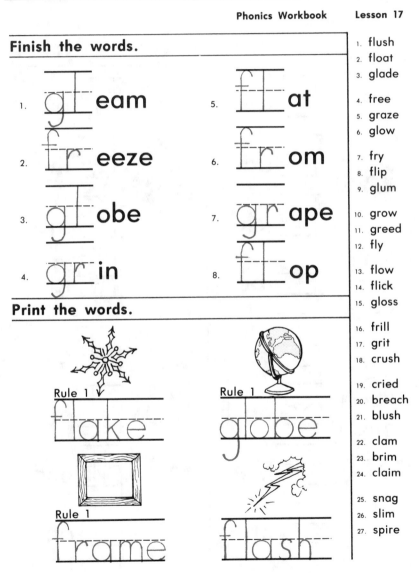

1. gl eam
2. fr eeze
3. gl obe
4. gr in
5. fl at
6. fr om
7. gr ape
8. fl op

Print the words.

Rule 1 flake

Rule 1 globe

Rule 1 frame

flash

1. flush
2. float
3. glade
4. free
5. graze
6. glow
7. fry
8. flip
9. glum
10. grow
11. greed
12. fly
13. flow
14. flick
15. gloss
16. frill
17. grit
18. crush
19. cried
20. breach
21. blush
22. clam
23. brim
24. claim
25. snag
26. slim
27. spire

39

LESSON 18
Consonant Blends: pl, pr tw, tr

Be prepared
1. Daily drill
    Vowel flash cards (Review the rules.)

Lesson 18   Unit 2

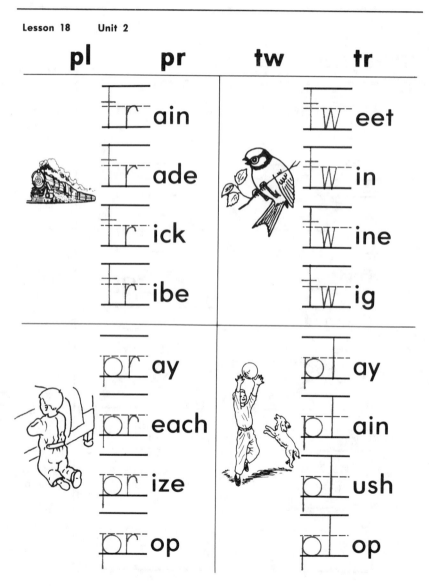

pl	pr	tw	tr

Tr ain

Tr ade

Tr ick

Tr ibe

Tw eet

Tw in

Tw ine

Tw ig

pr ay

pr each

pr ize

pr op

pl ay

pl ain

pl ush

pl op

Consonant digraph flash cards
Blends from the wall charts
Alphabet recitation

2. Make wall charts for the new blends with vowels.

Phonics Workbook **Lesson 18**

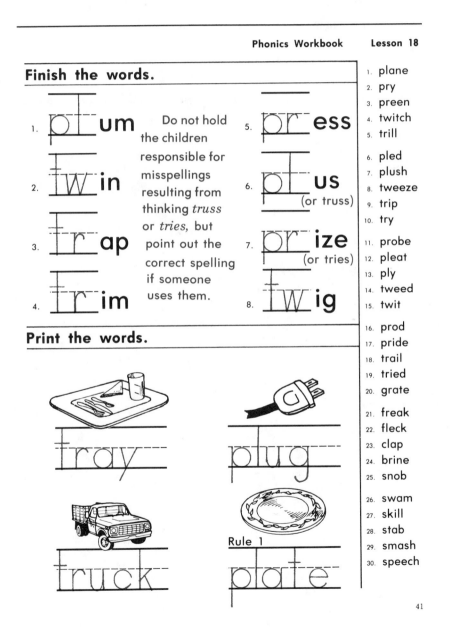

Finish the words.

1. plum
2. twin
3. trap
4. trim
5. press
6. plus (or truss)
7. prize (or tries)
8. twig

Do not hold the children responsible for misspellings resulting from thinking *truss* or *tries*, but point out the correct spelling if someone uses them.

Print the words.

tray

plug

truck

Rule 1

plate

1. plane
2. pry
3. preen
4. twitch
5. trill
6. pled
7. plush
8. tweeze
9. trip
10. try
11. probe
12. pleat
13. ply
14. tweed
15. twit
16. prod
17. pride
18. trail
19. tried
20. grate
21. freak
22. fleck
23. clap
24. brine
25. snob
26. swam
27. skill
28. stab
29. smash
30. speech

A. Introducing the blends

"What words can you make with ____*ay?* What do you hear when I say *play?* What do you hear in *pray?* What do you hear in *tray?*" Use the word *twin* to introduce *tw* in the same way. Print the new blends on the board and let the children list other words that begin with these blends.

Seatwork   workbook, page 40

B. Using the blends   workbook, page 41 (top)

C. Reading

Proceed with the edge list as usual.

D. Spelling

Dictate some words and have the children do workbook, page 41 (bottom).

LESSON 19
Review

Be prepared

Daily drill

    Vowel flash cards—Include the short vowels and macrons again.

    Consonant sound flash cards

    Consonant digraph flash cards

    Blends from the wall charts (Skip around with the pointer and have each
        child say just the blend and vowel sound to which you are pointing.)

    Alphabet recitation

A. Consonant blends

Print various blends on the board or show cards with blends and have
the children say words that begin with those blends.

Seatwork workbook, page 42

Have the children circle the correct blend for the initial sound of each
picture.

B. Vowel sounds workbook, page 43 (top)

Have the children print the correct vowel symbol in the blank after each
word.

C. Reading workbook, page 43 (edge and bottom)

Proceed with the edge list as usual, and have the children match the
rhymes at the bottom of page 43. Let them draw lines, then print the letters
in the blanks.

D. Spelling

Pronounce words for the children to spell.

Lesson 19   **Unit 2**   Gradebook: 20 points for this page

Circle the correct blends.

snake	clock	scooter	tree
(sn) sp sk	gr (cl) br	sn sl (sc)	gl (tr) pl

fruit	smile	pretzel	blueberries
tw cl (fr)	sn fl (sm)	(pr) sp sc	tw (bl) sm

crown	switch	steps	grasshopper
(cr) cl tr	(sw) sl fr	pr (st) sm	(gr) cr sc

gloves	skunk	twelve	flowers
(gl) bl br	sw pl (sk)	(tw) st tr	pr (fl) fr

sling	bread	spinning wheel	platter
(sl) cr sk	gl st (br)	gr bl (sp)	sw fl (pl)

| Phonics Workbook | Lesson 19 |

a ā e ē i ī o ō u ū

1. flow ō
2. faze ā
3. whip ī
4. track a
5. shoal ō
6. crutch u
7. prone ō
8. stew ū
9. clot o

10. clay ā
11. snub u
12. steam ē
13. fret e
14. hue ū
15. stain ā
16. try ī
17. chock o
18. tweet ē

19. go ō
20. dash a
21. she ē
22. toe ō
23. quite ī
24. flit i
25. cute ū
26. then e
27. pried ī

1. brass
2. whine
3. smash
4. still
5. grade
6. match
7. slime
8. bleat
9. each
10. snitch
11. plain
12. skin
13. faith
14. sweep
15. frail
16. twin
17. shake
18. stock
19. clan
20. glass
21. while
22. hatch
23. scope
24. treat
25. peach
26. spike
27. pry
28. spite

Match the words that rhyme.

d 1. preach a. slave
b 2. sneeze b. breeze
c 3. pleat c. sweet
e 4. green d. teach
a 5. clave e. clean

43

LESSON 20
Consonant Blends: dr, scr, str, spr

Be prepared
1. Daily drill
   Vowel flash cards—Include short vowels and macrons.

Lesson 20   Unit 2

dr	scr	str	spr

s**tr**etch   d**r**um
s**tr**eet   d**r**op
s**tr**ap   d**r**eam
s**tr**ipe   d**r**ain

s**pr**ain   s**cr**atch
s**pr**ee   s**cr**ape
s**pr**ig   s**cr**een
s**pr**y   s**cr**eam

44

Consonant digraph flash cards

Consonant blend flash cards—Find the other blends studied in set 6.
(Let the children say words beginning with the blends that you flash.)

Alphabet recitation

2. Make wall charts combining these blends with the vowels.

Phonics Workbook   Lesson 20

Finish the word.

1. dr__ ag

2. s t r __ eak

3. spr __ ig

4. scr __ eam
   (or stream or dream)

5. scr __ eech

6. spr __ ay
   (or stray)

7. dr __ ied

8. s t r __ uck

Print the word.

scrub

strike
Rule 1

spray

dress

Lesson 20

1. spry
2. stress
3. stream
4. drill
5. scrub
6. spree
7. stride
8. dry
9. strip
10. scruff
11. strive
12. strove
13. spry
14. sprat
15. drip
16. drug
17. drive
18. drove
19. scrape
20. sprain
21. drape
22. scribe
23. strain
24. stray
25. sprig
26. scream

45

A. Introducing the blends

Let the children make words with ____ess, then identify the blend in *dress*. Have them say other words they can think of with the same beginning blend.

"What words can you make with this ending? [Print ____eam on the board, and let them suggest some words.] What blend do you hear in *cream*? You have already studied that blend. Now listen carefully. What do you hear in *scream*? [Print the three letters on the board and circle them.] This is a blend with three letters. Can you think of any other words that begin with this blend?" Practice combining the blend with short and long vowels. Then print a few words on the board for the children to read.

scram   scrap   scrape   scratch   scribe   scrub

Show the ending ____ay, and let the children make words. If someone suggests the blend *tr* or *pr*, use it as part of another three-letter blend. The children may be able to say the word if you simply print the *s* before *tray* or *pray* and let them try it. Practice *str* and *spr* with vowel sounds, and print some words for the class to read.

strain	stroke	struck	street	strap
sprig	sprain	sprite	spry	spree

Seatwork   workbook, page 44

Have the children select the correct blends and print them in the blanks.

B. Using the blends   workbook, page 45 (top)

Have the children choose the correct blend for each word by sounding the different possibilities.

C. Reading

Do not be surprised if the children are slower on the triple blends.

D. Spelling

Pronounce some words from the edge list to spell.

Seatwork   workbook, page 45 (bottom)

"Print the word for each picture."

LESSON 21

Consonant Blends: spl, squ, shr, thr

Be prepared

1. Daily drill

> Consonant digraph flash cards
> Alphabet flash cards (Identify vowels as you come to them.)
> Blends from the wall charts
> Alphabet recitation

2. Make wall charts combining the new blends with vowels.

A. Introducing the blends

Use the ending ____*ay* to make words and go from *play* to *splay*. You may want to define the word to the children as meaning "spread out, as having the feet turned out extremely far." Give a few words for them to practice reading: *splash, split, spleen.*

Qu is not a consonant blend, but it has the sound of two consonants (*kw*). Form the word *squill* from *quill.* (Squill is a plant used for medicine.) Give a few words with the *squ* beginning for the children to read: *squeak, squeeze, squish.*

Print the ending ____*ub* for the children to make words. Print *rub.* "This blend is made with a digraph and a consonant. We will put the digraph *sh* before the *r*." Let someone say the word and practice the blend with vowel sounds. Print a few words to sound out: *shred, shrill, shrine, shrug.*

Using another digraph, go from ____*ob* to *rob* to *throb.* Practice the blend with vowels and practice some words: *thrill, throat, throw, throne, thrush.*

Seatwork   workbook, page 46

Have the children choose the correct blend for each word and print it in the blank. The children may notice that the pictures are labeled with letters instead of numbers. The letter has nothing to do with the answer that is to go in the blank.

B. Reading   workbook, page 47 (top and edge)

Let someone read the first sentence. Let another read it, and another, until the words are that familiar the children can think about what the sentence is saying rather than concentrating only on sounding the words. Then point out that all the pictures in the lesson are labeled by letters in boxes. "Can you find a picture that would be a good one for the sentence that we read? What is the letter for that picture? Print it on the blank before the sentence."

Study the next sentence together. Continue working with the children until you think they can handle the activity on their own. That may mean leaving only one or two sentences for them to do alone, or doing them all as a class activity.

Proceed with the edge list in the usual way.

C. Spelling

Pronounce some words from the edge list to spell.

Seatwork   workbook, page 47 (bottom)

Have the children print the words for the pictures. The letters with the pictures have nothing to do with the spelling.

Lesson 21   Unit 2

spl   squ   shr   thr

a. squeak

b. three

c. split

d. throw

e. shrub

f. squeeze

46

Phonics Workbook **Lesson 21**

Read the sentence. Find a picture.

b 1. The three did squeal and play.

f 2. Squeeze it till it is not wet.

g 3. The men thresh the wheat.

j 4. Do not scratch my throat.

e 5. We can trim the little shrub.

h 6. The fish can splash in the stream.

c 7. He will split something thick.

Print the words.

g.

thresh

h.

splash

i.
Rule 1

throne

j.
Rule 2

throat

1. squeal
2. shrug
3. shrine
4. thrill
5. throb
6. squish
7. split
8. thrush
9. shrill
10. squire
11. thrash
12. shred
13. squeak
14. splay
15. thrive
16. thrum
17. shrug
18. splat
19. squib
20. three
21. splash
22. throw
23. thrill
24. squeal
25. split

47

LESSON 22
Review

Be prepared
Daily drill
Consonant digraph flash cards

Lesson 22   Unit 2

Finish the words.

	gr pr	
	tr tw	

tr ee   Tr ap

pr ess   pr ick   gr ade
                  (or trick)   (or trade)

Tw ig   pr op   gr ow

	sw sp	
	st sk	

st ep   SW eet

sp eck   sp eak   sk ip

st ake   SW ine   st em
(or spake)   (or spine)

	cl bl	
	gl fl	

cl ack   cl ock
(or black)   (or block or flock)

cl ean   gl eam   cl ay
                        (or flay)

gl ad   bl ess   fl ow
(or clad)   (or glow or blow)

48

Vowel flash cards, without the short vowels and macrons
  (Review the rule and its number for each card.)
Alphabet recitation
Blends from the wall charts

Phonics Workbook   Lesson 22

Draw the pictures.

The breeze will dry the dress on the line.

Did she drop the dish that broke?

Fred got a frog from the stream.

1. splash
2. squeeze
3. shrine
4. stroke
5. fled
6. spray
7. frock
8. spleen
9. squish
10. slot
11. drill
12. gray
13. screech
14. throb
15. shrill
16. drone
17. throne
18. scrap
19. flee
20. drag
21. gloat
22. strife
23. thrush
24. strut
25. froth
26. squire
27. plead
28. spry
29. glaze
30. scrub

49

A. Consonant blends   workbook, page 48

"Try the blends given in the box in each section to make words. When you find a blend that fits, print it in the blank. Be sure to read your words after you have printed the blends."

Accept variations if they are words made with the blends given for the section.

B. Comprehending sentences workbook, page 49

Have the children read the sentences and draw a picture for each one.

C. Reading

Proceed with the edge list as usual.

D. Spelling

Pronounce some words from the edge list for spelling practice.

LESSON 23
Final Blends: lt, lk, lp, lf

Be prepared

1. Daily drill
   Vowel flash cards (Review rules.)
   Consonant sound flash cards
   Consonant digraph flash cards
   Consonant blend flash cards—Find the newly studied blend cards.
      (Let the children say words for the blends you flash.)
   Alphabet recitation
2. Make wall charts combining vowels and the final blends.

A. Introducing the blends

Print *fell* on the board and let someone say the word. Point to the double *l.* "These two letters make one sound at the end of the word. I will change the one letter and make a blend at the end of the word. We hear the sound of both letters in a blend. In a blend we never use two letters alike. [Erase the last *l* and replace it with *t.*]

"Can someone sound the new word?" List a few more words with the same ending for practice:

belt	stilt	cult
melt	wilt	
welt	quilt	

Print *mill* and form a blend by changing it to *milk.* Print these words for practice: *elk, silk, bulk, hulk, sulk.*

Print *gull* and change it to *gulp.* Print these words for practice: *help, yelp, scalp, pulp.*

Print *sell* and change it to *self.* Print these words for practice: *elf, shelf, gulf.*

Seatwork   workbook, page 50

This page is similar to those pages in lessons 13 to 20, except that all the words in one part end alike instead of beginning alike. Have the children print the correct blend at the end of each word.

B. Reading   workbook, page 51 (top and edge)

Help the children with the sentences and finding pictures.
Proceed with the edge list as usual.

C. Spelling

Pronounce some words from the edge list for the children to spell.

Seatwork   workbook, page 51 (bottom)

"Print the words for the pictures at the bottom of the page."
The row of pictures in the middle of the page may be ignored.

Lesson 23   Unit 2

lt   lk   lp   lf

be

me

ti

sti

a.

he

gu

ye

sca

b.

she

go

gu

se

c.

mi

su

hu

bu

d.

50

Phonics Workbook   **Lesson 23**

Find the pictures.

f 1. He felt a welt on his scalp.

d 2. Do not gulp the milk.

c 3. Put the quilt on the shelf.

e 4. Can you help me with the stilt?

g 5. I can tilt the stack my-self.

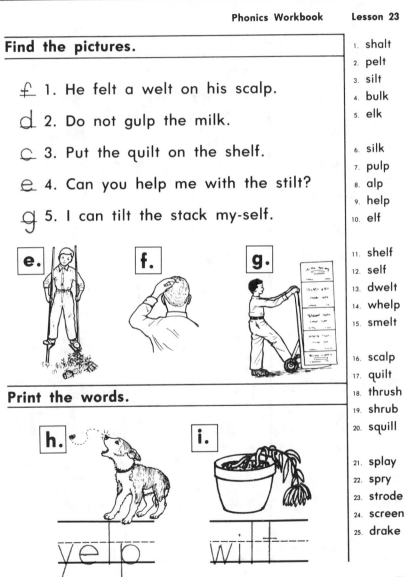

e.   **f.**   **g.**

Print the words.

h.   **i.**

yelp   wilt

1. shalt
2. pelt
3. silt
4. bulk
5. elk

6. silk
7. pulp
8. alp
9. help
10. elf

11. shelf
12. self
13. dwelt
14. whelp
15. smelt

16. scalp
17. quilt
18. thrush
19. shrub
20. squill

21. splay
22. spry
23. strode
24. screen
25. drake

51

LESSON 24
Final Blends: xt, sp, st, sk

Be prepared
1. Daily drill
   Vowel flash cards (Review rules.)

Lesson 24   Unit 2

xt   next   text

sp	st	sk
asp	list	ask
gasp	fast	husk
lisp	past	desk
wisp	vast	risk
grasp	twist	cask
crisp	rest	brisk

crisp

twist

?

ask

grasp

list

husk

52

Blends on the wall charts
Alphabet recitation
2. Make wall charts combining vowels and the final blends.
3. Look ahead to the general plan for unit 3 on page 118 of this manual. Plan and prepare for edge list charts if you want to use some.

Phonics Workbook   **Lesson 24**

Draw the pictures.

(individual preference)

The next thing to eat will be the best.

It is my task to dust the desk.

I see rust on the clasp of the belt.

1. disk
2. text
3. lest
4. blast
5. cast
6. hasp
7. quest
8. crest
9. flask
10. dusk
11. rasp
12. wisp
13. mast
14. best
15. pest
16. just
17. must
18. tusk
19. next
20. cask
21. test
22. west
23. bask
24. text
25. zest
26. rasp
27. mist
28. dust
29. crisp
30. task
31. last

A. Introducing the blends

Print *next* and *text* on the board. Hold your hand over the *t* and let the children sound the first three letters. Then expose the *t* and have them say it again and add the final sound. "There are not very many words that end with this blend. You can remember it by sounding the letters that you see in it."

Introduce the other blends by printing sample words for the children to sound.

In the workbook, have the children read the two words for the *xt* blend, then read the words under each of the other blends.

Seatwork workbook, page 52

Find a word in the lists for each picture and copy it on the lines.

B. Reading workbook, page 53

Have the children read the sentences and illustrate each one.

Proceed with the edge list as usual.

C. Spelling

Pronounce some words from the edge list for spelling practice.

Extra activity

Many of the words the children are sounding out are probably not a part of their vocabulary. Have them go through the edge list and list on writing paper all the words they know, or all the words they don't know. If listing all the words they know, you may have them give oral sentences using those words to you or an older student who has time to listen. If listing the ones they don't know, have a session when the meanings can be discussed.

LESSON 25

Final Blends: nt, ft, pt, ct

Be prepared

1. Daily drill

   Alphabet flash cards (Identify vowels.)

   Consonant digraph flash cards

   Blends from the wall charts

   Alphabet recitation

2. Make wall charts combining vowels with the new blends.

A. Introducing the blends

Print *ant, aft, apt,* and *act* on the board and see if the children can identify the one you say as they listen to the ending blend. Print additional words for them to practice sounding.

pant	raft	kept	fact
slant	shaft	wept	tact
sent	draft	slept	tract
mint	left	script	duct
grunt	swift	rapt	pact

Seatwork   workbook, page 54

Have the children find the correct blend for each section and print it in each of the blanks.

B. Reading   workbook, page 55 (top and edge)

Have the children find a picture for each sentence.

Proceed with the edge list as usual.

C. Spelling

Practice some of the words in the edge list.

Seatwork   workbook, page 55 (bottom)

Have the children print the words for the pictures.

Lesson 25   Unit 2

nt	**ft**	**pt**	**ct**

we**pt**

sle**pt**

cre**pt**

ke**pt**

a.

gi**ft**

le**ft**

shi**ft**

dri**ft**

b.

te**nt**

sla**nt**

pri**nt**

hu**nt**

c.

fa**ct**

tra**ct**

du**ct**

a**ct**

d.

$$2$$
$$\underline{+2}$$
$$4$$

Phonics Workbook **Lesson 25**

Find the pictures.

h 1. The raft may drift in the stream.

e 2. We had to squint in the sun.

b 3. I kept the gift you gave me.

g 4. God sent the rain for the plant.

f 5. The swift dog had to pant.

c 6. We slept in the tent.

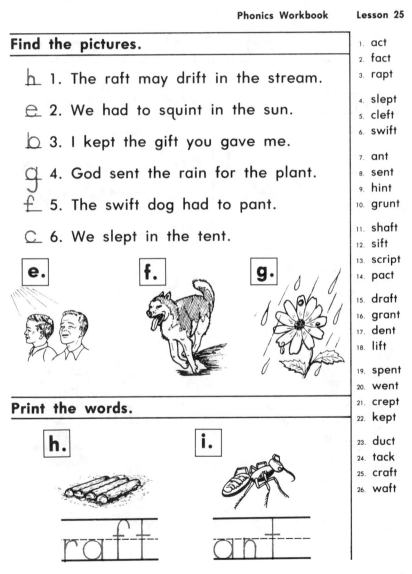

e. **f.** **g.**

Print the words.

h. **i.**

raft   ant

1. act
2. fact
3. rapt
4. slept
5. cleft
6. swift
7. ant
8. sent
9. hint
10. grunt
11. shaft
12. sift
13. script
14. pact
15. draft
16. grant
17. dent
18. lift
19. spent
20. went
21. crept
22. kept
23. duct
24. tack
25. craft
26. waft

LESSON 26
Endings: mp, nd, nk, ng

Be prepared

1. Daily drill

Vowels—Include short vowels and macrons.

Lesson 26   Unit 2

mp	**nd**	**nk**	**ng**

ha n̄d̄

spe n̄d̄

sa n̄d̄

me n̄d̄

ta n̄k̄

cra n̄k̄

thi n̄k̄

tru n̄k̄

wi n̄ḡ

si n̄ḡ

ba n̄ḡ

bri n̄ḡ

la m̄p̄

ju m̄p̄

da m̄p̄

li m̄p̄

Blends from the wall charts
Alphabet recitation
2. Make wall charts combining vowels with the new endings.

A. Introducing the endings
Pronounce the sample words *lamp* and *land* slowly, dwelling on the

---

Phonics Workbook   Lesson 26

Draw the pictures.

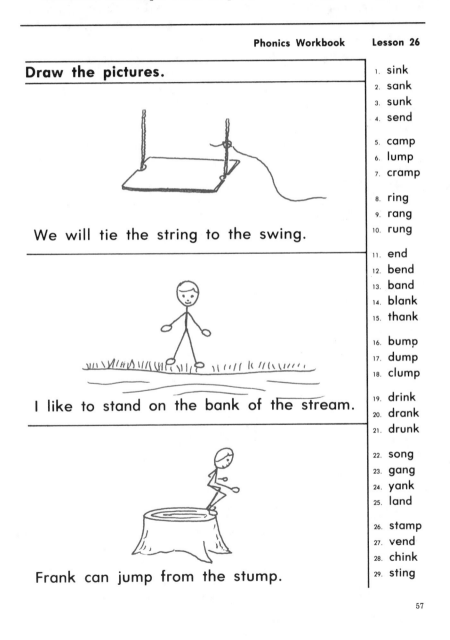

We will tie the string to the swing.

I like to stand on the bank of the stream.

Frank can jump from the stump.

1.	sink
2.	sank
3.	sunk
4.	send
5.	camp
6.	lump
7.	cramp
8.	ring
9.	rang
10.	rung
11.	end
12.	bend
13.	band
14.	blank
15.	thank
16.	bump
17.	dump
18.	clump
19.	drink
20.	drank
21.	drunk
22.	song
23.	gang
24.	yank
25.	land
26.	stamp
27.	vend
28.	chink
29.	sting

endings and see if the children can identify the letters in the blends. Print a few words for the children to practice sounding.

camp	limp	sand	bend
bump	pump	mend	pond

Print *think* and *thing* on the board and pronounce them for the children to identify according to the ending sound. Notice that you do not hear a separate /n/ and /g/ sound in the last ending. *Ng* is a digraph. Print some words for the children to practice.

sank	blank	bang	clang
pink	blink	song	strong
skunk	junk	hung	spring

Seatwork workbook, page 56

B. Reading workbook, page 57

Have the children illustrate each sentence and read the edge list.

C. Spelling

Practice some words from the edge list.

LESSON 27
Review

Be prepared

Daily drill

    Digraph flash cards, consonant and vowel

    Consonant blend flash cards—Include all the newly studied ones from
        set 6.

    Alphabet recitation

A. Comprehending sentences   workbook, page 58

Have the children read the sentences and match a picture to each one.

B. Forming words

Print the following arrangement of letters on the board.

d	a	mp
f	e	sk
l	i	ct
n	o	lt
r	u	xt

"We will make some words with these parts of words. [Point to the first
list.] This list of consonants is for the beginning of our words. The vowels
in the middle list are for the middle, and the last list is for the endings to
our words. [Slide your finger from *d* to *a* to *mp*.] We can make the word *damp*.
[Print that word to one side of the columns.] We can use the *d* again and
make *d-e-sk*. [Connect the letters with your finger and print the word under
damp.] We can use the *sk* again and make *disk*. [Connect the letters with
your finger and add the word to the list.] We can use any of the letters again.
We can make *dusk*." Compose a few words beginning with *f* then give the
children a chance to show with their fingers any words they see they can
make.

Seatwork   workbook, page 59

Have the children print the words they can make by combining the letters
at the top of the page.

C. Reading

Proceed with the edge list as usual.

D. Spelling

Pronounce some words from the edge list for the children to spell.

Extra activity

Let the children list on paper other words that they can make with the
letters on page 59 of the workbook after the spaces on the page are filled.

Lesson 27   Unit 2

Match the pictures and sentences.

c 1. We like to romp and jump.

f 2. He left his soft bed.

a 3. The quilt felt good.

g 4. The bump made a lump on his leg.

d 5. She did spill the milk on the silk.

b 6. I like to see them rest in the nest.

h 7. We will help to fill the shelf.

e 8. I will ask to sit at the next desk.

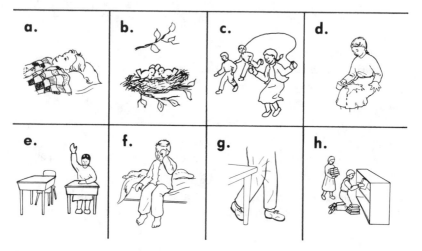

a.   b.   c.   d.

e.   f.   g.   h.

Phonics Workbook   **Lesson 27**

Make words.

s	a	ng
b	e	nk
t	i	nt
p	o	st
l	u	nd

song

pong

sang	pest	pond
bang	tend	sung
sent	sing	sunk
pend	sink	bunk
tent	pink	lung
test	link	lust

1. clank
2. brand
3. next
4. fang
5. mink
6. squint
7. crust
8. hang
9. chest
10. scant
11. quest
12. slang
13. wend
14. sprint
15. cling
16. welt
17. champ
18. text
19. trust
20. ding
21. dong
22. frond
23. zest
24. brink

LESSON 28
Endings: nch, ild, ind

Be prepared
1. Daily drill
   Alphabet flash cards (Identify vowels.)

Lesson 28   Unit 2

nch	**īld**	**īnd**
inch	wild	find
bench	mild	blind
finch	child	mind
bunch		

Mark the long vowels.

1. kīnd	9. blink	17. chīld
2. kill	10. blīnd	18. chill
3. king	11. wilt	19. chink
4. miss	12. wīld	20. grist
5. mīld	13. hint	21. grīnd
6. mīnd	14. hīnd	22. grill
7. ring	15. wīnd	23. fīnd
8. rīnd	16. wish	24. fist

lunch, branch

60

Consonant blend and consonant digraph flash cards mixed (Tell the
children to raise their hands every time they see a digraph card.
Then call on someone to say, "A digraph makes one sound.")
Alphabet recitation

2. Make a wall chart combining the *nch* ending with vowels, and one with
ild and *ind.*

Phonics Workbook   **Lesson 28**

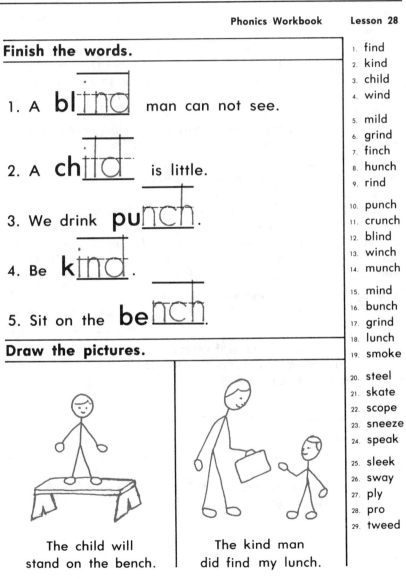

Finish the words.

1. A **bl**ind man can not see.

2. A **ch**ild is little.

3. We drink **pu**nch.

4. Be **k**ind.

5. Sit on the **be**nch.

Draw the pictures.

The child will
stand on the bench.

The kind man
did find my lunch.

1. find
2. kind
3. child
4. wind
5. mild
6. grind
7. finch
8. hunch
9. rind
10. punch
11. crunch
12. blind
13. winch
14. munch
15. mind
16. bunch
17. grind
18. lunch
19. smoke
20. steel
21. skate
22. scope
23. sneeze
24. speak
25. sleek
26. sway
27. ply
28. pro
29. tweed

A. Introducing the endings

Print *bun* on the board. "We are going to make a blend for the end of this word by putting a digraph with the *n*." Print *ch* at the end of the word and have the children say it adding the /ch/ sound at the end. Print a few more words for practice.

bench	finch	punch	winch
hunch	munch	pinch	crunch

Print *ild* and *ind* on the board and ask the children if these letters are consonants or vowels. "These are special endings. When you see *ld* or *nd* after vowel *i*, the word usually has a long *i* sound. When else does a word have the long vowel sound? [Print *wild* on the board.] This word does not have an *e* at the end. It does not have two vowels together. It does not have the only vowel at the end of the word. But because it has this special ending, the word has the long *i* sound. What is the word?" Use the word *kind* as another example. Have the children open their workbooks to page 60 and read the words under the long *i* endings for practice.

Seatwork workbook, page 60

The children are to find words in the lists on the page for each of the pictures and print them on the lines.

In the middle of the page, have the children find the words that will have the long *i* sound and mark those with a macron. If you think the children may have trouble with this exercise, have them first find all the words with the special endings shown at the top of the page and circle the *ld* or *nd* each time they find it. Then they should mark the *i* in those words with a macron.

B. Using the endings workbook, page 61 (top)

Have the children find the correct ending for each word and print it in the sentences.

C. Reading workbook, page 61 (bottom and edge)

"Read the sentences and draw the pictures."

Proceed with the edge list as usual.

D. Spelling

Practice some words from the edge list.

Extra activities

Have the children read the words listed in the middle of page 60 in the workbook.

Have the children print the words from numbers 19-29 in the edge list on a paper under headings according to long vowel rules 1, 2, and 3.

LESSON 29
Endings: old, olt, ost, oll

Be prepared

1. Daily drill

 Consonant digraph flash cards

 Vowel flash cards, without the short vowels and macrons
   (Review the rule for each spelling.)

 Blends from the wall charts

 Alphabet recitation

2. Make a wall chart with the *old, olt, ost, oll* endings.

A. Introducing the endings

"There are a number of special endings for long *o* as well as for long *i*. [Print *cold* on the board.] This word does not have an *e* at the end. It does not have two vowels together. It does not have the only vowel at the end of the word, but it has the long vowel sound. What is the word?" Tell the children to open their workbooks to page 62 and let them practice the words in the column under ōld. Show them the other two-consonant endings that make the long *o* sound and have them practice reading those words.

"For every rule that we study in phonics, there are some words that do not follow the rule. You have learned some words like that already in reading. And you will find more such words as you learn to read more. [Print *cost* on the board.] This word breaks the rule. It says *cost*. [Print *doll*.] This word breaks the rule. It says *doll*."

"Use the rule and say long *o* for all the words with these endings in your lesson today."

Seatwork   workbook, page 62

For each picture, have the children print a word from the list above.

B. Using the endings   workbook, page 63

If they need the help, have the children again circle the endings given in the rule before they mark the vowels.

Have the children find the right ending to finish the words in the sentences at the bottom of the page.

C. Reading

Proceed with the edge list as usual.

D. Spelling

Pronounce some words from the edge list for the children to spell.

ōld

bold

told

mold

cold

sold

fold

scold

hold

gold

ōlt

jolt

bolt

colt

molt

ōll

roll

toll

droll

stroll

troll

scroll

boll

ōst

most

post

host

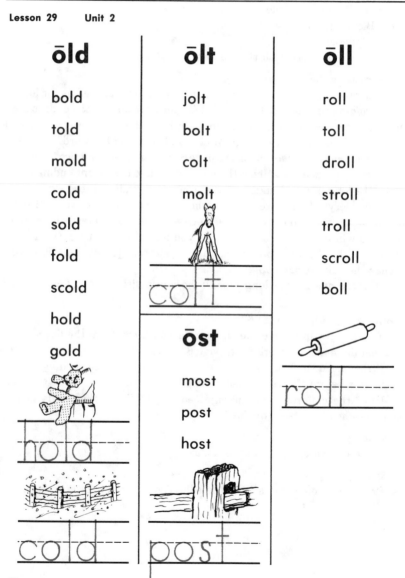

Phonics Workbook   Lesson 29

Mark the long vowels.

1. fōld	8. trot	15. jolt
2. crop	9. pōst	16. most
3. scōld	10. boll	17. from
4. smock	11. bōlt	18. gold
5. scrōll	12. clock	19. blob
6. mōlt	13. bold	20. throb
7. flock	14. rōll	21. host

Finish the words.

1. It was a very **c o l d** day.

2. I like to **str o l l** on the path.

3. She ate the **m o s t** pie.

4. Mother **t o l d** me to help.

5. The **c o l t** can run.

1. bold
2. stroll
3. find
4. mild
5. molt
6. blind
7. cold
8. roll
9. scroll
10. host
11. fold
12. gold
13. jolt
14. kind
15. wind
16. scold
17. toll
18. pinch
19. post
20. bolt
21. crunch
22. wild
23. bold
24. colt
25. child
26. most

63

LESSON 30
Review

Be prepared
Daily drill
    Consonant blend flash cards

Lesson 30   Unit 2   Gradebook: 48 points

ā a   ē e   ī i   ō o   ū u

1. chaff	ă	13. mail	ā	25. roll	ō
2. post	ō	14. neck	ĕ	26. by	ī
3. way	ā	15. child	ī	27. chop	ŏ
4. rove	ō	16. foe	ō	28. bee	ē
5. thick	ĭ	17. much	ŭ	29. quack	ă
6. find	ī	18. hike	ī	30. die	ī
7. due	ū	19. lift	ĭ	31. sold	ō
8. cask	ă	20. mew	ū	32. shut	ŭ
9. jolt	ō	21. hoax	ō	33. bean	ē
10. cure	ū	22. shock	ŏ	34. when	ĕ
11. self	ĕ	23. bill	ĭ	35. lame	ā
12. ye	ē	24. row	ō	36. so	ō

Vowel flash cards—Include the short vowels and macrons.
Special endings from the wall charts
Alphabet recitation

Phonics Workbook   Lesson **30**

Underline the correct word.

1. The egg will ___ if you drop it.
   <u>smash</u>   flash   slash

2. He ___ the old truck.
   grove   stove   <u>drove</u>

3. Mother will ___ the cream from the milk.
   <u>skim</u>   swim   snip

4. Did the cat ___ your hand?
   scotch   <u>scratch</u>   speech

5. We like ___ peaches.
   brush   blush   <u>fresh</u>

6. We will ___ to do good work.
   fly   spry   <u>try</u>

7. She saw a ___ on the clean glass.
   squeak   <u>streak</u>   sneak

8. A new game will ___ the child.
   shrill   <u>thrill</u>   twill

9. Mother will ___ the hole in my sleeve.
   melt   milk   <u>mend</u>

10. Did you ___ up your coat?
    help   hasp   <u>hang</u>

11. We will ___ God to help us.
    <u>ask</u>   ant   act

12. The ___ day we had rain.
    <u>next</u>   kept   camp

65

A. Vowel sounds   workbook, page 64

Have the children sound each word and print the symbol for the vowel sound in the blank.

B. Comprehending sentences   workbook, page 65

"Underline the best word for the blank in each sentence."

C. Reading

Part or all of the words on page 64 may be used as the edge list.

D. Spelling

Any of the words in the lesson may be used for spelling practice.

Extra activity

Have the children choose one of the sentences from page 65 and copy it on a paper and illustrate it.

Phonics
Unit 3

GENERAL PLAN

Continue to drill, drill, drill. Following the suggested review schedule at the beginning of each lesson in the teacher's guide will insure coverage of the material you should be reviewing. Aim to review all of the suggested sets in the day, but they need not be done all in one session. Conduct short drill sessions at various times during the day.

Continue the routine reading of the edge list. Review the suggestions given on page 16 of this manual and evaluate your system. Are you being as efficient as possible?

Do the children enjoy the challenge of increasing their speed? You may spark fresh inspiration by providing a new type of chart. In art class, let each child prepare a paper on which may be pasted seals with the theme of your choice. Give each child a seal for each lesson in which he succeeds *his own* record established in unit 2. The chart at the end of the workbook may be kept up as usual to serve as a reference for the chart with seals.

The children will become acquainted with oral spelling in the process of this unit if you follow the suggestions given for spelling in each lesson. Occasionally pronounce a list of words for the children to print on paper, and do not have them spelled orally. Check the papers yourself and enter the scores in the gradebook as part of the phonics grade.

Phonics Lessons   Unit 3

Lesson   **Page**

1. Digraph: o͞o 120
2. Digraph: oo 123
3. Other Spellings for /o͞o/ and /oo/ 126
4. Diphthongs: oi, oy 129
5. Diphthongs: ou, ow 132
6. Review 136
7. Modified Vowel: ėr (er, ir, ur) 139
8. Modified Vowel: är 142
9. Modified Vowel: ôr 145
10. Review of Modified Vowels 148
11. Vowel Sound: ô 151
12. Digraph aw = /ô/ 154
13. Other Spellings for /ô/ 157
14. Sometimes s = /z/ 160
15. Suffixes in Plurals: s, es 163
16. Suffixes in Verbs: s, es 166
17. Suffix: ed 169
18. Suffix: ing 172
19. Review of Suffixes 175
20. Two-Syllable Words 178
21. Sometimes y = /ē/ 181
22. Sometimes c = /s/ 184
23. Sometimes g = /j/ 187
24. The Letters dge = /j/ 190
25. Review Long Vowel Rules 193
26. Review o Sounds and Diphthongs 196
27. Review Modified Vowels 199
28. Review Consonant Blends 202
29. Review Sounds of s and y 205
30. Review Sounds of c and g 208

Be prepared
Daily drill
    Wall charts (Practice blends

Lesson 1   Unit 3

o̅o̅

Draw the pictures.

| room | bloom | stool |

Print the words.

a.

coon

b.

food

c.

boot

d.

spool

e.

broom

f.

spoon

68

Vowel flash cards—Separate into two packs. Put the short vowels and the vowels marked with macrons into one pack which will be referred to as *vowel sounds*. The other pack containing the long vowel spellings will be called *vowel spellings*. (Drill the vowel spellings, having the children identify the rule number and quote the rule for each one.)

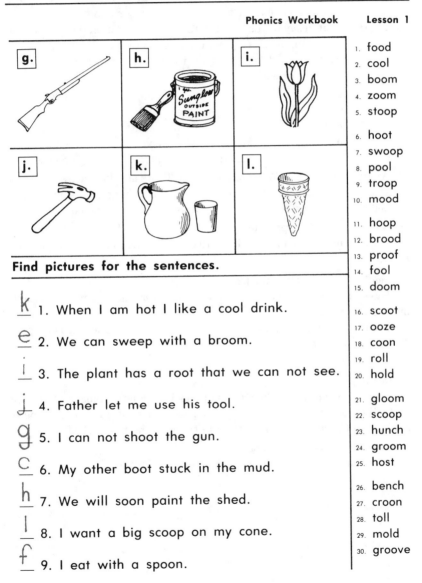

Phonics Workbook   **Lesson 1**

g.	1. food
h.	2. cool
i.	3. boom
	4. zoom
	5. stoop
	6. hoot
	7. swoop
j.	8. pool
k.	9. troop
l.	10. mood
	11. hoop
	12. brood
	13. proof
	14. fool

Find pictures for the sentences.

15. doom

<u>k</u> 1. When I am hot I like a cool drink.   16. scoot

<u>e</u> 2. We can sweep with a broom.   17. ooze
                                                 18. coon
<u>i</u> 3. The plant has a root that we can not see.   19. roll
                                                 20. hold
<u>j</u> 4. Father let me use his tool.

<u>g</u> 5. I can not shoot the gun.   21. gloom
                                        22. scoop
<u>c</u> 6. My other boot stuck in the mud.   23. hunch
                                        24. groom
<u>h</u> 7. We will soon paint the shed.   25. host

<u>l</u> 8. I want a big scoop on my cone.   26. bench
                                        27. croon
<u>f</u> 9. I eat with a spoon.   28. toll
                                        29. mold
                                        30. groove

A. Introducing the sound

"What is the word at the top of page 68 in your phonics book? What sound do you hear in the middle of *moon*? What letter do you think makes the /o͞o/ sound?

"We use two letters together to say /o͞o/." Print o͞o on the board and tell the children that it is also a long vowel sound so we mark it with a macron. Print ū as well and have the children compare the two sounds. The sound /ū/ is the same as /o͞o/ except that we begin it by saying /y/.

Let the children say words they can think of that contain the /o͞o/ sound.

If you have a capable class, you may want to test them on hearing the difference between /ū/ and /o͞o/ by saying these words and letting them point to the vowel sound for each one.

mew	moo	pew	pool
hew	who	cool	cute
food	few	beauty	bootie
fuel	fool	coon	cubic
hoop	human	music	moose

Avoid stressing the /ū/ sound if your students are slow in grasping new material. Emphasize /o͞o/ and practice words containing that sound. After the children have mastered /o͞o/ you may profitably compare the two sounds.

Seatwork   workbook, page 68 (middle)

Let the children figure out the words in the boxes and draw pictures for them.

B. Reading   workbook, page 69

Have the children read the sentences and print the letter of a suitable picture before each sentence.

Let the children read the edge list in lesson 1. Use the words on page 64 for the timed drill.

C. Spelling

Pronounce words for the children to spell with letter blocks or to print on the board. After each word is arranged or printed, call on someone to read aloud the names of the letters in the word he has spelled.

Seatwork   workbook, page 68 (bottom)

Have the children print the words for the pictures.

LESSON 2

Digraph: oo

Be prepared

Daily drill

> Vowel sound flash cards, as separated in lesson 1—Include /o͞o/ from
> set 5.

> Consonant digraph flash cards

A. Introducing the sound

"What is the picture at the top of page 70 in your phonics workbook?
What sound do you hear in the middle of *book*? This is another new sound,
but we do not have a new letter for the sound. How do we write the sound?
We use the same two letters we used to write /o͞o/. The sound /oo/ is the
short sound for those two letters."

Play the listening game as in unit 1, listening for the medial /oo/ sound,
or let the children think of words in which they hear /oo/.

good	hoop	shook	rule
book	wood	hook	fishhook
goat	wooly	cool	crooked
hood	stone	spoon	mustard
hot	look	stood	puddle
foot	food	homemade	bookmark
cook	but	rush	foolish

Seatwork workbook, page 70 (middle)

Let the children figure out the phrases in the boxes and draw pictures
for them.

B. Reading workbook, page 71

The children are to read the first sentence saying "blank" for the blank
space, then re-read it, trying words from the list at the top until they find
one that makes sense. They are to print the correct word in the blank and
proceed to do each sentence in the same way.

Have each child read the edge list to someone, then give timed tests of
30 seconds on the list in lesson 1. The scores may be marked in the space
for lesson 2 on the chart at the back of the workbook.

C. Spelling

"What is the rule for the /k/ sound at the end of a short vowel word?"
Have the children spell *lock* with their letter blocks. Then ask them how we
should spell the vowel sound for *look*. "Although /oo/ is a short vowel sound,
we do not use *ck* after two o's. When you spell words with the /k/ sound
after /oo/, use the *k* by itself. Spell *hook*."

Give additional words for spelling practice, and after each one have someone name the letters he used to spell the word.

124   *Unit 3   Phonics*

Seatwork   workbook, page 70 (bottom)
   Have the children print the words for the pictures.

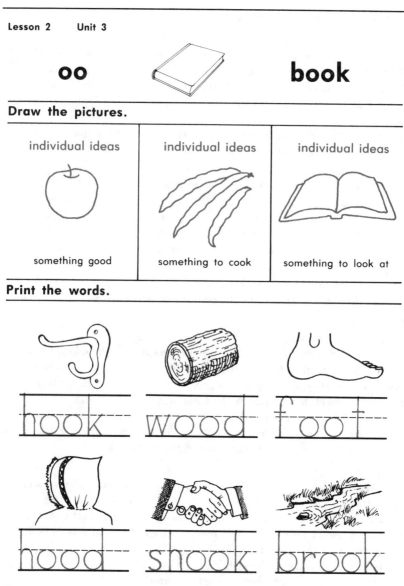

Lesson 2   Unit 3

oo   **book**

Draw the pictures.

individual ideas	individual ideas	individual ideas
something good	something to cook	something to look at

Print the words.

hook   wood   foot

hood   shook   brook

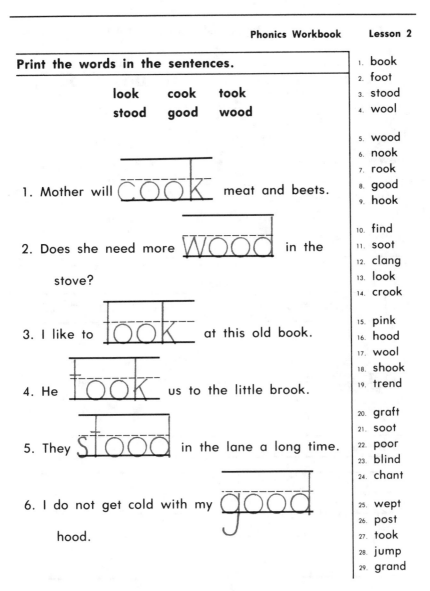

Phonics Workbook   **Lesson 2**

Print the words in the sentences.

look   cook   took
stood   good   wood

1. Mother will COOK meat and beets.

2. Does she need more WOOD in the stove?

3. I like to look at this old book.

4. He took us to the little brook.

5. They stood in the lane a long time.

6. I do not get cold with my good hood.

1. book
2. foot
3. stood
4. wool

5. wood
6. nook
7. rook
8. good
9. hook

10. find
11. soot
12. clang
13. look
14. crook

15. pink
16. hood
17. wool
18. shook
19. trend

20. graft
21. soot
22. poor
23. blind
24. chant

25. wept
26. post
27. took
28. jump
29. grand

71

LESSON 3
Other Spellings for /o͞o/ and /oo/

Be prepared
Daily drill
Vowel sound flash cards—Include /oo/ from set 5.

Lesson 3   Unit 3   Gradebook: 36 points for the whole lesson

o͞o

| ew = o͞o | | | ue = o͞o |

flew	grew	drew	true
screw	crew	brew	blue
chew	blew	slew	clue
shrew	threw	screw	flue
grew	strew	chew	glue

---

oo

| u = oo | ou or o = oo |

pull	would
full	could
bush	should
push	wolf
put	

Finish the words.

grew   glue   drew

threw   bush   put

Vowel spelling flash cards—Include *ild, ind, old, oll, olt, ost,* from set 9.
(Let the children say, "Rule 4, special endings" for those cards.)
Blends from the wall charts.

A. Introducing the spellings

Help the children to read the equations in the four boxes.

Phonics Workbook   Lesson 3

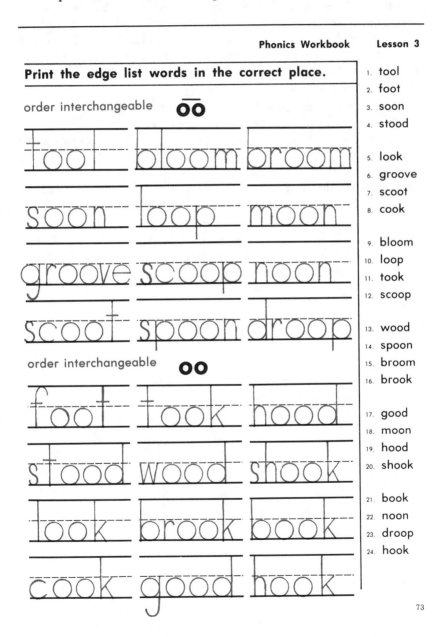

Print the edge list words in the correct place.

order interchangeable $\overline{OO}$

tool   bloom   broom

soon   loop   moon

groove scoop   noon

scoot   spoon   droop

order interchangeable   OO

foot   took   hood

stood   wood   shook

look   brook   book

cook   good   hook

1. tool
2. foot
3. soon
4. stood
5. look
6. groove
7. scoot
8. cook
9. bloom
10. loop
11. took
12. scoop
13. wood
14. spoon
15. broom
16. brook
17. good
18. moon
19. hood
20. shook
21. book
22. noon
23. droop
24. hook

73

You may tell them to circle the letter combinations in the words listed under the pictures. Have them practice sounding the words and underline the one in each list that best fits with the picture above it. Notice that the *ou* words contain a silent *l*. These words are all reading vocabulary words.

Seatwork workbook, page 72 (bottom)

The list of words to finish is a hunt-and-find exercise. Each of the words appears in one of the lists on the page. The children will need to find the words and print the correct vowel combinations to finish them. If you have an exceptional class you may have them try filling in the words before they find them on the page to see if they can spell them correctly. They should then change any that they have misspelled.

B. Reading workbook, page 73

Tell the children to try the words in the edge list with /o͞o/ and with /oo/ to decide what the word is. Print each word in the correct part of the page.

If you wish to avoid the trial and error pronunciation when reading the edge list, have the children read the words from the columns they have printed. Give the 30-second timed reading from lesson 2.

C. Spelling

Pronounce some words from the edge list for the children to spell. Also give some words in which *ck* follows a short vowel. Let someone spell each word aloud after it has been arranged or printed.

LESSON 4
Diphthongs: oi, oy

Be prepared

1. Daily drill

Vowel sound flash cards—Include *ue* from set 5.

Alphabet flash cards (Have the children identify the vowels as you come to them, telling when it is a vowel in the case of *y* or *w*.)

Wall charts (Practice the special endings, referring to them as *rule 4*.)

2. Locate *oi* and *oy* flash cards in set 7.

A. Introducing the sound

Say the following sentence while the children listen. "Roy spoiled the boys' joy with annoying noise." Can they tell you what recurring sound they heard? Let them list other words if they can which contain the same sound. Show the flash card with the diphthong *oi* and tell the children that these two letters together stand for the /oi/ sound.

Have the children open their phonics workbooks to page 74 and print the words for the two pictures at the top of the page.

Direct attention to the *oy* spelling at the edge of the page. Tell the children that this is another way to spell the /oi/ sound. The letter *y* is a vowel again when it is used to help spell the /oi/ sound. We use *oi* when /oi/ is in the middle of a word and *oy* when /oi/ is at the end of a word.

Let the children print the words for the second row of pictures.

Review with the children the times when *y* and *w* are vowels. (ay, -y, ow, ew, oy)

Seatwork workbook, page 74

Have the children choose the best word in the row for each picture and circle it.

At the bottom of the page, have them find and circle all the vowels including *y* and *w* when they are vowels.

B. Reading workbook, page 75 (bottom and edge)

The children are to read the sentences at the bottom of the page and find a picture in the lesson to fit with each sentence. Have them print the letter of the picture in the blank before the sentence. Number 2 could have more than one correct letter. If someone realizes that and asks what to do, encourage them to use both letters.

Let each child read the edge list, then give him a timed test from lesson 3, using the edge list or his printed columns as you decide.

C. Spelling

Ask the children to give several ways to spell the /ā/ sound. Print *ai* and *ay* on the board when you get those responses, then ask them which spelling is used for the end of a word. Circle or underline *ay*.

Then ask the children if they can give the spellings for /oi/. Print *oi* and *oy* on the board and ask which should be used at the end of a word. Circle or underline *oy* and ask the children if they notice anything alike about the two rules. In each case it is the *y* spelling that belongs at the end.

Lesson 4   Unit 3

oi

oi

a.

b.

coin

point

Circle the correct word.

join   foil   spoil   (soil)   hoist

oy

c.   **d.**   **e.**

joy   boy   toy

Circle the correct word.

soy   (Roy)   coy   toy   joy

Circle all the vowels.

spr(ay)	sto(o)p	h(ue)	st(y)	g(o)
wh(ea)t	tr(ay)	gr(ow)	st(oo)d	fr(ai)l
pr(y)	l(oo)m	bl(ue)	thr(ew)	b(e)
sh(oo)k	p(u)ll	f(u)ll	fl(ow)	cr(ew)

74

Pronounce words from the edge list for the children to spell individually calling for oral spelling after each word.

Seatwork workbook, page 75 (top and middle)

Following the rule that *oy* and *ay* are used at the end of words, have the children print the letter combinations in the blanks.

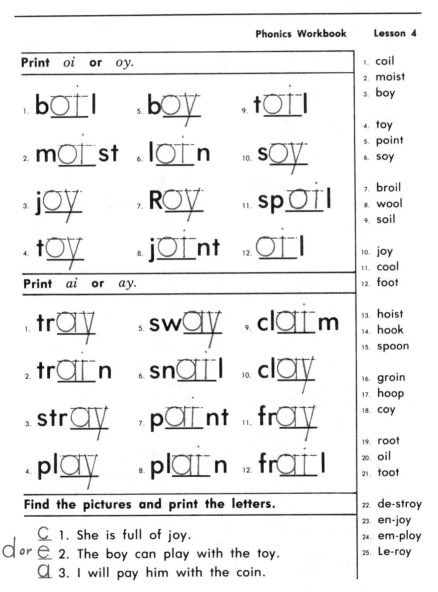

	Phonics Workbook	Lesson 4

Print *oi* **or** *oy*.

1. b_oi_l   5. b_oy_   9. t_oi_l

2. m_oi_st 6. l_oi_n 10. s_oy_

3. j_oy_   7. R_oy_   11. sp_oi_l

4. t_oy_   8. j_oi_nt 12. _oi_l

Print *ai* **or** *ay*.

1. tr_ay_   5. sw_ay_ 9. cl_ai_m

2. tr_ai_n 6. sn_ai_l 10. cl_ay_

3. str_ay_ 7. p_ai_nt 11. fr_ay_

4. pl_ay_   8. pl_ai_n 12. fr_ai_l

Find the pictures and print the letters.

_C_ 1. She is full of joy.

d or _e_ 2. The boy can play with the toy.

_a_ 3. I will pay him with the coin.

Edge list:
1. coil
2. moist
3. boy
4. toy
5. point
6. soy
7. broil
8. wool
9. soil
10. joy
11. cool
12. foot
13. hoist
14. hook
15. spoon
16. groin
17. hoop
18. coy
19. root
20. oil
21. toot
22. de-stroy
23. en-joy
24. em-ploy
25. Le-roy

LESSON 5

Diphthongs: ou, ow

Be prepared

1. Daily drill

Vowel sound flash cards—Include *oi* and *oy*.

Lesson 5   Unit 3

OU

OU

1 2 3 4 5

cloud mouth count

Circle the correct word.

house   sour   (mouse)   stout   loud

OW

cow   town   crown

Circle the correct word.

(frown)   growl   fowl   brown   how

OW   1.   2.   3.

n ow   h ow l   d ow n

76

Consonant digraph flash cards
Blends from the wall charts

2. Find the *ou* and *ow* cards in set 7.
3. Plan to spend more time than usual with the spelling section of this lesson.
4. Prepare the wall chart for the *ow* spelling rule as shown on page 10 of this manual.

Phonics Workbook   Lesson 5

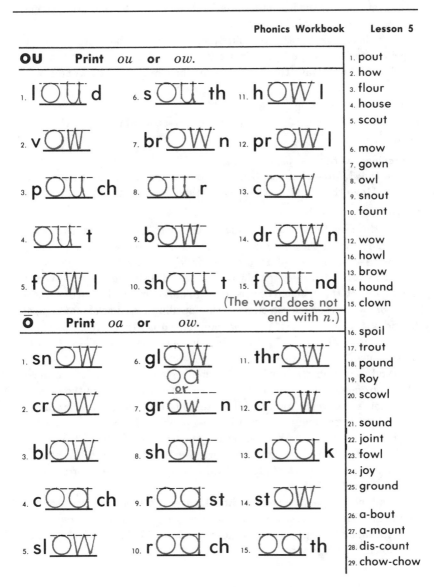

	OU Print *ou* or *ow*.	
1. l OU d	6. s OU th	11. h OW l
2. v OW	7. br OW n	12. pr OW l
3. p OU ch	8. OU r	13. c OW
4. OU t	9. b OW	14. dr OW n
5. f OW l	10. sh OU t	15. f OU nd

(The word does not end with *n*.)

	Ō Print *oa* or *ow*.	
1. sn OW	6. gl OW / OQ *or*	11. thr OW
2. cr OW	7. gr OW n	12. cr OW
3. bl OW	8. sh OW	13. cl OQ k
4. c OQ ch	9. r OQ st	14. st OW
5. sl OW	10. r OQ ch	15. OQ th

1. pout
2. how
3. flour
4. house
5. scout
6. mow
7. gown
8. owl
9. snout
10. fount
12. wow
16. howl
13. brow
14. hound
15. clown
16. spoil
17. trout
18. pound
19. Roy
20. scowl
21. sound
22. joint
23. fowl
24. joy
25. ground
26. a-bout
27. a-mount
28. dis-count
29. chow-chow

77

A. Introducing the sound

Ask the children what they say when they stub a toe, or get a bee sting or a scratch. Show them the card with the diphthong *ou* and tell them that these two letters stand for the /ou/ sound. Solicit words with the /ou/ sound from the class.

Have the class open their phonics books to page 76 and name the pictures in the first row. Let them print the words, then direct attention to the second spelling at the edge of the page.

W is also a vowel in this combination. The children have studied *ow* as a spelling for the long *o* sound, but tell them that it also makes the /ou/ sound sometimes. Have the children print the words for the second row of pictures.

Seatwork workbook, page 76

Let the children choose and circle the correct word in each row for the small pictures.

B. Reading workbook, page 77 (edge)

Tell the children that *ow* spells the /ou/ sound whenever it appears in the list. Have them read the words and take the timed test in lesson 4.

C. Spelling

Ask the class for various spellings of the long *o* sound. Print *oa* and *ow* on the board when they are given. Let the children tell you which spelling is to be used at the end of a word and circle or underline *ow*.

Then ask for two spellings of the /ou/ sound. Print *ou* and *ow*. "Which spelling do you think should be used for the /ou/ sound at the end of a word? [Mark *ow* when the children suggest that spelling.] We use *ow* for /ou/ at the end of a word. But we use *ow* for /ou/ some other times, too. Open your phonics workbook to page 76. At the bottom of the page we will study three rules for using the *ow* spelling.

"Find the number *1*. The blank for number *1* is at the end of the word. When /ou/ comes at the end of a word, we use *ow*. Print *ow* in the blank." Give a few more words for individuals to go to the board and print, using *ow* for /ou/ at the end of the word. (how, plow, vow)

"Find the number *2*. What letter do you see after the blank? When we hear /l/ at the end of an /ou/ word, we use *ow*. Print *ow* in the blank." Pronounce a few more words for individuals to print on the board, ending with *owl*. (fowl, growl, owl)

"Find the number *3* on your workbook page. What letter do you see after the blank? When we hear *n* at the end of an /ou/ word, we use *ow*. Print *ow* in the blank." Pronounce a few more *own* words for the children to practice. (town, frown, gown)

List again the three rules for using *ow* to spell the /ou/ sound:

1. at the end of a word
2. when the word ends with *l*
3. when the word ends with *n*

Pronounce an assortment of words for the children to spell with letter blocks or to print, some to be spelled with *ow* and some with *ou*. Practice until the children can apply the rule to a word they hear.

If they need the help, print -*ow*, -*owl*, and -*own* on the board for their reference.

Have each word spelled orally after the children have arranged or printed it on their own.

Seatwork   workbook, page 77

Following the three *ow* rules, the children are to print *ou* or *ow* in each blank for the /ou/ sound at the top of the page. Following the rule that *ow* is used at the end of a word the children are to print *oa* or *ow* in each blank for the /ō/ sound at the bottom of the page.

25

LESSON 6
Review

Be prepared
Daily drill
   Vowel spelling flash cards (Have the children refer to the special endings

---

Lesson 6   Unit 3   Gradebook: 64 points for the whole lesson

Review

Match the words and sounds.

could	ōō	boy	ōō	pull	ōō
owl	oo	true	oo	cow	oo
tool	ou	proud	ou	joy	ou
toil	oi	cook	oi	threw	oi

chew	ōō	coy	ōō	glue	ōō
hood	oo	out	oo	broil	oo
hoist	ou	should	ou	town	ou
mouse	oi	food	oi	full	oi

Mark the long vowels. Circle the other words.

pōol	smōoth	lōath	(joy)
thrōw	hūe	mūle	grāve
(desk)	(moist)	smōke	spōol
(good)	(crutch)	vīe	(loin)
shē	(stood)	prīze	spēech
swāy	(wax)	jāil	(toy)
(hit)	Jōe	(nook)	chēap
(buzz)	(flock)	prō	(quick)

as *rule 4.)*

Vowel sound flash cards—Include *ou* and *ow*. Your set will now contain two *ow* cards. (You may train the children to say "/ou/ or /ō/" every time you come to one of them.)

Phonics Workbook **Lesson 6**

Print the words in the sentences.

found   cow   spoil   growl   oil

1. Our brown C OW gives good milk.

2. Did the dog growl at the crowd?

3. We will oil the joint so it does not squeak.

4. Do not spoil our new toy.

---

book   bush   hook   moo   chew

5. The sound a cow makes is moo .

6. She gave me a good book to read.

7. Stand on the stool to reach the hook .

8. You should chew your food well.

A. Vowel sounds

Print some /o͞o/ and /oo/ words on the board and teach the children to mark /o͞o/ with a macron that covers both letters. All the other long vowel sounds are marked with a macron over just one letter. Emphasize the importance of exactness in these markings. The sounds /ou/ and /oi/ are not long vowel sounds.

Seatwork workbook, page 78

Discuss the directions and assign the page.

B. Reading workbook, page 79

Have the children read the sentences with blanks, then find the word that fits each sentence and print it in the blank.

Proceed with the edge list as usual.

C. Spelling

See how many vowel spellings the children can think of that are to be used at the end of words. (ay, -e, ee, ea, -y, ie, -o, ow, oe, ew, oy, ow)

Pronounce these words for the children to spell with letter blocks or printing, then orally.

way	fly (rule 3)	go (rule 3)	how
few	pie (rule 2)	she (rule 3)	shout
joy	toil		

Extra activity

Have the children print the circled words from the exercise at the bottom of page 78 in alphabetical order.

LESSON 7
Modified Vowel: ėr (er, ir, ur)

Be prepared
Daily drill
  Alphabet flash cards (Identify vowels.)
  Vowel sound flash cards
  Blends from the wall charts

A. Introducing the sound and symbol

If you have been using ėr in pronunciations for the reading vocabulary words, the symbol will not be altogether new to the children.

Let the children list all the vowel sounds they can think of: long, short, and diphthongs. "Sometimes there is a vowel sound in a word that you can hardly hear at all. It is not one of the long sounds or one of the short sounds or one of the other sounds you have learned. Listen to the words I say and see if you can tell me what vowel sound is in the words." Pronounce *her, sir,* and *fur.* The children may readily identify the initial and final consonants. Print them on the board leaving a gap between them for the vowels later.

"Each time there was an *r* after the vowel in the word. We will learn that *r* is a strong letter that changes a vowel beside it. We call a vowel that is changed by *r* a modified vowel. [Print *e* in the blank to spell the word *her*. The children should recognize it as a reading word.] Is it a long *e*? Is it a short *e*? It is a modified *e*. [Put a dot over the *e* and tell the children that we mark the modified *e* with a dot.] Modified *e* usually has an *r* right after it, and we hardly hear any sound for the *e* so we will print them together." Print *er* on the board and have the children practice saying /ėr/, then ask them for words in which you hear /ėr/.

Have the children open their workbooks to page 80 and let them read the sentence at the top of the page. Discuss /ėr/ as the sound a rooster makes and notice the letters on each rooster picture. The letter *r* does the same thing to *i* and to *u* when it is beside them, and they sound just like *er*. "They all say /ėr/ . We do not mark the *i* and the *u* differently, but we use the dotted *e* symbol for all three spellings when we want to show the sound."

Spell the words in part 1 with *er*. Use *ir* for the words in part 2, and *ur* for the words in part 3. Print the vowel in the remaining words on the board as you discuss each spelling.

Seatwork workbook, page 80

Have the children sound the row of words in each section and circle the one that best fits the picture.

B. Reading workbook, page 81

Have the children read the sentences and find a picture for each one.
Proceed with the edge list as usual.

C. Spelling

Review the rule to use *c* before *a, o, u; k* before *e, i;* and *ck* after short vowels. Remind the children to use only *k* after *oo*, and tell them to use only *k* after a modified vowel and *r*.

Print *er, ir,* and *ur* on the board and label them *1, 2, 3.* When giving spelling

Lesson 7   Unit 3

ėr   We all say ėr.

1
er

a.   b.   c.

her   fern   clerk

Circle the correct word.

herb   perk   term   (perch)   stern

2
ir

d.   e.   f.

skirt   shirt   stir

Circle the correct word.

squirm   (squirt)   birth   first   swirl

3
ur

g.   h.   i.

curl   burn   church

Circle the correct word.

hurt   curb   (purse)   fur   turn

80

words, tell the children to use *modified vowel 1, modified vowel 2,* or *modified vowel 3* so they will know which spelling to use.

Another procedure would be to give only *er* words for a while, then tell the children to use *ir* and give only *ir* words until you tell them to use *ur.*

Have each word spelled orally after it is arranged or printed.

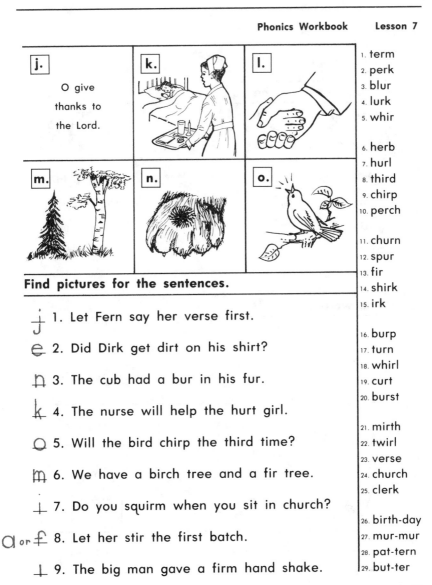

Phonics Workbook   **Lesson 7**

1. term
2. perk
3. blur
4. lurk
5. whir

6. herb
7. hurl
8. third
9. chirp
10. perch

11. churn
12. spur
13. fir
14. shirk
15. irk

16. burp
17. turn
18. whirl
19. curt
20. burst

21. mirth
22. twirl
23. verse
24. church
25. clerk

26. birth-day
27. mur-mur
28. pat-tern
29. but-ter

Find pictures for the sentences.

j. 1. Let Fern say her verse first.

e. 2. Did Dirk get dirt on his shirt?

n. 3. The cub had a bur in his fur.

k. 4. The nurse will help the hurt girl.

o. 5. Will the bird chirp the third time?

m. 6. We have a birch tree and a fir tree.

l. 7. Do you squirm when you sit in church?

a or l. 8. Let her stir the first batch.

l. 9. The big man gave a firm hand shake.

81

LESSON 8
Modified Vowel: är

Be prepared
Daily drill
  Vowel sound flash cards—Include *ėr* from set 4.

Lesson 8   Unit 3

är   car

Circle *ar*. Underline the correct word.

cart	lark	far	farm
harm	scarf	scar	bark
card	march	arch	tart
hard	shark	smart	chart
part	harp	sharp	charm

Print the words.

star   jar   car

arm   cart   barn

Vowel spelling flash cards—Include *er, ir,* and *ur* from set 9.
Consonant digraph flash cards

A. Introducing the sound and symbol

Let the children give the three modified vowels they studied in the last
lesson and say the sound of each vowel with *r*.

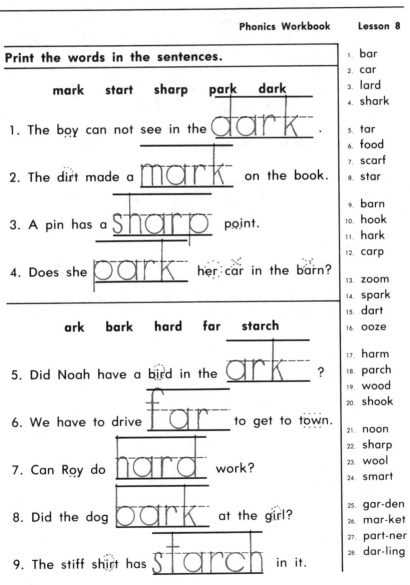

Phonics Workbook   **Lesson 8**

Print the words in the sentences.

mark   start   sharp   park   dark

1. The boy can not see in the ⎓dark⎓ .

2. The dirt made a ⎓mark⎓ on the book.

3. A pin has a ⎓sharp⎓ point.

4. Does she ⎓park⎓ her car in the barn?

---

ark   bark   hard   far   starch

5. Did Noah have a bird in the ⎓ark⎓ ?

6. We have to drive ⎓far⎓ to get to town.

7. Can Roy do ⎓hard⎓ work?

8. Did the dog ⎓bark⎓ at the girl?

9. The stiff shirt has ⎓starch⎓ in it.

1. bar
2. car
3. lard
4. shark
5. tar
6. food
7. scarf
8. star
9. barn
10. hook
11. hark
12. carp
13. zoom
14. spark
15. dart
16. ooze
17. harm
18. parch
19. wood
20. shook
21. noon
22. sharp
23. wool
24. smart
25. gar-den
26. mar-ket
27. part-ner
28. dar-ling

83

"The letter *r* modifies the other vowels too. Today we will study the modified *a.*" Print reading vocabulary words that have the /är/ sound and circle *ar.* (ark, stars)

Let the children say the sounds and think of other words containing /är/. Print *a* with two dots and tell the children that is how we mark the modified *a.*

Seatwork workbook, page 82.

Have the children open their workbooks to page 82 and notice the symbol at the top. Circling the *ar* in each word should help them to see the *ar* together rather than as the two sounds /a/ and /r/. Tell the children to sound the words in the lists and underline the one that best fits with the picture above it.

B. Reading workbook, page 83

Discuss the directions with the children and assign the page.

Proceed with the edge list as usual.

C. Spelling

Pronounce words from the edge list for the children to print or arrange, and then spell orally.

Seatwork workbook, page 82 (bottom)

Have the children follow the directions.

Extra activity workbook, page 83

Search the sentences on page 83.

Circle all the letter groups that say /ėr/.

Put a box around all the letter groups that say /ou/.

Underline all the letter groups that say /oi/.

Put a cross over all the letter groups that say /är/.

The set of directions may be printed on the board for reference.

LESSON 9

Modified Vowel: ôr

Be prepared

1. Daily drill

Vowel spelling flash cards—Include *är* from set 9.

(When reviewing rules with this set, say *modified vowels* for *er, ir, ur,* and *ar.*)

Vowel sound flash cards—Include *är* from set 4.

Consonant blend flash cards—Divide into 3 packs to cover all the blends with regular frequency rather than repeating the same ones. The initial blends should be separated equally into 2 packs and will be referred to as *initial blends a* and *initial blends b.* The third pack will include only *final blends.* (Flash the pack of *initial blends a* and have each child think of a word for the blend flashed to him. You may give clues if the children need help, such as saying "The opposite of *fast*" to help someone with the blend *sl.*)

2. Option

Due to variations of speech in different geographical areas, you may prefer to teach ôr as ōr. The pupil's books can be changed by using opaquing fluid or by pasting a paper patch over the symbol. That may be a teacher job or you may direct the children to make the change. Give the simple explanation, "In our area, we say it this way."

Alter the flash card to match your teaching.

Tailor the procedures in the teacher's instructions to suit what you want to teach.

A. Introducing the sound and symbol

Print the word *or* on the board and let the children say it. Pronounce the word with the long *o* sound and with the short *o* sound. "This is not a long or short vowel. It is another modified vowel." Let the children say some words that have the /ôr/ sound. Show the symbol used to mark the modified vowel.

Seatwork workbook, page 84 (top)

Have the children circle *or* in each word, then sound the words and underline the one in each column that best fits the picture above.

B. Reading workbook, page 85

Follow the directions and read the edge list.

C. Spelling

Pronounce words from the edge list for the children to arrange or print, then spell.

Seatwork workbook, page 84 (bottom)

Print the word for each picture.

ôr

Circle *or*. **Underline the correct word.**

ford	Lord	horn	for
shorn	scorn	fort	pork
sort	torn	stork	dorm
form	snort	morn	port
storm	born	sport	scorn

Print the words.

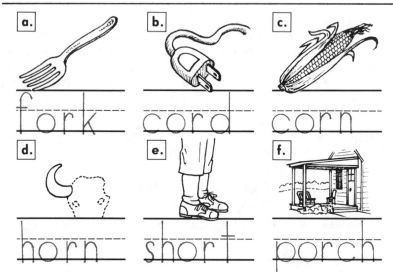

a. fork

b. cord

c. corn

d. horn

e. short

f. porch

84

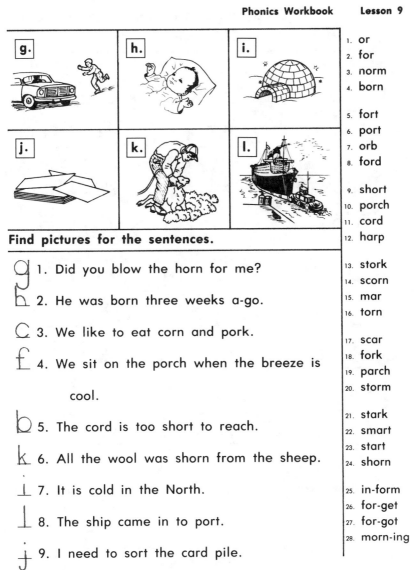

Phonics Workbook   **Lesson 9**

g.	**h.**	**i.**
j.	**k.**	**l.**

Find pictures for the sentences.

1. Did you blow the horn for me?

2. He was born three weeks a-go.

3. We like to eat corn and pork.

4. We sit on the porch when the breeze is cool.

5. The cord is too short to reach.

6. All the wool was shorn from the sheep.

7. It is cold in the North.

8. The ship came in to port.

9. I need to sort the card pile.

1. or
2. for
3. norm
4. born

5. fort
6. port
7. orb
8. ford

9. short
10. porch
11. cord
12. harp

13. stork
14. scorn
15. mar
16. torn

17. scar
18. fork
19. parch
20. storm

21. stark
22. smart
23. start
24. shorn

25. in-form
26. for-get
27. for-got
28. morn-ing

85

LESSON 10
Review of Modified Vowels

Be prepared
Daily drill
  Consonant sound flash cards

Lesson 10   Unit 3 Gradebook: 34 points for the whole lesson
Review

Print *ar* **or** *or*.

1. j ar
2. c or n
3. m ar k
4. t or n
5. h or n
6. d ar k
7. f or k
8. h ar d

9. ar k
10. s or t
11. y ar d
12. sm ar t
13. st or m
14. st ar t
15. m ar ch
16. sp or t

17. ar m
18. d ar t
19. sn or t
20. y ar n
21. sh ar p
22. sh or t
23. st ar ch
24. sc or n

Circle the correct word. Print it in the blank.

1. Will you wait for me?   (for) far

2. There are many animals on the farm .
                firm (farm)

86

Vowel sound flash cards—Include *ôr* from set 4.

Initial blend *b* flash cards (Have the children say words for the blends.)

A. Modified vowels

Introduce the first exercise in the workbook by printing words with blanks on the board.

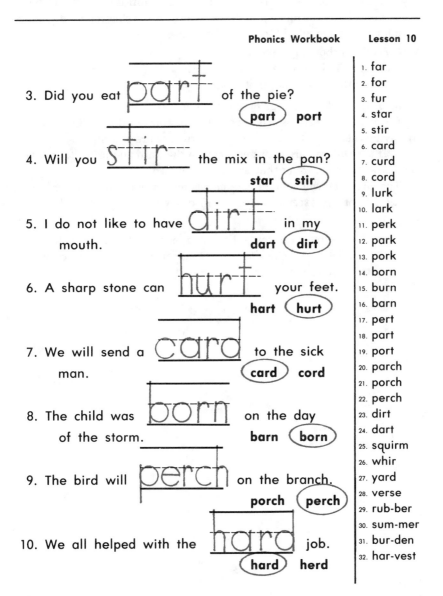

Phonics Workbook   **Lesson 10**

3. Did you eat ⎅⎅⎅⎅⎅ of the pie?
   (**part**) **port**

4. Will you ⎅⎅⎅⎅⎅ the mix in the pan?
   star (**stir**)

5. I do not like to have ⎅⎅⎅⎅⎅ in my mouth.
   dart (**dirt**)

6. A sharp stone can ⎅⎅⎅⎅⎅ your feet.
   hart (**hurt**)

7. We will send a ⎅⎅⎅⎅⎅ to the sick man.
   (**card**) **cord**

8. The child was ⎅⎅⎅⎅⎅ on the day of the storm.
   barn (**born**)

9. The bird will ⎅⎅⎅⎅⎅ on the branch.
   porch (**perch**)

10. We all helped with the ⎅⎅⎅⎅⎅ job.
    (**hard**) **herd**

1. far
2. for
3. fur
4. star
5. stir
6. card
7. curd
8. cord
9. lurk
10. lark
11. perk
12. park
13. pork
14. born
15. burn
16. barn
17. pert
18. part
19. port
20. parch
21. porch
22. perch
23. dirt
24. dart
25. squirm
26. whir
27. yard
28. verse
29. rub-ber
30. sum-mer
31. bur-den
32. har-vest

sh___t   d___k   st___m   f___m

Print *ar* in the first blank and have someone sound the word. Replace *ar* with *or* and let someone say that word. Repeat the two results and ask, "Which one is a word?" Do the next word in the same manner. Then see if the children can sound the next one both ways without seeing the letters in print in the blank. "What is the word? Which modified vowel do you hear in the word?" Give as much practice as you think the children need, taking samples from page 86 of the phonics workbook.

Seatwork   workbook, page 86 (top)

Have the children sound the words with both /är/ and /ôr/, then fill in the blank with the spelling that makes a word.

B. Reading   workbook, page 86 (bottom) and 87

Discuss the directions. The work could be shortened for a limited class by having them only circle the correct word. Be sure your instructions are clear. If the children are expected to circle the word and print it, answers should be counted wrong that are not completed.

The edge list will require careful reading as many of the words are identical to others except for the modified vowel.

C. Spelling

Have the children spell words that you pronounce. Use the *1, 2, 3* system to tell them which /ėr/ spelling to use, or tell them to use *er* for all /ėr/ words until you tell them to use *ir* or *ur*.

Have each word spelled orally.

LESSON 11
Vowel Sound: ô

Be prepared

1. Daily drill

    Vowel sound flash cards

    Final blend flash cards (Have the children say words.)

2. Option

    If you and your school constituency make no difference in the pronunciations of *caught* and *cot,* you may not want to teach the /ô/ sound and symbol.

    You can go to the work of covering the circumflex in the next few lessons including the pronunciations in matching exercises, or simply tell the children, "We will use the same sound for these words that we use for short *o* which has no marking above it," and let them cross out or ignore the circumflex.

A. Introducing the sound

Review the modified vowels and their markings. Print each of the pronunciations as you discuss them, then erase all but ôr. Erase the *r* and let ô stand alone. "We use this symbol for an *o* sound that is not long or short, but it can stand alone in a word without the letter *r.*"

Say the sound for the children and have them practice saying it. Let them say words containing the sound or play the listening game.

lost	loaf	nose	moss
fog	wrong	cost	hope
smoke	dock	moth	frost
cloth	soft	comb	strong
moon	wood	rob	off
shot	cross	dog	crop

Have the children turn to page 88 in their phonics books and sound out the words in the columns at the top of the page.

Seatwork   workbook, page 88

Discuss the directions and do some samples in each part of the page with the children.

Some of the matching exercises are to be done by drawing lines to avoid the confusion that could be produced by printing one letter to represent another letter sound.

B. Reading   workbook, page 89 (top)

C. Spelling

Pronounce words from the edge list for the children to print or arrange, then spell.

Seatwork   workbook, page 89 (bottom)

Lesson 11   Unit 3

ô

Underline the correct words.

<u>log</u>	hog	broth	<u>long</u>
fog	toss	cloth	strong
cloth	<u>off</u>	cost	moth
lost	fog	frost	lost
moss	gloss	<u>soft</u>	moss

Match the words and sounds.

1. look	o	6. job	ô
2. yoke	ō	7. lost	o
3. spoon	oo	8. food	oo
4. soft	ô	9. shook	ō
5. stop	oo	10. roast	oo

Match the words with the way they sound.

C	1. were	a. spärk	j	6. cross	f. skär
d	2. toss	b. fėrl	i	7. verse	g. chėrp
b	3. furl	c. wėr	h	8. curse	h. kėrs
a	4. spark	d. tôs	f	9. scar	i. vėrs
e	5. hog	e. hôg	g	10. chirp	j. krôs

Phonics Workbook   Lesson 11

Print the words in the sentences.

hog   cloth   strong   moss   frost

1. Use a soft cloth to wipe the glass dish.

2. A green frog sat on the moss on the log.

3. The cold frost made the grass white.

4. A strong man can toss the wood on the pile.

5. The hog ran into the corn and got lost.

Print the words.

dog   moth   cross

1. log
2. fog
3. off
4. dog
5. hog
6. joy
7. gloss
8. fork
9. toss
10. frost
11. join
12. cord
13. broth
14. moth
15. spoil
16. cross
17. short
18. boy
19. cloth
20. moss
21. moist
22. lost
23. soft
24. cost
25. long
26. strong
27. be-long
28. song-book
29. song-bird
30. dust-cloth

89

LESSON 12
Digraph *aw* = /ô/

Be prepared
Daily drill
  Vowel sound flash cards—Include ô from set 3.

Lesson 12   Unit 3

aw = ô   saw

Circle *aw*. Underline the correct words.

sh(aw)l	l(aw)	c(aw)	l(aw)n
tr(aw)l	r(aw)	m(aw)	f(aw)n
th(aw)	d(aw)n	cr(aw)l	fl(aw)
sl(aw)	h(aw)k	b(aw)l	br(aw)l
p(aw)n	str(aw)	th(aw)	squ(aw)

Match the words and vowel sounds.

1. crew	ô	or
2. caw	ô	
3. cost	ōō	
4. crow	ō	
5. cow	ou	

6. flew	ô	or
7. crowd	ô	
8. flow	ōō	
9. fawn	ou	
10. fog	ō	

Match the words with the way they sound.

C 1. flaw	**a.** flō		h 6. drew	**f.** bôl
e 2. thaw	**b.** flōō		g 7. draw	**g.** drô
a 3. flow	**c.** flô		f 8. bawl	**h.** drōō
d 4. throw	**d.** thrō		j 9. dawn	**i.** droun
b 5. flew	**e.** thô		⊥ 10. drown	**j.** dôn

90

Consonant digraph flash cards
Initial blend *a* flash cards

A. Introducing the spelling
Let the children figure out the word at the top of page 90 and analyze its sounds. Discuss the equation $aw = \hat{o}$. Have the children circle the *aw*

Phonics Workbook   Lesson 12

Print the words in the sentences.

dawn   lawn   draw   straw   crawl

1. He cut the grass on the ̲l̲a̲w̲n̲ .

2. The little child can not yet ̲c̲r̲a̲w̲l̲ .

3. We saw her ̲d̲r̲a̲w̲ a big tree on the card.

4. I can drink with a ̲s̲t̲r̲a̲w̲ .

Print the words.

paw   saw   jaw

claw   draw   yawn

1. jaw
2. law
3. raw
4. thaw
5. slaw
6. claw
7. farm
8. draw
9. star
10. bawl
11. flaw
12. smart
13. march
14. straw
15. squaw
16. yarn
17. fawn
18. cross
19. spark
20. yawn
21. shawl
22. dark
23. strong
24. scarf
25. hawk
26. law-yer
27. flaw-less
28. craw-fish
29. haw-thorn

91

in the lists of words to aid the habit of seeing the two letters together as one sound.

Seatwork   workbook, page 90

Discuss the directions and assign the page.

B. Reading   workbook, page 91 (top and edge)

C. Spelling

Pronounce words from the edge list for the children to spell. Have them give the letters orally after they have spelled the words.

Seatwork   workbook, page 91 (bottom)

LESSON 13
Other spellings for /ô/

Be prepared

1. Daily drill

   Vowel spelling flash cards—Include the modified vowel *or* from set 9,
   and *au* and *aw* from set 5.

   Vowel sound flash cards

   Initial blend *b* flash cards

2. Make the wall chart for ô spellings as shown on page 10 of this manual.

A. Introducing the sounds

Tell the children to open their workbooks to page 92 and discuss the words
and pictures at the top of the page. Have them circle the letter or combination that represents the /ô/ sound in each word as you discuss it.

Seatwork   workbook, page 92

B. Reading   workbook, page 93 (top and edge)

Do a few samples with the class when explaining the exercise on page
93. They are to sound each word, then print one of the three sounds given
above to show which one they hear in the word.

C. Spelling

Tell the class which spelling to use in the words you pronounce. After
some practice, change to another spelling for a few words. Have the children
print or arrange, and then spell the words.

Seatwork   workbook, page 93 (bottom)

Extra activities

1. Find the names in the exercise on page 93 and print some sentences
using them.

2. Print sentences or draw pictures for some of the words in the exercise
on page 92 (top).

Lesson 13   Unit 3

ô

saw   Paul   salt

Circle *aw* **and** *au.* **Circle** *a* **before** *l.*

paw	haunt	fall	mall
halt	jaw	squaw	pawn
thaw	salt	maul	Paul
haul	hall	small	slaw
raw	caul	yawn	tall
stall	hawk	call	Saul
lawn	straw	malt	law
trawl	all	dawn	flaw

Match the words and sounds. Gradebook: 12 points for the

salt ——— ô
spray ——— a
smash ——— ā

grab ——— ô
chain ——— a
fall ——— ā

chap ——— ô
draw ——— a
wave ——— ā

frail ——— ô
hatch ——— a
stall ——— ā

matching exercise

Phonics Workbook   Lesson 13

Print the sounds.

ô   a   ā

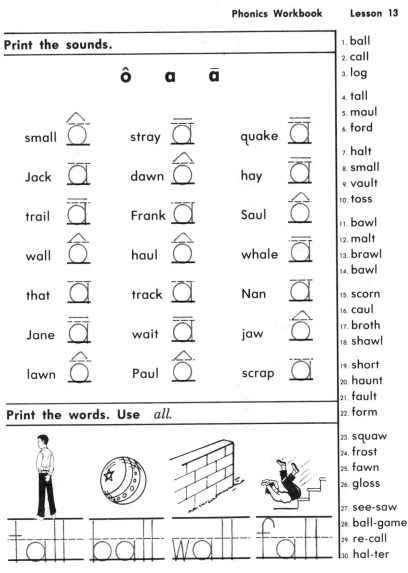

small	stray	quake
Jack	dawn	hay
trail	Frank	Saul
wall	haul	whale
that	track	Nan
Jane	wait	jaw
lawn	Paul	scrap

Print the words. Use *all*.

fall ball wall fall

1. ball
2. call
3. log
4. tall
5. maul
6. ford
7. halt
8. small
9. vault
10. toss
11. bawl
12. malt
13. brawl
14. bawl
15. scorn
16. caul
17. broth
18. shawl
19. short
20. haunt
21. fault
22. form
23. squaw
24. frost
25. fawn
26. gloss
27. see-saw
28. ball-game
29. re-call
30. hal-ter

LESSON 14
Sometimes s = /z/

Be prepared
Daily drill
  Alphabet flash cards (Let each child say the name of the preceding letter,

---

Lesson 14   Unit 3

S = Z

Z buzzes
like a bee.
Sometimes S
buzzes, too.

order interchangeable

joins

tools

joys

jaws   birds   rooms

yawns   frogs   cows

curls   towns   spoons

toys   clouds   walls

Print each word with an s that buzzes.

jaws	birds	joys	spoons
books	frogs	rooms	walls
yawns	towns	roots	hawks
curls	clouds	faults	charts
marks	joins	hurts	crops
toys	tools	cows	boats

94

the letter he sees, and the following letter when you flash a card to him.)

Final blend flash cards

Vowel sound flash cards

Phonics Workbook   **Lesson 14**

Match the words with the way they sound.

  c 1. fawn   **a.** toiz

  d 2. stools   **b.** kroudz

  f 3. squaw   **c.** fôn

  a 4. toys   **d.** stoolz

  e 5. perch   **e.** perch

  b 6. crowds   **f.** skwô

Print the words.

boy   cow   cloud

boys   cows   clouds

pins   Rule 1 nose   Rule 1 rose

1. rise
2. hose
3. his
4. days

5. ease
6. wise
7. fuse
8. balls

9. coins
10. brooms
11. pools
12. crowns

13. girls
14. cars
15. turns
16. storms

17. squaws
18. cheese
19. those
20. these

21. noise
22. tease
23. please
24. grooves

25. wis-dom
26. ros-in
27. pris-on
28. poi-son

A. Introducing the sound   workbook, page 94

Have the children read the sentences in the beehive. The words that have a *z* sound for *s* are to be printed on the bee lines. *S* following a vowel sound or voiced consonant buzzes, and *s* following a voiceless consonant hisses. The children will probably do best by sounding each word both ways to decide which is correct.

B. Reading   workbook, page 95 (top and edge)

C. Spelling

Pronounce words from the edge list for the children to spell using *s* for the /z/ sound. Have each word spelled orally.

Seatwork   workbook, page 95 (bottom)

Notice that rule 1 is to be followed for the last two pictures in spelling the long vowel sound.

Extra activity

Let the children print some of the words from the edge list then try to print the pronunciation symbols for the word beside it.

LESSON 15
Suffixes in Plurals: s, es

Be prepared
1. Daily drill
     Vowel sound flash cards
     Initial blend *a* flash cards
2. Make a wall chart for the *s, es* rule as shown on page 10 of this manual.

A. Introducing the rule
Hold up a pencil. "What is this? [Hold up several pencils.] What do I have now? What changed in the word you said?" Do the children realize that the difference is adding an *s* at the end? Say some more words for them to respond with the word that means more than one.

hat	cuff	cup	bell	rib
road	sock	rag	ear	lip

Turn to page 96 in the phonics books. Let the children say the words for the pictures of more than one at the top of the page. Discuss what they are to print in the blanks. Discuss whether *s* buzzes in the words they will print.

"Look at the bottom of the page. Sometimes when we want a word to mean more than one, we need to add *es* and not just *s*. We will look at these words to learn when we should add *es*. What is the last letter in the word *fox*? When we see an *x* at the end of a word, we must add *es* to make it mean more than one. Circle the *x*. What is the last letter in the word *dress*? When we see an *s* at the end of a word, we also need to add *es* to make it mean more than one. Circle the *s*. What is at the end of the other two words? Circle the consonant digraph in each of these words. When a word ends with *sh* or *ch*, we need to add *es* to make it mean more than one."

Let the children say the plural words for the bottom of the page. Pronounce the words with a distinct syllable separation and point out that the words change from one syllable to two syllables. Note also that *s* buzzes in each one.

Seatwork workbook, page 96
Have the children print the plural words.

B. Reading workbook, page 97 (top and edge)
Review the four endings that require *es* for plurals. Direct the children to circle the word endings that indicate the need for *es* rather than *s*. They are not to circle those letters at other places in the words.

Proceed with the edge list as usual.

C. Spelling
Pronounce words for the children to spell, giving first a singular word,

then its plural form. After they have printed or arranged the plural form, have the word spelled orally.

Seatwork   workbook, page 97 (bottom)

Lesson 15   Unit 3

Print words that mean more than one.

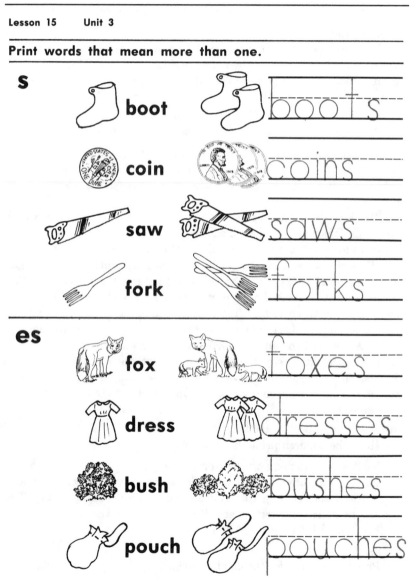

s

boot — boots

coin — coins

saw — saws

fork — forks

es

fox — foxes

dress — dresses

bush — bushes

pouch — pouches

Extra activity

Have the children print a certain number of words from page 97 and add *s* or *es* to each one.

Phonics Workbook   **Lesson 15**

Circle *x, s, sh, ch.*

1. broom	9. glass	17. thrush	25. wax
2. cross	10. point	18. bench	26. moss
3. mouth	11. box	19. sound	27. skirt
4. porch	12. truss	20. thorn	28. bunch
5. brush	13. bird	21. tax	29. speech
6. charm	14. switch	22. rose	30. clerk
7. fox	15. pound	23. church	31. lunch
8. grass	16. flash	24. storm	32. class

Print the words.

brushes   lips

benches   boxes

grasses   cats

1. tax
2. taxes
3. finch
4. finches
5. train
6. trains
7. couch
8. couches
9. block
10. blocks
11. stress
12. stresses
13. crotch
14. crotches
15. crosses
16. porches
17. heaps
18. springs
19. lunches
20. flashes
21. switches
22. trees
23. crutches
24. classes
25. churches
26. in-dex-es
27. bul-rush-es

LESSON 16
Suffixes in Verbs: s, es

Be prepared
Daily drill
 Vowel sound flash cards

Lesson 16   Unit 3

Print the words with *es.*

es

They mix.   She mixes .

We miss.   He misses .

We push.   She pushes .

They march.   He marches .

Initial blend *b* flash cards
Consonant digraph flash cards

A. Introducing the rule

"Why do we sometimes add *s* to words? [to make them mean more than one] When do we add *es* instead of *s*?" Review the wall chart with the children.

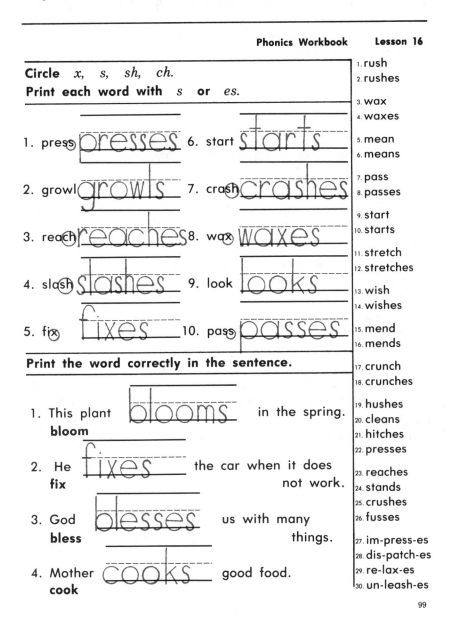

Phonics Workbook   **Lesson 16**

Circle *x, s, sh, ch.*
Print each word with *s* or *es.*

1. press   presses   6. start   starts

2. growl   growls   7. crash   crashes

3. reach   reaches   8. wax   waxes

4. slash   slashes   9. look   looks

5. fix   fixes   10. pass   passes

Print the word correctly in the sentence.

1. This plant   blooms   in the spring.
   bloom

2. He   fixes   the car when it does
   fix   not work.

3. God   blesses   us with many
   bless   things.

4. Mother   cooks   good food.
   cook

1. rush
2. rushes
3. wax
4. waxes
5. mean
6. means
7. pass
8. passes
9. start
10. starts
11. stretch
12. stretches
13. wish
14. wishes
15. mend
16. mends
17. crunch
18. crunches
19. hushes
20. cleans
21. hitches
22. presses
23. reaches
24. stands
25. crushes
26. fusses
27. im-press-es
28. dis-patch-es
29. re-lax-es
30. un-leash-es

99

"There are other times we add *s* to a word too." Print some sentences on the board to illustrate the verb change for plural and singular subjects.

We sing.   He sings.

We work.   She works.

Point to *sings* and *works*. "These words do not mean more than one, but we need to add *s* to say the sentences correctly." Give some oral sentences for the children to repeat using *he* or *she* with the *s* form of the verb. Print the *s* form of the verb on the board after each response. If your class can handle the exercise without confusion or distraction, have them consider whether the *s* buzzes or hisses.

We sleep.   We read.

We run.   We eat.

We fix.

"Did you notice that your word *fix-es* has two syllables?" Print *fix* and ask the children how they think *fixes* is spelled. Continue in like manner with these sentences:

We pass.   We rush.   We catch.

"We follow the same rule for adding *s* to these words as we do when we make words mean more than one." Review the rule again.

Seatwork workbook, page 98

B. Reading workbook, page 99 (top and edge)

Have the children follow the directions and read the edge list.

C. Spelling

Pronounce words from the edge list giving first the root word, then the *s* form. Have the words spelled orally after they are printed or arranged.

Seatwork workbook, page 99 (bottom)

Tell the children to read each sentence with the word as it is given, then read it with *s* on the end of the word. "Print the word the way it belongs to say the sentence correctly. Make sure you spell the word correctly."

Extra activity

Let the children make sentences using some *s* or *es* words from page 99.

LESSON 17
Suffix: ed

Be prepared
1. Daily drill
   Vowel sound flash cards
   Vowel spelling flash cards
   Final blend flash cards
   Wall chart (Review the *es* rule.)
2. Make the *ed* wall chart as shown on page 11 of this manual.

A. Introducing the sounds
Print a list of verbs on the board, and tell the children these are things they can do. Have someone read the list.

| look | dump | kick | smell | wail |
| fill | clean | trust | print | hunt |

"Sometimes we change such words to make them mean that these things were done in the past. If you did all these things yesterday, how would you say the words?" Say some of the words in the past tense for an example, then let the children finish the list.

"Notice the different sounds that are put on the end of the words to make them mean it has been done already. [Have someone repeat the list again just to listen to the difference of the added sounds. Print *ed* on the end of each word in the list.] That is how we print these words to make them mean these things were done already. We use the same ending for all these words, but they sound different when we say them." Identify the three different sounds of the suffix. Notice that one of them is an added syllable. Have the children practice the two-syllable words.

Seatwork workbook, page 100
The children are to print the suffix *ed* after each word and sound the words to themselves. You may want to have them read the words and make oral sentences with some of them.

B. Reading workbook, page 101
The children are to use the word given in each section for both sentences. In one sentence they will print the word as it appears, and in the other they will add *ed*.

In reading the edge list the children will need to decide which pronunciation to give *ed*. The correct sound will probably come naturally.

The suffix is sounded /t/ after voiceless consonants and digraphs (k, s, f, p, sh, ch).

It is sounded /d/ after vowel sounds and voiced consonants.

And it sounds /ed/ following the /t/ or /d/ sound.

C. Spelling

Pronounce words from the edge list for the children to spell. Give only the first principal part of the verb at first, then pronounce it in the past tense for them to add *ed*. Have each word spelled orally after the children have printed or arranged it.

Lesson 17   Unit 3

ed

Print *ed* **on the end of each word. Read the words.**

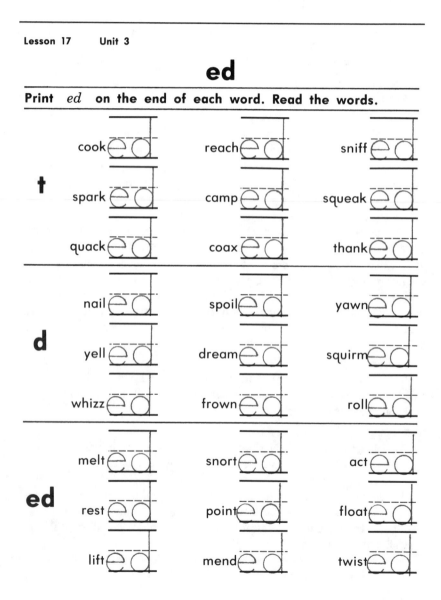

t

cook◯◯ reach◯◯ sniff◯◯

spark◯◯ camp◯◯ squeak◯◯

quack◯◯ coax◯◯ thank◯◯

d

nail◯◯ spoil◯◯ yawn◯◯

yell◯◯ dream◯◯ squirm◯◯

whizz◯◯ frown◯◯ roll◯◯

ed

melt◯◯ snort◯◯ act◯◯

rest◯◯ point◯◯ float◯◯

lift◯◯ mend◯◯ twist◯◯

Phonics Workbook   **Lesson 17**

Print the word correctly in each sentence.

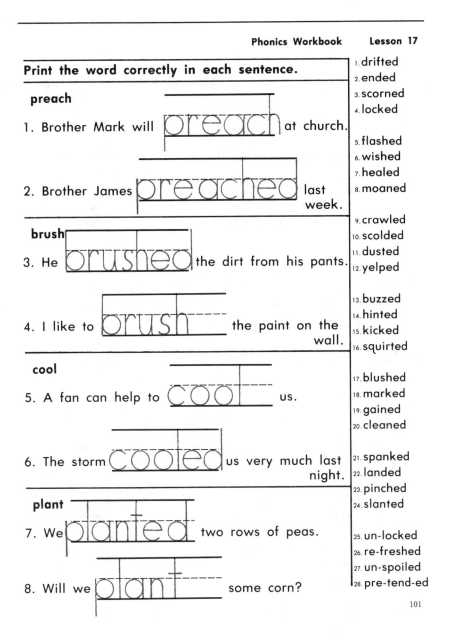

preach

1. Brother Mark will �⎪preach⎪ at church.

2. Brother James ⎪preached⎪ last week.

brush

3. He ⎪brushed⎪ the dirt from his pants.

4. I like to ⎪brush⎪ the paint on the wall.

cool

5. A fan can help to ⎪cool⎪ us.

6. The storm ⎪cooled⎪ us very much last night.

plant

7. We ⎪planted⎪ two rows of peas.

8. Will we ⎪plant⎪ some corn?

1. drifted
2. ended
3. scorned
4. locked

5. flashed
6. wished
7. healed
8. moaned

9. crawled
10. scolded
11. dusted
12. yelped

13. buzzed
14. hinted
15. kicked
16. squirted

17. blushed
18. marked
19. gained
20. cleaned

21. spanked
22. landed
23. pinched
24. slanted

25. un-locked
26. re-freshed
27. un-spoiled
28. pre-tend-ed

101

LESSON 18
Suffix: ing

Be prepared
Daily drill
   Vowel sound flash cards

Lesson 18   Unit 3

ing

Print the words.

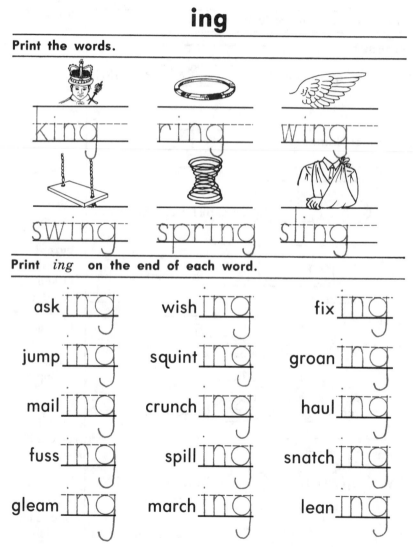

king   ring   wing

swing   spring   sling

Print *ing* on the end of each word.

ask ing   wish ing   fix ing

jump ing   squint ing   groan ing

mail ing   crunch ing   haul ing

fuss ing   spill ing   snatch ing

gleam ing   march ing   lean ing

Consonant sound flash cards
Initial blend *a* flash cards
Wall charts for *es* and *ed*

A. Introducing the suffix
Let the children name the words for the pictures at the top of page 102

| Phonics Workbook | Lesson 18 |

| **Print the word correctly in each sentence.** | 1. handing |

fish

1. They were _fishing_ all day.

2. May we _fish_ in the little pond?

count

3. He is _counting_ the birds in the tree.

4. Can you _count_ to 100?

bloom

5. Did the plant _bloom_ last summer?

6. It is _blooming_ now.

catch

7. We all helped to _catch_ the pig.

8. He thinks _catching_ animals is hard work.

Word list:
1. handing
2. farming
3. clutching
4. ticking
5. vending
6. smacking
7. training
8. slashing
9. filling
10. boiling
11. sounding
12. draining
13. stuffing
14. hissing
15. checking
16. starching
17. leaking
18. bumping
19. grasping
20. rusting
21. tending
22. forming
23. blessing
24. puffing
25. dis-play-ing
26. ex-tend-ing
27. pro-test-ing
28. re-heat-ing

103

and say other rhyming words. Then explain that the ending sound given
at the top of the page is often added to words that name things we can do.
Let the children say the list of verbs at the bottom of the page, adding *ing*.
Have them pronounce two distinct syllables.

Seatwork   workbook, page 102 (bottom)

B. Reading   workbook, page 103

The children are to use the word given in each section for both sentences.
One sentence is to have the word in its given form, and the other should
have the suffix *ing* added.

Proceed with the edge list as usual.

C. Spelling

Pronounce words from the edge list for the children to spell giving first
the root word, then repeating it with the suffix. Have each word spelled orally.

Seatwork   workbook, page 102 (top)

Extra activity

Have the children print sentences using some of the words at the bottom of page 102 with the *ing* suffix.

Have the children print the words at the bottom of page 102 with the
suffixes *ed* and *s* or *es*.

LESSON 19
Review of Suffixes

Be prepared

Daily drill
    Vowel sound flash cards
    Vowel spelling flash cards
    Initial blend *b* flash cards

A. Adding Suffixes

Use the words on page 104 or other samples and have the children say them orally with each of the suffixes given. Notice the number of syllables and the different sounds of *ed*. Review the rule for using *s* or *es*.

Seatwork   workbook, page 104

Have the children print each root word with three suffixes.

B. Reading   workbook, page 105

Have the children follow the directions.
Read the edge list as usual.

C. Spelling

Use the edge list for spelling practice as usual.

Extra activity

On page 104 have the children print the sound of the suffix after each *ed* word, or print after each word the number of syllables.

Review

Print each word with three endings.

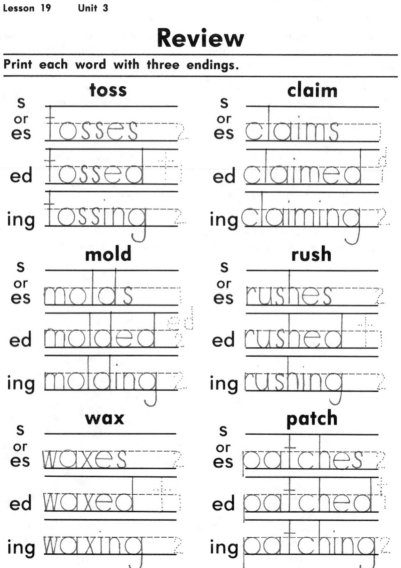

toss
s or es fosses
ed fossed
ing fossing

claim
s or es claims
ed claimed
ing claiming

mold
s or es molds
ed molded
ing molding

rush
s or es rushes
ed rushed
ing rushing

wax
s or es waxes
ed waxed
ing waxing

patch
s or es patches
ed patched
ing patching

Phonics Workbook   **Lesson 19**

Circle the sound of *ed* in each word.

1. killed	t (d) ed	7. pushed	(t) d ed
2. ended	t d (ed)	8. prayed	t (d) ed
3. picked	(t) d ed	9. sniffed	(t) d ed
4. buzzed	t (d) ed	10. trusted	t d (ed)
5. kissed	(t) d ed	11. counted	t d (ed)
6. parted	t d (ed)	12. snowed	t (d) ed

Match the words with the way they sound.

C 1. heaped   **a.** trāld
d 2. trailed   **b.** snēkt
e 3. passed   **c.** hēpt
b 4. sneaked   **d.** klāmd
d 5. claimed   **e.** past

f 6. loafing   **f.** lōf-ing
i 7. spraying   **g.** sōk-ing
j 8. counting   **h.** shok-ing
h 9. shocking   **i.** sprā-ing
g 10. soaking   **j.** kount-ing

m 11. splashes   **k.** pēch-ez
k 12. peaches   **l.** pres-ez
o 13. perches   **m.** splash-ez
n 14. stitches   **n.** stich-ez
l 15. presses   **o.** pėrch-ez

1. peas
2. ways
3. churches
4. stamped
5. parked
6. dresses
7. pins
8. spools
9. picked
10. jailed
11. beamed
12. crosses
13. hose
14. granted
15. coiled
16. joints
17. wailed
18. hunted
19. listed
20. shirts
21. flashes
22. licked
23. crowded
24. fizzed
25. shoots
26. fin-ished
27. ham-mered
28. har-ness-es
29. sor-row-ing

LESSON 20
Two-Syllable Words

Be prepared
Daily drill
    Vowel sound flash cards

Lesson 20   **Unit 3**

Syllables

Print the number of syllables.
Underline a word for each picture.

planted 2 ed	ribbon 2	spilled 1 d
magnet 2	shifted 2 ed	swished 1 †
pumped 1 †	cracked 1 †	kitten 2
basket 2	missed 1 †	turnip 2
spelled 1 d	tinted 2 ed	scratched 1 †
number 2	master 2	lumber 2
crushed 1 †	sprayed 1 d	carpet 2
sounded 2 ed	smashed 1 †	supper 2
servant 2	mocked 1 †	latched 1 †
fizzed 1 d	martin 2	melted 2 ed
ladder 2	member 2	smelled 1 d
thunder 2	mitten 2	lantern 2

Consonant digraph flash cards
Final blend flash cards
Wall charts for *es* and *ed*

Gradebook: 13 points for this page

	Phonics Workbook	**Lesson 20**

Match the words and the way they sound.

b 1. yellow   **a.** blis-tėr

d 2. husband   **b.** yel-ō

a 3. blister   **c.** sud-en

C 4. sudden   **d.** huz-band

e 5. bitter   **e.** bit-ėr

i 6. better   **f.** win-tėr

h 7. burden   **g.** mas-tėr

f 8. winter   **h.** bėr-den

j 9. pillow   **i.** bet-ėr

k 10. happen   **j.** pil-ō

g 11. master   **k.** hap-en

Draw the pictures.

a basket of turnips | a sunset in winter

1. pilgrim
2. fellow
3. gander
4. until
5. lesson
6. cockpit
7. fender
8. hamlet
9. harpoon
10. barber
11. sinner
12. compass
13. bitter
14. golden
15. submit
16. summer
17. portray
18. imply
19. extend
20. carmel
21. marvel
22. rubber
23. kingdom
24. person
25. spectrum
26. silver

A. Introducing the words

Print the first list below on the board.

dreamed	trumpet
napkin	slanted
rusted	number
silver	yawned
mended	matter
shocked	pillow

The children have been reading two-syllable words with suffixes. Let them find words in the list that have the *ed* ending. You may cover the *ed* and let someone say the root word, then the complete word. How many syllables does the whole word have? Print the number after the word.

Then look at the other words. Let someone start at the beginning to sound one of the words. He may stall in the middle of the word with the consonant sounds. Accept the first part of the word and repeat the syllable that was sounded. Then cover that part and have the child try the last part. Repeat the second syllable after him and point out that this is a word to say in two parts. Let the class practice the word and print the number of syllables after it. Attack the next word and proceed through the list.

Print the other list given above and begin with the first word. Do the children recognize the *ed* suffix and use it for a key when they come to an *ed* word?

Seatwork workbook, page 106

Have the children sound the words and print the number of syllables for each one. In each box the word that fits to the picture is to be underlined.

B. Reading workbook, page 107

Have the children follow the directions on the page.

The children will be reading two-syllable words in the edge list.

C. Spelling

Pronounce two-syllable words for the children to spell. Say the syllables separately so they can hear each one distinctly and pronounce all the vowel sounds clearly. You may tell the children that any /ėr/ sound in these words is spelled *er*.

Have each word spelled orally.

Extra activity

Have the children find all the *ed* words on page 106 and print the sound of the suffix after the number that tells how many syllables.

LESSON 21

Sometimes $y = /\bar{e}/$

Be prepared

1. Daily drill

 Vowel spelling flash cards

 Initial blend *a* flash cards

 Wall charts for *es* and *ed*

2. Make the wall chart for sounds of *y* as shown on page 11 of this manual.

A. Introducing the rule

"What kind of shoes do you have if you get mud on them? [muddy] What kind of fingers do you have if things stick to them? [sticky] What kind of room do you have if you leave it in a mess? [messy] What kind of child are you if you fuss a lot? [fussy] There are a lot of words we say with an $/\bar{e}/$ ending like that. I will show you how we spell some of them."

Print *hand, trick, flash,* and *mist* on the board. Pronounce one of the words, then add a *y* to the word and pronounce the new word. Do that to the rest of the words or let the children do some of the samples. Point out that *y* on the end of these words says $/\bar{e}/$ rather than $/\bar{i}/$ as in the words in which it is the only vowel.

Seatwork workbook, page 108

B. Reading workbook, page 109

C. Spelling

Pronounce words from the edge list for the children to spell. Point out that each word has two consonants between the vowel in the word and the *y* on the end. If they do not hear two consonants in that part of the word, they are to print two letters for the sound they do hear.

Have each word spelled orally.

Lesson 21   Unit 3

y = ē

Print each word and add *y.*

dust	dusty	puff	puffy
rock	rocky	fuzz	fuzzy
fuss	fussy	sand	sandy
hill	hilly	bump	bumpy
trash	trashy	milk	milky

Match the words with the way they sound.

b 1. happy	**a.** jel-ē	j 8. thy	**h.** flash-ē
a 2. jelly	**b.** hap-ē	n 9. sticky	**i.** diz-ē
d 3. try	**c.** krus-tē	h 10. flashy	**j.** thī
f 4. misty	**d.** trī	l 11. dizzy	**k.** frī
c 5. crusty	**e.** shī	l 12. penny	**l.** pen-ē
e 6. shy	**f.** mis-tē	k 13. fry	**m.** mī
g 7. inky	**g.** ing-kē	m 14. my	**n.** stik-ē

Phonics Workbook   **Lesson 21**

Print the words in the sentences.

taffy   cloudy   rocky   lumpy   fuzzy

1. We played on a <u>rocky</u> hill.

2. Polly has a <u>fuzzy</u> kitten.

3. Can you sleep on a <u>lumpy</u> bed?

4. Who made this sweet <u>taffy</u> ?

Circle *ed* **if it sounds like** *t.*
Put a box around *ed* **if it sounds like** *d.*
Underline the whole word if *ed* **sounds like** *ed.*

dress(ed)	jolted	pray[ed]
wicked	dream[ed]	mended
frown[ed]	sifted	weeded
petted	clean[ed]	snow[ed]
needed	brush(ed)	dash(ed)
breath[ed]	roasted	milk(ed)
climb[ed]	bak(ed)	pouted

1. baggy
2. sorry
3. Billy
4. crispy
5. hilly
6. handy
7. Timmy
8. Sally
9. glassy
10. sloppy
11. holly
12. husky
13. Becky
14. silly
15. puppy
16. fifty
17. buggy
18. scratchy
19. crafty
20. Betty
21. Peggy
22. tricky
23. bunny
24. soggy
25. Randy
26. kitty
27. forty

109

LESSON 22
Sometimes *c* = /s/

Be prepared

1. Daily drill

    Vowel sound flash cards

Lesson 22   Unit 3

c = s

Print the words in the correct column. Say the words.

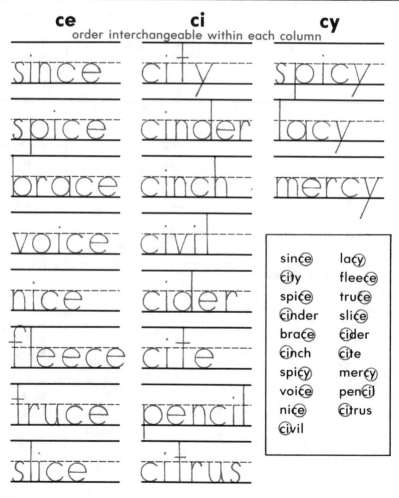

ce	ci	cy
since	city	spicy
spice	cinder	lacy
brace	cinch	mercy
voice	civil	
nice	cider	
fleece	cite	
truce	pencil	
slice	citrus	

order interchangeable within each column

since	lacy
city	fleece
spice	truce
cinder	slice
brace	cider
cinch	cite
spicy	mercy
voice	pencil
nice	citrus
civil	

Initial blend *b* flash cards
Alphabet flash cards
Wall charts
2. Make the *soft c* wall chart as shown on page 11 of this manual.

| Phonics Workbook | Lesson 22 |

Match the words with the way they sound.

d 1. face   **a.** thrīs
b 2. grace   **b.** grās
a 3. thrice   **c.** sins
c 4. since   **d.** fās
e 5. ounce   **e.** ouns

h 6. bounce   **f.** trās
f 7. trace   **g.** plās
j 8. glance   **h.** bouns
g 9. place   **i.** īs
i 10. ice   **j.** glans

Print the words in the sentences.

mice   cent   price   fence   race

1. Some vines are growing on the

fence .

2. A penny is one cent .

3. A fast boy won the race .

4. He found three mice in the traps.

5. Did you pay a big price for the
book?

1. lace
2. cell
3. prince
4. voice
5. chance
6. rice
7. dunce
8. vice
9. cent
10. quince
11. trace
12. twice
13. slice
14. fleece
15. lice
16. splice
17. choice
18. grace
19. space
20. mince
21. nice
22. cinch
23. pace
24. cir-cus
25. cis-tern
26. re-joice
27. cy-clone

111

A. Introducing the rule

Print the letter *c* on the board. "What is the sound of this letter? What other letter makes that sound? When do we use *c* and when do we use *k*?" List on the board the combinations *ca, ke, ki, co,* and *cu.*

Beside the combination *ke* print *ce.* "Sometimes we have these letters together in a word, but when you find that, *c* does not say /k/. It has the sound of another letter. When *c* has an *e* after it, *c* says /s/." Print *nt* after the *ce* combination and let the children sound the word *cent.*

Print *ci* beside the combination *ki.* "Sometimes we have a *c* before *i* in words too. Can you guess what happens? When *c* has *i* after it, *c* says /s/ again." Use your *ci* combination to build the word *city.* Tell the children that *y* says /ē/ to help them say the word.

"Turn to page 110 in your phonics book. Look at the words in the box. Find the *c* in the first word. What letter comes right after the *c*? What sound does that *c* make? Why? Circle the *c* and the *e* together. Find the *c* in the next word. What is the letter right after the *c*? Circle that letter with the *c.* Do that in each word. Make sure you circle the letter after the *c* and not the letter before the *c.*

"What other letter did you find after the *c* a few times? *C* sounds like *s* when it has an *e,* an *i,* or a *y* right after it. Notice the letters at the head of the columns on your page. Print the words you have marked in the correct columns. Try to pronounce the words. Some of them are two-syllable words."

Short cut for slow students: Put a large *1* beside the first column heading, *2* beside the second, and *3* beside the third. Have the child put the correct number before each word in the list to indicate where it belongs.

B. Reading   workbook, page 111

C. Spelling

Pronounce words for the children to spell. Tell them that the words will all have the letter *c* for the /s/ sound. After they have spelled such words as *lace* or *vice,* discuss the fact that the *e* gives the word a long vowel sound and also makes the *c* sound like *s.*

Have each word spelled orally.

LESSON 23
Sometimes *g* = /j/

Be prepared

1. Daily drill

   Final blend flash cards

   Vowel sound flash cards

   Wall charts

2. Make the wall chart for *soft g* as shown on page 11 of this manual.

A. Introducing the rule

Print the letter *c* on the board. "What are the two sounds of this consonant? We call /k/ the hard sound of *c*, and /s/ the soft sound of *c*. When does *c* have the soft sound?" Print *ce, ci,* and *cy* as the children respond.

"There is another consonant that has a hard and a soft sound. [Print the letter *g* on the board.] We learned the hard sound of this letter. What is it? [Under *ce, ci,* and *cy*, print *ge, gi,* and *gy*.] Just like the letter *c*, *g* makes its soft sound when it comes before *e, i,* or *y*. The soft sound of *g* is /j/." Print a list of words on the board for the children to find those in which *g* is followed by *e, i,* or *y*. Let them circle the two letters and pronounce the word.

gem	game	stage	gyp
cage	gym	gin	gum
shrug	gun	good	greet

Discuss the effect of adding *e* to such words as *wag, rag, sag,* and *hug*. The vowel becomes long and the *g* becomes soft.

Seatwork workbook, page 112

Have the children circle the *g* and the following letter in each word of the list in the box. Then have them print the words in the correct column according to the letters at the head of each column and try to pronounce the words.

By applying the rule that *g* sounds like *j* when followed by *e, i,* or *y*, have the children print *g* or *j* on the line after each word at the bottom of the page.

B. Review workbook, page 113

Follow the *ce, ci, cy* rule to print the sound of *c* in the words at the top of page 113. Challenge the children to try to read the words after they have decided the sound of *c*.

Proceed with the edge list as usual.

C. Spelling

Pronounce some words from the edge list for the children to spell. Have each word spelled orally.

Lesson 23   Unit 3

g = j

Print the words in the correct column. Say the words.

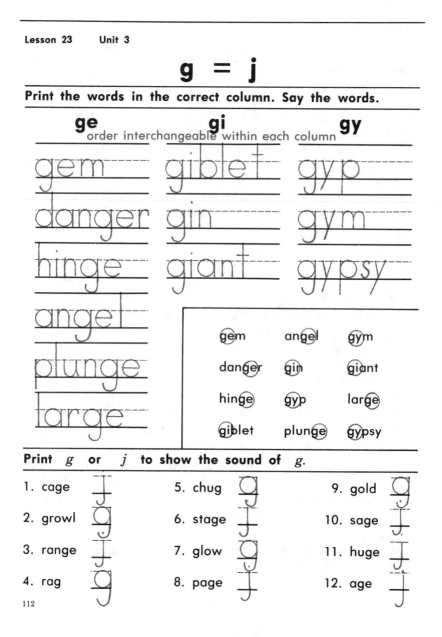

ge	**gi**	**gy**
gem	giblet	gyp
danger	gin	gym
hinge	giant	gypsy
angel		
plunge		
large		

order interchangeable within each column

gem	angel	gym
danger	gin	giant
hinge	gyp	large
giblet	plunge	gypsy

Print *g* or *j* to show the sound of *g.*

1. cage   j
2. growl g
3. range j
4. rag   g

5. chug   g
6. stage j
7. glow   g
8. page   j

9. gold   g
10. sage j
11. huge j
12. age   j

112

Gradebook: 30 points for this page

Phonics Workbook   **Lesson 23**

Print *k* **or** *s* **to show the sound of** *c.*

1. cell	S	7. cart	K	13. cob	K
2. cord	K	8. icy	S	14. cite	S
3. prince	S	9. pace	S	15. Alice	S
4. cool	K	10. Lucy	S	16. count	K
5. cry	K	11. coin	K	17. spruce	S
6. Bruce	S	12. center	S	18. civil	S

Print *t,* *d,* **or** *ed* **to show the sound of** *ed.*

1. mashed	t	7. stretched	t
2. twisted	ed	8. blended	ed
3. chilled	d	9. harmed	d
4. clawed	d	10. splashed	t
5. switched	t	11. frosted	ed
6. rained	d	12. folded	ed

1. gem
2. cage
3. sage
4. gin
5. huge
6. page
7. nice
8. cent
9. stage
10. vice
11. age
12. prance
13. change
14. twice
15. Jimmy
16. strange
17. jiffy
18. skinny
19. fussy
20. rage
21. Molly
22. quince
23. stretchy
24. fluffy
25. scrubby
26. cloudy
27. twenty

113

LESSON 24
The Letters *dge* = /j/

Be prepared
Daily drill
    Consonant digraph flash cards

Lesson 24   Unit 3

dge = j

Print the correct ending for each word.

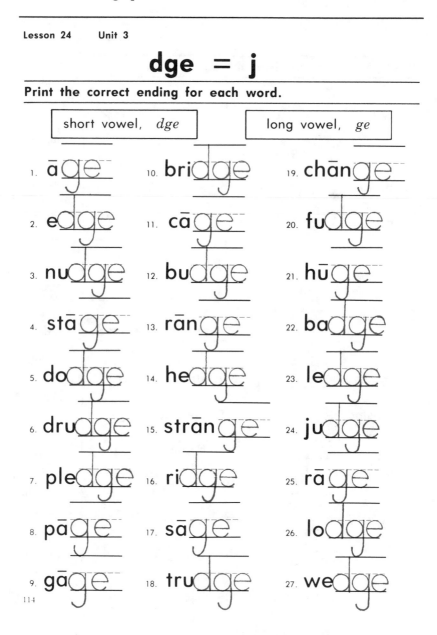

short vowel, *dge*		long vowel, *ge*

1. āge
2. edge
3. nudge
4. stāge
5. dodge
6. drudge
7. pledge
8. pāge
9. gāge

10. bridge
11. cāge
12. budge
13. rānge
14. hedge
15. strānge
16. ridge
17. sāge
18. trudge

19. chānge
20. fudge
21. hūge
22. badge
23. ledge
24. judge
25. rāge
26. lodge
27. wedge

114

Initial blend *a* flash cards
Vowel sound flash cards
Wall charts

| | **Phonics Workbook** | **Lesson 24** |

Match the words to the way they sound.

<table>
<tr><td>b</td><td>1. ledge</td><td>**a.** drej</td></tr>
<tr><td>d</td><td>2. hinge</td><td>**b.** lej</td></tr>
<tr><td>f</td><td>3. range</td><td>**c.** chānj</td></tr>
<tr><td>c</td><td>4. change</td><td>**d.** hinj</td></tr>
<tr><td>a</td><td>5. dredge</td><td>**e.** wāj</td></tr>
<tr><td>e</td><td>6. wage</td><td>**f.** rānj</td></tr>
</table>

Print the words in the sentences.

page   cage   bridge   budge   hedge

1. We stood on the bridge and looked at the stream.

2. He did the last page in his book.

3. Father planted a hedge by the lane.

4. We could not budge the big rock.

5. They have a little yellow bird in the cage .

1. edge
2. wedge
3. judge
4. ridge
5. age

6. lodge
7. dredge
8. large
9. budge
10. hedge
11. dodge
12. stage
13. fudge
14. nudge
15. trudge
16. plunge
17. bridge
18. ledge
19. range
20. pledge
21. change
22. angel
23. stranger
24. manger
25. danger

115

A. Introducing the rule

"What is the soft sound of *g*? [Print *edge* on the board.] The letters *dge* are a common ending for words that end with the /j/ sound. The three letters together make only that one sound. The *d* is just as silent as the *e* on the end."

Print a few of the *dge* words on the board and circle the last three letters of each. Let the children say the words.

hedge   ridge   dodge   fudge

"The *dge* ending is usually found on a short vowel word. If the word has a long vowel, it is usually spelled with *ge*. Sometimes we have *nge* after a long vowel, but the *n* is not silent like the *d*."

Seatwork   workbook, page 114

Help the children to understand the guide in the boxes at the top of page 114. They are to finish the short vowel words on the page with *dge,* and the long vowel words with *ge.*

B. Reading   workbook, page 115

Have the children follow the directions and read the edge list.

C. Spelling

Pronounce some long vowel words and some short vowel words with /j/ endings for the children to spell. Have each word spelled orally after the letters have been printed or arranged.

LESSON 25
Review Long Vowel Rules

Be prepared

Daily drill

Vowel spelling flash cards—Include *soft c* and *g* from set 9.

Initial blend *b* flash cards

Vowel sound flash cards

A. Long vowel sounds

find	best	late	heat	fly
plug	rain	lot	slow	think
tune	by	boat	cry	flat

Print a list of words on the board. Have the children consider the vowel sound of the first word and let someone mark it with a macron. On deciding that the second word has a short vowel sound, let someone circle the word. When you come to a word in which *y* makes the /ī/ sound, teach the children to print *i* after the word and put the macron over the *i*.

Seatwork   workbook, page 116

B. Long vowel rules

Let the children identify the long vowel rule for each of the words you have printed on the board.

Seatwork   workbook, page 117

Have the children identify the rule for each of the long vowel words on page 116, then print each word in the section with that number on page 117.

Proceed with the edge list as usual.

C. Spelling

Pronounce words from the edge list. Give the rule number when it is needed to indicate the correct long vowel spelling. Have each word spelled aloud.

Extra activity

Have the children copy onto a paper in alphabetical order the short vowel words from page 116.

Long Vowels

1. We see an *e* at the end.

2. We see 2 vowels together.

3. We see 1 vowel. It is at the end.

4. Special endings: īld, īnd, ōld, ōll, ōlt, ōst

Mark the long vowels. Circle the words with short vowels.
Print *ī* for words like *by*.

1. strēam	10. (drench)	19. jōke	28. cōach
2. (much)	11. scōld	20. (blink)	29. (jet)
3. (pluck)	12. shē	21. blīnd	30. grāy
4. bē	13. plāte	22. (last)	31. (chop)
5. (egg)	14. (ash)	23. sprȳ	32. strīve
6. fūme	15. (king)	24. mōst	33. strōll
7. (ox)	16. chīld	25. (flip)	34. (next)
8. (ink)	17. shȳ	26. prīze	35. grēet
9. crīed	18. (gruff)	27. gō	36. (hatch)

Phonics Workbook | **Lesson 25**

Print the words from page 116 with the correct rule number.

1 fume
plate
joke
prize
strive

2 stream
cried
coach
gray
greet

3 be
she
shy
spry
go

4 scold
child
blind
most
stroll

1. we
2. jeep
3. bone
4. fire
5. mule
6. game
7. grind
8. say
9. faith
10. screen
11. tie
12. roast
13. jolt
14. stray
15. tune
16. streak
17. grow
18. reach
19. wove
20. chain
21. woe
22. hue
23. stripe
24. thy
25. lo
26. wild
27. trade
28. scroll
29. post
30. mew
31. cold

order interchangeable within each section   117

LESSON 26
Review *o* Sounds and Diphthongs

Be prepared
Daily drill
   Consonant sound flash cards

Lesson 26   **Unit 3**   Gradebook: 42 points for this page

Sounds of O

Print $\overline{oo}$ or oo.

1. food	OO	8. scoop	OO	15. screw	OO
2. full	OO	9. put	OO	16. bush	OO
3. could	OO	10. room	OO	17. wool	OO
4. threw	OO	11. shook	OO	18. spoon	OO
5. roof	OO	12. spool	OO	19. stood	OO
6. cook	OO	13. shoot	OO	20. crew	OO
7. cool	OO	14. pool	OO	21. moon	OO

Print *oi* or *ou*.

1. spoil	OI	8. boy	OI	15. noise	OI
2. proud	OU	9. house	OU	16. cow	OU
3. vow	OU	10. crown	OU	17. joy	OI
4. Roy	OI	11. toy	OI	18. round	OU
5. howl	OU	12. pouch	OU	19. owl	OU
6. voice	OI	13. town	OU	20. hoist	OI
7. growl	OU	14. south	OU	21. frown	OU

Final blend flash cards
Wall charts

A. Vowel sounds workbook, page 118
Have the children print the vowel sound for each word.

Phonics Workbook   **Lesson 26**

Gradebook: 44 points for this page

$$o = \hat{o}$$ $$aw = \hat{o}$$

$$a = \hat{o} \text{ before } l$$ $$au = \hat{o}$$

1. mood
2. true

Circle the letters that say ô.

hall	hawk	malt	frost
haunt	cloth	fault	thaw
gloss	maul	cross	cost
small	salt	jaw	halt
Paul	fog	crawl	squaw
strong	fawn	shawl	vault

5. dawn
6. brook
7. fool
8. fowl
9. law
10. clown
11. gloom
12. grew
13. foot
14. toss
15. broil
16. ground

Match the words with the sounds.

1. broth_____ ô	11. poise ô
2. foil ōo	12. call ōo
3. push oo	13. scoot oo
4. hoot oi	14. bull oi
5. mount_____ ou	15. now_____ ou

17. stall
18. proof
19. hood
20. pull
21. soil
22. raw
23. lost

6. drew ô	16. yawn_____ ô
7. Saul ōo	17. soy ōo
8. coin oo	18. bound oo
9. brown oi	19. flew oi
10. took ou	20. would ou

24. glue
25. prowl
26. shout
27. chew
28. haul
29. moist

119

B. More vowel sounds   workbook, page 119

Go over the guide at the top of page 119 with the children, then have them circle the letter or combination that makes the /ô/ sound in each word.

Have them follow the directions for the bottom of the page.

Proceed with the edge list as usual.

C. Spelling

Pronounce words from the edge list for the children to spell. Perhaps by this time they are ready for the challenge of spelling a word orally without first printing it or arranging the letters.

Extra activity

1. Prepare a list of pronunciations for some of the /ô/ words on page 119. Let the children find the words in the workbook and print each one beside the pronunciation.

2. Let the children copy some words from page 119 and beside each one, try to print the pronunciation using the /ô/ symbol.

LESSON 27
Review Modified Vowels

Be prepared
Daily drill
 Vowel sound flash cards
 Initial blend *a* flash cards
 Wall charts

A. We all say ėr   workbook, page 120

Have the children use the /ėr/ spelling given at the head of each list for all the words in that list, then choose from any of the lists to fill in the sentences below.

B. Sounds of *ar* and *or*   workbook, page 121

Have the children finish all the words in the first column with *ar* and all the words in the second with *or*, then choose from either column to complete the sentences.

Proceed with the edge list as usual.

C. Spelling

Pronounce words from the edge list for the children to spell. Tell them which spelling to use for the /ėr/ words. Give opportunity again for the children to spell words orally without first printing or arranging them.

Lesson 27   Unit 3

We all say ėr.

er	ir	ur
t**er**m	st**ir**	c**ur**l
f**er**n	b**ir**d	b**ur**n
p**er**ch	th**ir**d	n**ur**se
v**er**se	g**ir**l	t**ur**n
cl**er**k	squ**ir**m	ch**ur**ch

Print words in the sentences.

1. I can say a Bible verse .

2. He made a fire to burn the trash.

3. Wait for your turn to get a drink.

4. A bird made a nest in our tree.

5. A fern is a green plant.

6. The nurse helps sick people. (or girl)

120

Phonics Workbook **Lesson 27**

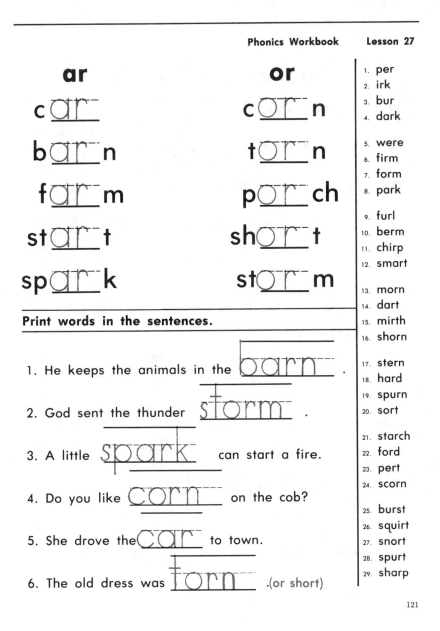

ar

c ar

b ar n

f ar m

st ar t

sp ar k

or

c or n

t or n

p or ch

sh or t

st or m

Print words in the sentences.

1. He keeps the animals in the barn .

2. God sent the thunder storm .

3. A little spark can start a fire.

4. Do you like corn on the cob?

5. She drove the car to town.

6. The old dress was torn .(or short)

1. per
2. irk
3. bur
4. dark
5. were
6. firm
7. form
8. park
9. furl
10. berm
11. chirp
12. smart
13. morn
14. dart
15. mirth
16. shorn
17. stern
18. hard
19. spurn
20. sort
21. starch
22. ford
23. pert
24. scorn
25. burst
26. squirt
27. snort
28. spurt
29. sharp

121

LESSON 28
Review Consonant Blends

Be prepared
Daily drill
   Consonant digraph flash cards

Lesson 28   Unit 3

Consonant Blends

Print the correct words in the sentences.

1. We had popcorn and drink for our **snack** .	1. stack 2. snack 3. slack
2. The people in the ark did not **drown** in the flood.	4. brown 5. frown 6. drown
3. How hard did the wind **blow** ?	7. blow 8. flow 9. glow
4. He could not pay the **price** for the house.	10. twice 11. price 12. spice
5. Did you see the duck **splash** ?	13. plash 14. clash 15. splash
6. The animals sleep on **straw** .	16. squaw 17. straw 18. sprawl
7. He **threw** the ball on the roof.	19. threw 20. screw 21. shrew

Initial blend *b* flash cards
Wall charts

A. Initial blends workbook, page 122

Have the children print the correct word from the box at the right of
each sentence.

Phonics Workbook   Lesson 28

Print the correct words in the sentences.

1. Mother has a nice ____quilt____ on the bed.

   1. quilt
   2. wilt
   3. tilt

2. We should ____help____ each other.

   4. yelp
   5. help
   6. whelp

3. The jar is on the ____shelf____ .

   7. shelf
   8. self
   9. pelf

4. Sally gave me a ____crisp____ cookie.

   10. crisp
   11. wisp
   12. lisp

5. Andy helped to ____lift____ the big box.

   13. drift
   14. swift
   15. lift

6. Can you ____jump____ from the edge of the porch?

   16. lump
   17. jump
   18. stump

7. Draw a rabbit in the ____blank____ space.

   19. drank
   20. blank
   21. shrank

   22. next
   23. task
   24. vest
   25. squint
   26. crept
   27. duct

123

Short cut for slow students: Circle or underline the correct choice.

B. Final blends workbook, page 123

This page is to be done in the same way as page 122. Encourage the children to do what the last sentence tells them to do.

Use the words in the boxes as the usual edge list. You may want to include the lists from both pages.

C. Spelling

Pronounce words for the children to spell orally and/or to print or arrange.

LESSON 29

Review Sounds of *s* and *y*

Be prepared

Daily drill

    Vowel spelling flash cards

    Final blend flash cards

    Vowel sound flash cards

A. Sounds of *s* workbook, page 124

To help the children concentrate on the *s* in the words, you may want to direct them to go through the list and circle the *s* in each word before printing the sound on the blank. You may have them go over the list the third time to determine the number of syllables in each word, rather than trying to handle all the items at one time.

At the bottom of the page, have the children follow the rule to spell the *s* form of the words given.

B. Sounds of *y* workbook, page 125

You may have the children first of all find and circle the *y* in each word, then print the sound of the letter on the first blank, and the number of syllables on the second.

Have the children follow the directions at the bottom of the page.

Proceed with the edge list as usual.

C. Spelling

Pronounce some of the simpler words from the edge list for oral spelling. Let the children print or arrange some of the others. Give root words first and repeat them with the *y* or *s* ending. Give any long vowel rule numbers that may be needed. (*Flies* could be given as a word for *rule 2* rather than *fly* with a suffix). You may want to remind the children that words with the *y* ending will have two consonants before the *y*, meaning the consonant is doubled if they hear only one.

Extra activity

Let the children print the sound of *s* and the number of syllables for the words at the bottom of page 124.

Lesson 29   Unit 3

Sounds of s

Print s or z. Print the number of syllables.

1.	missed	S	1	9.	six	S	1
2.	teams	Z	1	10.	horse	S	1
3.	pits	S	1	11.	obeys	Z	2
4.	preachers	Z	2	12.	scrape	S	1
5.	mouse	S	1	13.	kittens	Z	2
6.	yokes	S	1	14.	rabbits	S	2
7.	caps	S	1	15.	peels	Z	1
8.	gates	S	1	16.	wisdom	Z	2

Print each word with s or es.

1. peach peaches z 2
2. boot boots s 1
3. tax taxes z 2
4. dress dresses z 2
5. sleep sleeps s 1
6. mix mixes z 2
7. sing sings z 1
8. rush rushes z 2

Phonics Workbook   **Lesson 29**

Sounds of y

Print *y*, *ē*, **or** *ī*. **Print the number of syllables.**

1.	candy	ē	2	9.	good-by	ī	2
2.	your	y	⊥	10.	yes	y	⊥
3.	my	ī	⊥	11.	berry	ē	2
4.	fly	ī	⊥	12.	yelled	y	⊥
5.	cherry	ē	2	13.	fuzzy	ē	2
6.	yarn	y	⊥	14.	try	ī	⊥
7.	carry	ē	2	15.	dusty	ē	2
8.	shy	ī	⊥	16.	curly	ē	2

Match the words with the way they sound.

f	1. thirty	**a.**	plen-tē
e	2. furry	**b.**	sprī
b	3. spry	**c.**	yon-der
d	4. yawned	**d.**	yônd
c	5. yonder	**e.**	fer-ē
a	6. plenty	**f.**	ther-tē

1. toes
2. rusty
3. yank
4. ties
5. ply
6. pays
7. hobby
8. sharks
9. goes
10. grouchy
11. bees
12. speedy
13. books
14. rugs
15. dry
16. flies
17. spoils
18. funny
19. poise
20. drafty
21. sleepy
22. please
23. parts
24. oily
25. pies
26. trashy
27. yard

LESSON 30
Review Sounds of *c* and *g*

Be prepared
Daily drill
   Alphabet flash cards

Lesson 30   Unit 3

Sounds of c

Print *k* or *s*. Print the number of syllables.

1.	stick	k	1	9.	cloth	k	1
2.	icy	s	2	10.	cider	s	2
3.	pencil	s	2	11.	vice	s	1
4.	fence	s	1	12.	clean	k	1
5.	crusty	k	2	13.	spicy	s	2
6.	corn	k	1	14.	since	s	1
7.	clover	k	2	15.	city	s	2
8.	center	s	2	16. scream	k	1

Add *ed* and *ing*. Print the number of syllables.

	ed	1 or 2	ing	1 or 2
stack	stacked	1	stacking	2
plant	planted	2	planting	2
bloom	bloomed	1	blooming	2
test	tested	2	testing	2

126

Wall charts

A. Sounds of *c* and suffixes workbook, page 126

You may want to have the children first of all find the *c* in each word and circle it with the letter that follows it. Then according to the rule, *c = s* when followed by *e, i,* or *y,* have them print the sound of the letter on the

---

Phonics Workbook   Lesson 30

Sounds of g

Print *g* **or** *j*. **Print the number of syllables.**

1.	greedy	g	2	9.	ginger	j 2
2.	stage	j	1	10.	graze	g 1
3.	dingy	j	2	11.	hinge	j 1
4.	gravy	g	2	12.	gather	g 2
5.	wage	j	1	13.	forgot	g 2
6.	danger	j	2	14.	bridge	j 1
7.	greeted	g	2	15.	manger	j 2
8.	magic	j	2	16.	change	j 1

Print the vowel sound for each word.

1. age ā 7. budge ŭ 13. page ā 19. joy oi

2. edge ĕ 8. nudge ŭ 14. cage ā 20. grew oo

3. badge ā 9. hedge ĕ 15. ridge ĭ 21. foot oo

4. bridge ĭ 10. sage ā 16. wedge ĕ 22. fall ô

5. stage ā 11. gage ā 17. thaw ô 23. boil oi

6. huge ū 12. dodge ŏ 18. mouse ou 24. true oo

1.	face
2.	dice
3.	cell
4.	gem
5.	gym
6.	race
7.	glance
8.	gin
9.	place
10.	bounce
11.	cage
12.	cent
13.	prance
14.	thrice
15.	rage
16.	prince
17.	brace
18.	sledge
19.	cite
20.	large
21.	price
22.	drudge
23.	mice
24.	voice
25.	badge
26.	page
27.	since
28.	gypsy
29.	cinder
30.	center
31.	pencil
32.	
	hodgepodge

127

first blank. Have them sound the words and print the number of syllables in the second blank.

At the bottom of the page, have the children print the given words with *ed* and *ing*, then show how many syllables the new words have.

B. Sounds of *g* and vowel sounds   workbook, page 127

You may again have the children circle the letter under consideration and the letter that follows it before filling in the blanks.

The first sixteen words at the bottom of the page are based on the rule that *dge* follows a short vowel. The rest of the words review some of the variant vowel sounds.

Proceed with the edge list as usual.

C. Spelling

Use words from the edge list for spelling and printing or arranging the letters.

Reading
Unit 2

GENERAL PLAN

The vocabulary review schedule lists flash cards by words rather than by lesson number to give more practice to those particular words which are used less frequently in the reader or workbook.

The Bible lesson is contained in the reading lesson and will be studied by discussing what the children have read.

The reader lists the new words for each lesson at the end of the lesson. They are categorized as *Key* words, *Sound* words, and *Learn* words. The children should be able to figure out the *Key* and *Sound* words on their own. Help them to learn the *Learn* words by applying some phonics (using simplified pronunciations which may differ from a dictionary), and by printing the words in sentences for the children to consider context.

The children should also develop acquaintance with the table of contents and learn where to find the Bible memory verses as you proceed through the book.

Reading Lessons   Unit 2

LESSON 1

What God Gave—Father and Mother

Be prepared

1. Vocabulary flash cards

    New words: 2:1

    Review words: want, was, obey, love, punished

    Phrases: 2:1

2. Make provision for storing the worksheet items until after lesson 7, when they will be taken home as a packet.

Introduce the new reader.

Help the children read the title. It is just like the title of their first book except for the word *more.* Help them to find the table of contents and observe the story numbers and page numbers. Have them turn to page 14 to find story number one. Notice the heading *Lesson 1* and the title below it. Notice that the lesson continues at the top of the next page.

A. Vocabulary

1. In the readers, direct attention to the bottom of page 15. Have the children find the three bold print headings and tell you with what sounds they begin. Print *Key* on the board and tell the children that it says *key.* "The words you will have in this part of your lesson have a key for you to unlock them. A key helps you to get in somewhere or do something that you could not do otherwise. What is the first word in the *key* part of your page? That word is a key for you. If you did not know that word, you probably could not say the word beside it. But because you know it, you can probably say the other one. Look at the word beside *want.* What word is the new word?"

2. Print *Sound* on the board and tell the children that it says *sound.* "You can say the word in this part of the lesson because you know the sounds of the letters. Look at the word under *sound* in your book. What does the *e* at the end of the word tell you? What is the word?"

3. Print *Learn* on the board and see if anyone recognizes it from the title of the book. "The words in this part do not sound just like the letter sounds as you have studied them. You will need to learn what each word is and remember it without only sounding the letters. Letter sounds will help you to learn and remember these words though. Look at the first word under *learn* in your book. What is the beginning sound of the word?" Print *Father is a man.* on the board and underline *Father.* "What do you think this word is?" Give them additional clues or tell them the word. Print *fathers* directly under *father* and suggest that they use the one new word for a key to the other one. Print the sentence *Mother can help Father.* for a clue to the word *mother* and use that word for a key to *mothers. Our fathers and mothers love us.* can help the children to guess the word

our. Let the three sentences remain on the board for the children to refer to if they need a reminder.

4. Drill with flash cards the new and review words and phrases.

B. Reader

Review the meaning of the question mark and period.

Put an exclamation mark on the board and ask the children to find one like it in the lesson. "This is called an exclamation mark. When we have an exclamation mark after some words, we read those words a bit louder and say them as though it is something very important or exciting." Let someone practice reading the line with the exclamation marks.

Have the children read the story silently two or three times.

If the class is large, have a few individuals stand to read orally before discussing the Bible lesson and others at a later point in the discussion or at the end.

C. Bible lesson

"Did anybody ever give you something? What was given to you? Who gave it? Does it make you happy when someone gives you something?

"Turn to the page before the lesson we read. What does it say? All of our stories for a few days will be about what God gave. What did God give us? The title of the story we read tells one thing that God gave.

"God gave you a father and mother. Did you ever think of them as a gift from God? What would you ever do without them? What are some of the things they do for you? What does the lesson say they do?

"What does the lesson say we want to do for them? Why do we obey them?" Have the children read the third to last sentence on page 14.

Dwell on the last two sentences of page 14. "Sometimes children get the idea they don't like to obey. They wish they could do what they want to do instead of obeying. Did you ever see some children that did not obey and their parents did not make them obey? Such children are not happy children. Even when it seems hard to obey, we want to obey because that is the way to be happy, and that is what God likes."

Have the class read the last three lines of the lesson again with you.

"Our new Bible verse is about the things that God gives us. 'Every good gift and every perfect gift is from above' (James 1:17a)."

Practice the verse with the class a few times.

D. Workbook

page 6

The new words are repeated on the workbook page. In the first exercise, the children are to complete the word by filling in the missing letters. At the bottom of the page, the words are to be chosen by the context of the sentence.

page 7

Have the children tell you what the directions say. For the bottom of
the page, make sure they understand how to decide what should be the *next*
figure in the *sequence*.

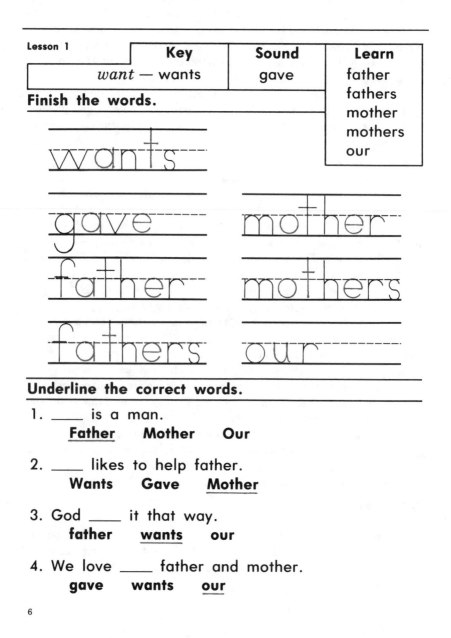

Lesson 1

Key	Sound	Learn
want — wants	gave	father

Finish the words.

father
fathers
mother
mothers
our

wants

gave   mother

father   mothers

fathers   our

Underline the correct words.

1. ____ is a man.
   Father   Mother   Our

2. ____ likes to help father.
   Wants   Gave   **Mother**

3. God ____ it that way.
   father   **wants**   our

4. We love ____ father and mother.
   gave   wants   **our**

6

E. Worksheet

The worksheets for this unit are to be done each day and kept at school to make a packet to take home at the end of each section.

"God gave us fathers and mothers."

"Color the pictures of the father and mother, paste them on construction

---

Reading Workbook   **Unit 2**   **Lesson 1**

Underline the correct words.

1. Adam was the first ____.   <u>father</u>   mother

2. Eve was the first ____.   father   <u>mother</u>

3. God ____ us fathers.   <u>gave</u>   want

4. ____ gave us mothers.   We   <u>He</u>

5. ____ fathers love us.   <u>Our</u>   Obey

6. God ____ us to obey our fathers. <u>wants</u>   was

7. We want to obey. Yes, we ____.   <u>do</u>   to

Circle the correct shape.

7

paper, and cut them out." Have the children save them in a workbook, or collect them and keep them until the end of the section.

Extra activity

Have the children start a list on writing paper of the things God gave. Tell them which sentences to copy from the reader, or print the sentences on the board for them to copy.

God gave us fathers.

God gave us mothers.

Have them keep this paper with the cut out figures.

LESSON 2
What God Gave—Children

Be prepared

Vocabulary flash cards

New words: 2:2

Review words: wants, all, love, gave, father, fathers, mother, mothers, our

Phrases: 2:2

Review phrases: 2:1

A. Vocabulary

1. Explain the *Sound* and *Learn* sections again and do it daily until the children recognize the words and understand their meaning. You may want to comment that none of the new words for this lesson are key words.
2. Have the children tell you what the sound word says.
3. Print *We are children.* on the board and see if the class can guess the word *children.*
4. Print *be* on the board and let the children tell you what it is. Add the letters *cause* and print the sentence *We love Him because He loves us.*
5. Print the word *of* and tell the children that this word does not sound like the letters they see in the word. You may let them sound the letters; then print *uv* in parentheses beside the word and let them sound that.
6. Print *does* and put *duz* in parentheses beside it.
7. Use the pair of sentences *He wants some.* and *I want some, too.* as a clue for the word *too.*
8. Let the sentences and pronunciations remain on the board for reminders as you drill the words and phrases.

B. Reader

Review the meaning of the question mark, exclamation mark, and period. Have the children study the lesson silently; then conduct oral reading.

C. Bible lesson

Turn to the beginning of the section again and read the title, *What God Gave.* "What did we read about in lesson 1 that God gave? What does this lesson tell us that God gave?

"One day God gave your parents a very special gift. They loved their gift, and it made them very happy. Do you know what that gift was? It was you! God gave you to your parents. How many other gifts like that did God give to your parents?

"To whom else did God give such gifts? You can find an answer in the lesson we read.

"Who loves the children? What kind of children does God love?

"Why do we love God?"

Practice James 1:17a.

D. Workbook

page 8

Discuss the directions with the children.

page 9

Let the children read the directions at the top of the page and notice

Lesson 2

Sound	**Learn**
him	too
	because
	children
	does
Finish the words.	of

h i m   c h i l d r e n

t o o   d o e s

b e c a u s e   o f

Underline the correct phrase.

all are on
<u>some are on</u>

all are in
some are in

all are good
some are good

all are children
<u>some are children</u>

all are little
<u>some are little</u>

all are big
some are big

that the answers to the first four questions are different forms of the same word.

Read the directions at the bottom of the page and have someone read both sentences with each of their possible endings.

Reading Workbook   Unit 2   Lesson 2

Underline the correct words.

1. God ____ children.	love	<u>loves</u>
2. He ____ all the children.	love	<u>loves</u>
3. We ____ God.	<u>love</u>	loves
4. God ____ us first.	love	<u>loved</u>
5. Does God love us?	<u>yes</u>	no
6. Does God love big children?	<u>yes</u>	no
7. Does God love little children?	<u>yes</u>	no
8. Are all the children big?	yes	<u>no</u>
9. Are all the children little?	yes	<u>no</u>
10. Did God love us first?	<u>yes</u>	no

Underline the correct phrase.

1. God loves
   a. <u>all the children.</u>
   b. some of the children.
   c. some fathers and mothers.

2. We love Him
   a. because He made Adam.
   b. <u>because He loved us first.</u>
   c. because He made light.

9

E. Worksheet

Color, paste, and cut out the pictures of the children.

Extra activity

Have the children compose the sentence *God gave children.* from words in the reader, or print it on the board for them to copy. Have them put it on the same paper as they did the two sentences about parents.

LESSON 3
What God Gave—the Home

Be prepared

Vocabulary flash cards

New words: 2:3

Review words: first, wants, our, him, too, because, children, does, of

Phrases: 2:3

Review phrases: 2:1-2:2

A. Vocabulary

1. Let the children say the key and sound words.
2. Print *It will make us happy to obey.* and underline *happy.* Put your hand over the last two letters of *happy.* Have the children sound the first syllable and then try to read the sentence.
3. Print *He is happy. She is happy. They are happy.* Can the children guess the last sentence? You may point out that the first two letters have the same beginning sound as *the.*
4. Print *We are happy when we obey.* for the word *when.*
5. From the new and review words ask the children which word(s)—
   a. have the /ā/ sound. (make, they, obeyed)
   b. rhymes with *then.* (when)
   c. rhymes with *buzz.* (does)
   d. means "a glad feeling." (happy)
   e. mean or refer to people. (children, they, him)
   f. means "also." (too)
   g. is a word we use when something belongs to us. (our)
6. Flash the words and phrases.

B. Reader

Have the children study the lesson silently; then conduct oral reading class.

See how quickly the children can find a sentence you read from the story.

C. Bible lesson

Turn to the table of contents in the front of the book. Let the children read the title of section 1 and give the names of the first three stories as you ask for number 1, number 2, and number 3. Review James 1:17a.

"God gave us homes. What is a home? It is not just the house you live in. It is the people you live with. You are part of the home, too.

"We like our homes. What makes a good home? Can you find some things in the lesson that make a good home?

"How can big children help to make a home happy? How can little children help to make a home happy?

"Who had the first home? Was it a happy home? What made it happy?"

Have the children read the last sentence again with you. "See what you can do when you get home tonight, to make your home happy."

D. Workbook

page 10

Have the children read and follow the directions.

page 11

Discuss the different meanings of the word *too* as used at the bottom

Lesson 3	Key	Sound	Learn
	help — helps	had	happy
	obey — obeyed	make	they
			when

Finish the words.

he lps   happy

obeyed   they

had   when

make

Circle the correct word.

1. He is happy because he ____.
   had   make   (helps)

2. They are happy because they ____.
   (obeyed)   when   happy

3. I like when I am ____.
   They   (happy)   helps

4. God can ____ us happy.
   (make)   They   when

of the page—"more than enough" and "also."

E. Worksheet

Proceed as for lessons 1 and 2. Discuss what it takes to make a home. It takes more than a house.

If the children have been listing on writing paper the things God gave, have them add the first sentence of this lesson.

Reading Workbook   Unit 2   Lesson 3

Underline the correct words.

1. A good father ____ to make a good home.   help   <u>helps</u>

2. A good mother ____ to make a good home.   help   <u>helps</u>

3. Children ____ make a happy home.   <u>help</u>   helps

4. We want to ____ make a happy home.   <u>help</u>   helps

5. Big children ____ to make a happy home.   help   <u>helps</u>

6. They are happy when they ____.   <u>help</u>   helps

Match the words to the pictures.
Color the pictures.

too big

too little

I want to see it.

I want to see it, too.

11

LESSON 4

What God Gave—a Time to Work

Be prepared
Vocabulary flash cards
New words: 2:4

Lesson 4	Key	Sound	Learn
day + *time* = daytime *make* — makes	so sun	should that work

Finish the words.

daytime should

makes that

so work

sun

Print the new word.

1. When is it light? daytime

2. What should we do? work

3. Father can do work that I can not do.

12

Review words: wants, him, because, children, does, of, helps, obeyed, had,
    make, happy, they, when
Phrases: 2:4
Review phrases: 2:1-2:3

Reading Workbook   Unit 2   Lesson 4

Underline the correct answers.

1. Should we work in the night?   **yes**   **<u>no</u>**

2. Should we work in the daytime?   **<u>yes</u>**   **no**

3. Should fathers and mothers work?   **<u>yes</u>**   **no**

4. Should children work?   **<u>yes</u>**   **no**

5. Should it make us happy to help?   **<u>yes</u>**   **no**

6. God gave work
   a. for the night.
   b. for all to see.
   <u>c. for fathers and mothers to do.</u>

7. The time to work is
   a. in the night.
   <u>b. in the daytime.</u>
   c. when we do not work.

Match the words to the pictures.

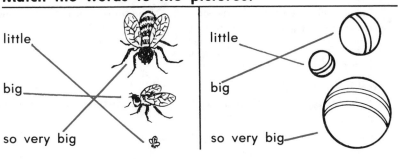

little   little

big   big

so very big   so very big

13

A. Vocabulary

1. Let the children say the key and sound words. If you have not yet had the phonics lesson for today, you will need to help them with the word *so*.
2. Print *the* and *they* on the board. Ask someone to say the words and to underline th in each word as he says it. Print *that* and underline th again. "This word begins with the same sound as *the* and *they*. Can you sound it?"
3. "When there are toys scattered on the floor and dirty dishes are on the table and the little children are fussy and mother has ironing to do, what should you do?" Print the sentence *You should help Mother.* and see if the children can guess the word *should*.
4. Add the word *work* to the end of the sentence and see if the children can read it.
5. Drill the words and phrases.

B. Reader

Have the children study silently and then read orally. See how quickly they can find a sentence you read.

C. Bible lesson

Let the children list from memory the things they have read about so far that God gave. "What did we read about today that God gave? [work and a time to work] God gave work. Did you ever think of your work as a gift from God? Do you like to work? Work is a good part of our lives. It gives us a satisfied feeling to do the work God gives us to do.

"To whom did God give work?

"What kind of work can you do? When do we do our work? Why do we work in the daytime?

"How can we help God?

"When we thank God for His gifts to us, let us remember to thank Him for the work He gave us to do."

Review James 1:17a.

D. Workbook

page 12

Help the children read the directions. At the bottom of the page they are to use one of the new words to answer the question or fill in the blank.

page 13

Help the children read the directions.

E. Worksheet

"Color the pictures. Cut out the sentences and paste them with the correct pictures."

Add to the printed list of things God gave:

God gave a time to work.

God gave work for all to do.

LESSON 5

What God Gave—a Time to Rest

Be prepared
Vocabulary flash cards

New words: 2:5

Review words: light, can, not, too, does, of, obeyed, make, they, daytime, makes, so, sun, that

Phrases: 2:5

Review phrases: he wants, when we are, because he, for mother, our fathers, should work

A. Vocabulary
1. Let the children tell you the key words.
2. Print these sentences on the board.

    I can see the *moon* in the sky.

    I can see the *stars* in the sky.

    Tell the children that both sentences tell something that we can see at night and see if they can guess the words by the beginning sounds.
3. Print *I can rest at night.* Hold your hand over the *t* in *rest* and have the children sound the first three letters of the word; then have them say it again and add the /t/ sound.
4. Print *It is quiet at night.* Put a macron over the *i* in *quiet* and if necessary cover the last two letters of the word as they sound the first part.
5. Drill the new and review words and phrases.

B. Reader
Review the table of contents again. At this point the children should be able to read all the titles in section 1.

After silent reading, conduct oral reading class, encouraging good expression especially in the questions and answers.

C. Bible lesson
"Do you like to be in the dark?

"Who made the dark time? Why do you think God made the night? Did He make that for a gift to us, too? Do we like His gift of the dark, quiet nighttime?

"What do we do at night? What would it be like if there was no time to rest? God was good to give us the nighttime. When we have a good night of sleep, we feel ready to do good work the next day.

"Why is the nighttime a good time to rest? What helps us to rest at night? What lights can we see at night?

"Let us name all of God's gifts that we have read about in the last five lessons."

Review James 1:17a.

230 *Unit 2 Reading*

D. Workbook
pages 14 and 15
 Help the children to read the directions.

E. Worksheet
 "Color the picture. Cut out the rectangles with words and paste them

Gradebook: 21 points

Lesson 5	**Key**	**Learn**
	light — lights	moon
	night + time = nighttime	quiet
		rest
Finish the words.		stars

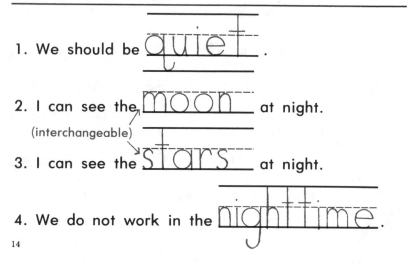

Print the new words.

1. We should be quiet .

2. I can see the moon at night.

(interchangeable)

3. I can see the stars at night.

4. We do not work in the nighttime.

14

under the picture so the complete sentence says, 'God gave us a time to rest.' "

The children may copy this sentence, adding it to their list of things God gave.

Underline the correct words.

1. The nighttime is a   **work**   <u>**rest**</u>   **help**

   time to ____.

2. It is ____ at night.   **big**   **happy**   <u>**quiet**</u>

3. We can see the ____.   <u>**moon**</u>   **day**   **sun**

4. It makes a little ____   **moon**   <u>**light**</u>   **stars**

   for us.

5. We can not see the   <u>**at**</u>   **on**   **in**

   sun ____ night.

Match the words to the pictures.

gave
happy

quiet
children

work
stars

LESSON 6
What God Gave—Day and Night

Be prepared
Vocabulary flash cards
   New words: 2:6

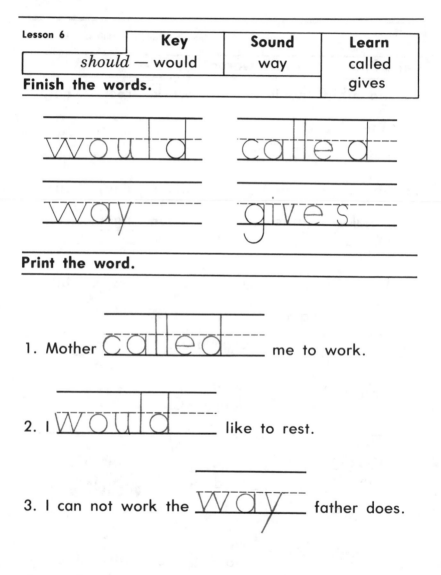

Lesson 6	Key	Sound	Learn
should — would		way	called
Finish the words.			gives

would   called

way   gives

Print the word.

1. Mother c̲a̲l̲l̲e̲d̲ me to work.

2. I w̲o̲u̲l̲d̲ like to rest.

3. I can not work the w̲a̲y̲ father does.

Review words: our, him, obeyed, had, happy, makes, so, lights, nighttime, rest

Phrases: 2:6

Review phrases: all the children, moon and stars, He does, they help,
quiet night, we should

Reading Workbook   Unit 2   Lesson 6

Underline the correct words.

1. What did God call the light?   <u>day</u>   night

2. When do we see the stars?   day   <u>night</u>

3. When do we see the sun?   <u>day</u>   night

4. When do we work?   <u>day</u>   night

5. When do we rest?   day   <u>night</u>

6. Would we want to work all

   the time?   yes   <u>no</u>

7. Would we want to rest all the time? yes   <u>no</u>

8. Do we like everything the way God

   made it?   <u>yes</u>   no

Match the words to the pictures.

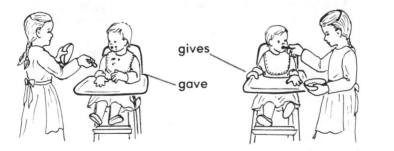

gives

gave

17

A. Vocabulary

1. Let the children say the key and sound words.
2. Print *all* on the board; then add the *c* at the beginning; then add the *ed* and see if someone can say the word and put it in a sentence.
3. Let someone sound the word *give* according to the phonics rules they have learned. Tell them that this word does not follow the rule, and the *i* has the short sound even if there is an e on the end. When they recognize the word, add the *s*.
4. Practice the word and phrase cards.
5. Let the children sound the words for *Extra Practice* in the reader by rhyming each word with the one at the top of the list.

B. Reader

Have the children read the lesson silently.

Teach the class how to read in unison. Let the boys read the first sentence in unison and the girls read the next sentence in unison, and so on, all the way through the story.

C. Bible lesson

"If you could choose something to eat right now, what would you ask for? It would be nice to eat some ____ [name the chosen food] now. Then suppose you opened your lunch box at noon and found it full of ____. Maybe you would be glad to eat ____ for lunch. But what if you were given more of it to eat when you got home from school? Then when you were hungry for supper, what if that were all you would have to eat—as much as you want, but only ____? What if that were the only thing you got to eat tomorrow? How soon would you wish you could have something else? ____ is good, but other things are good, too, and it is best to have a change.

"God knew it is best to have a change, and He made many things that way for us. He made many kinds of food. He made the seasons change from summer to autumn and winter and spring. What did you read in your lesson that is a change God made for us?

"What did God call the light? What did He call the dark time?

"What makes light in the daytime? What makes light at night?

"Why do we work in the daytime? Why would we not want to work all the time? Why would we not want to rest all the time?

"We are glad for God's good gift of changing day and night."

Review James 1:17a.

D. Workbook
pages 16 and 17

Discuss the tenses of *gives* and *gave*. Let the children make sentences for the words.

Have the children follow the directions.

E. Worksheet

Have the children notice that the 12 on the clock is straight up from the middle, where the hands are fastened, and the 6 is straight down. The 9 is to the left and the 3 to the right. Then the other numbers are filled in between them. Look at the classroom clock and tell the children what time it is if they cannot read the time. Tell them that we have that time in the day, and we also have that time in the night.

One clock on the worksheet shows a daytime hour, and one shows a nighttime hour. You may explain the *a.m.* and *p.m.* to them. The nighttime clock shows a good time for children to go to bed, and the daytime clock shows a good time for children to get up.

The children are to cut out the numbers and paste them on the second clock in the same order as they appear on the first clock.

This lesson is a review, so there are no new sentences to add to the list of things God gave. You may let the children add sentences of their own, naming other things God gave.

LESSON 7
What God Gave—Everything Good

Be prepared
Vocabulary flash cards
   New words: 2:7

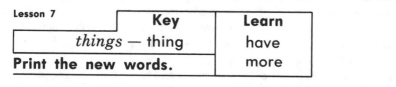

Lesson 7	**Key**	**Learn**
things — thing		have
Print the new words.		more

Underline the correct phrase.

1. God gives us
   a. every good thing we have.
   b. work that we can not do.
   c. what He does not want.

2. The daytime
   a. is too light to work.
   b. is the time to rest.
   c. is the time to work.

3. The nighttime
   a. is too quiet to rest.
   b. is the time to rest.
   c. is the time to work.

4. We can love God more and more
   a. when we are big.
   b. when we work.
   c. when we rest.

18

Review words: every, want, wants, because, does, helps, make, they,
  should, moon, quiet, stars, would, way, called
Phrases: 2:7
Review phrases: the sun gives, time to rest, for father, all of, are happy,
  He gave

Underline the correct answers.

1. Does God give us good things?   **yes** no

2. Does He give everything we want?   yes **no**

3. Does He give us what we should have?   **yes** no

4. Does He give us bad things?   yes **no**

5. Does He give us work to do?   **yes** no

6. Does He give the daytime for work?   **yes** no

7. Does He give us a quiet time to rest?   **yes** no

Match the words to the pictures.

some more   some more   more some

some more   more some   some more

A. Vocabulary

1. Let the children say the key word.
2. Let them sound the word *have* and discover that this is another word that breaks the long *e* rule.
3. Print these sentences for a clue to the word *more*. *We have some things. Do we want more things?*
4. Display the new and review words and let the children find the word(s) that—
   - a. means "did call." (called)
   - b. rhyme. (would, should)
   - c. can be used to tell the reason why. (because)
   - d. rhyme with *pay*. (way, they)
   - e. means "all." (every)
   - f. are lights in the sky. (stars, moon)
   - g. is the opposite of *loud*. (quiet)
   - h. mean "to wish." (want, wants)
   - i. makes you think of work. (helps)
   - j. is the opposite of *less*. (more)
   - k. means almost the same as *has*. (have)
5. Drill the phrase cards.
6. Practice reading the words under *Extra Practice* in the reader.

B. Reader

Turn to the table of contents and read the titles listed under *What God Gave*. Notice that this lesson is the last one in the section.

Have the children study silently; then conduct oral reading class, doing some reading in unison again.

C. Bible lesson

"Who gave you eyes? Who gave you hair? Who gave you health? Who gave you a home? Who gave you grass and trees to look at? Who gave you the blue sky? Who gave you air to breathe? Who gave you food to eat? Who gave you clothes to wear?" If the children do not see how some of these things are from God, help them to understand that God made the things grow or enabled their parents to obtain them.

Name the things in the following list and have the children find the sentence in the lesson that tells that God gives each thing. Call on someone to read each sentence.

fathers	nighttime	mothers
a home	work to do	daytime
	children	

Then ask them to find the sentences that answer these questions:
   What is the daytime for?
   What is the nighttime for?

What is the nighttime like?

When can we love God more?

Test the students on James 1:17a.

D. Workbook
pages 18 and 19

Have the children follow the directions.

E. Worksheet

This is the last exercise for this packet. Remove both sheets for this lesson, and let the children color the letters of the motto with crayon or colored pencil. To make the packet, lay the back on the reverse side of the motto. Fold the flaps around the back and paste.

They may put the items from the last six lessons in the packet to take home today, as well as the paper or papers with sentences if they have been printing the things God gave.

If the children have been printing these sentences, let them compose sentences for additional things that God has given.

LESSON 8
What God Likes—Happy Homes

Be prepared
Vocabulary flash cards
   New words: 2:8

Lesson 8	Key	Sound	Learn
	home — homes	be	family
	is — his	<u>th</u>em	
	see — sees	with	
	some + *day* = someday		

Print the new words.

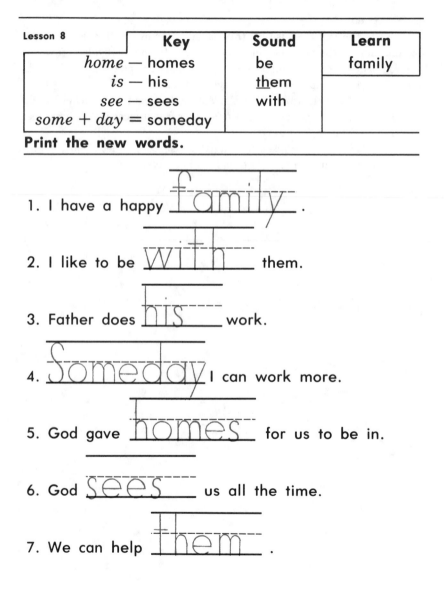

1. I have a happy _family_ .

2. I like to be _with_ them.

3. Father does _his_ work.

4. _Someday_ I can work more.

5. God gave _homes_ for us to be in.

6. God _sees_ us all the time.

7. We can help _them_ .

Review words: is, do, likes, too, obeyed, had, daytime, so, that, lights, have, more, thing

Phrases: 2:8

Review phrases: he called, to work, when we are, our mothers, we would, we should

---

Match the phrases to make sentences.

1. God likes to see a   **happy.**

2. He likes to see them   **family.**

3. He is our _____ **Father.**

4. We are His   **us.**

5. We like to be in   **children.**

6. God gave it to   **the family of God.**

7. We want to do   **His family.**

8. We like to be in   **our work.**

9. They gave it to _____ **them.**

Underline all the correct pictures.

What makes a family?

21

A. Vocabulary

1. Let the children say the key and sound words.
2. Sketch a group of stick figures on the board and print the sentence *This is a family.* As a help, have the children sound the first three letters of *family.*
3. Drill the words and phrases.

B. Reader

Turn to the table of contents. Have the children notice that they are beginning a new section, and read the title of the section. Look at the titles of the lessons for a preview of what they will read in the section.

Find the page of Bible verses after the table of contents. Have the children read the first verse, which they have learned. "Look at the verse where it says *Lesson 8.* Can you find any words you know?" Read the verse to the children and explain its meaning. "Cleave to that which is good" (Romans 12:9c). Practice saying the verse together; then ask the class what it means.

Have the children turn to lesson 8 in the reader and study silently; then conduct oral reading class.

C. Bible lesson

"Do you like to see little kittens playing? Do you like to watch the sunset? Do you like to see it snow? Do you like flowers? What else do you like? There are some things you do not like, too. You probably don't like to see animals fighting. Maybe you don't like snakes or thistles or bad storms."

Look at the title of section 2 on page 29 with the children. "There are some things God likes and some things He does not like, too. What does God like?" Let the children answer on their own; then point out that a number of the sentences in the lesson answer your question.

"What do a good father and mother do? What does God like to see children do? Who can help us to be a happy family? [Have them find the sentence in the reader that answers that question.] How does He help us to be happy?" Help the children to realize that the answer is in the next sentence.

"Who is the father in God's family? Where can we be with God someday? Do you know where His home is?"

D. Workbook

page 20

Follow the directions.

page 21

Do the top of the page with the children. Have the first sentence read with each of the possible endings before you let the children tell which one is right. Direct them to draw a line from the beginning phrase to the correct ending.

Discuss the directions for the bottom of the page.

E. Worksheet

This worksheet and the next six are to form a booklet of *What God Likes*. The children are to color the picture and cut out and paste under the picture the sentences that are true about a happy home. Collect the worksheets or have the children save them for the next six lessons.

LESSON 9

What God Likes—Happy Children

Be prepared

1. Vocabulary flash cards
   New words: 2:9

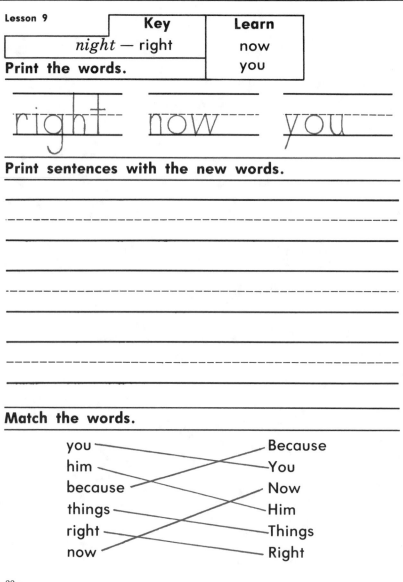

Lesson 9	Key	Learn
	night — right	now
Print the words.		you

Print sentences with the new words.

Match the words.

you   Because
him   You
because   Now
things   Him
right   Things
now   Right

22

Review words: obey, because, of, make, makes, should, nighttime, moon, rest, would, way, gives, thing, sees, someday, be, family, homes

Phrases: 2:9

Review phrases: he wants, our fathers, he does, more and more, we have, quiet night, they help, his children, with them

---

Reading Workbook   Unit 2   Lesson 9

Underline the correct words. Gradebook: 11 points for

1. You can obey God.   this page   **now**   **not now**

2. You can be big.   **now**   **not now**

3. You can be happy.   **now**   **not now**

4. You can help Mother.   **now**   **not now**

5. You can be a father.   **now**   **not now**

                                                      or

5. You can be a mother.   **now**   **not now**

6. You can do good work.   **now**   **not now**

7. You can see God.   **now**   **not now**

Match the words and pictures.

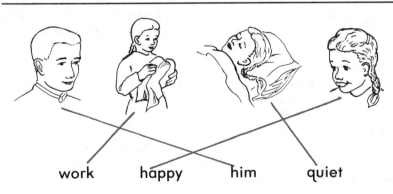

work   happy   him   quiet

23

2. Be a happy teacher. God likes to see happy adults, too. There are countless reasons to rejoice in Christ Jesus!

A. Vocabulary
1. Let the children say the key word.
2. Print *you* = $\bar{u}$ and let the children say the word. Point out the /y/ sound heard at the beginning of /ū/ and let the equation remain on the board for a reminder.
3. The children have studied *ow* as making the long *o* sound, and they will think it is a word if pronounced that way. Tell them that *ow* sometimes makes another sound. Print the sentence *God loves you now.* for a clue and for a reference.
4. Display the new and review words and ask which word(s)—
    a. means "to do what you are told to do."(obey)
    b. are two words put together. (nighttime, someday)
    c. tells what we do at night. (rest)
    d. means "not wrong." (right)
    e. is the opposite of *left*. (right)
    f. names a group of people. (family)
    g. tells where people live. (homes)
    h. has the /th/ sound. (thing)
    i. tells what a person does with his eyes. (sees)
    j. means "a person." (you)
    k. rhymes with *how*. (now)
    l. tells what a person does with a gift. (gives)
5. Drill the phrase cards.
6. Have the children sound the rhyming words under *Extra Practice* in the reader.

B. Reader
    Have the children read the lesson silently a few times.
    In oral reading, have the children stand by pairs and take turns reading sentences. Work for good expression in the questions and answers.
    Review Romans 12:9c and ask what the verse means.

C. Bible lesson
    "Who made all the things that we like? God made the sunsets and animals and flowers. He gave us many nice things. Wouldn't it be nice if we could give God something that He likes? What does God like? [happy children] So if we are happy, we are giving God something that He likes.
    "When are you happy?" Have the children find and read a sentence to answer, until all four answers have been given. Then let the children say the four answers in their own words.
    "Can you do all those things now? Then you can be happy now!"
    Discuss the fact that one does not need to have a lot of favors and fun

to be happy. "People who constantly get many new and special things become selfish, and selfish people are not happy. The real way to be happy is the way our lesson says. The other special things in life are gifts from God that we thank Him for. But we do not need them to have happiness."

D. Workbook
page 22

Read the directions with the children. Let them practice making original sentences with the new words. Then help them to spell any words they need help with. For spelling help, you can encourage them to find words in the reader.

If you think the children are not capable of getting sentences printed on their own, you may tell them to find and copy sentences from their reader with the new words.

Mention the capital letter at the beginning of every sentence, but do not require it if the children have not learned to print the capitals needed for their sentences. Tell them to end the sentences with periods or questions marks.

page 23

Notice that there are two number 5s. One is for the boys to do, and one is for the girls.

E. Worksheet

"Color the picture. Cut and paste under the picture the sentences that are true about happy children. Save the paper with the one from lesson 8."

LESSON 10
What God Likes—When We Work

Be prepared
Vocabulary flash cards
New words: 2:10

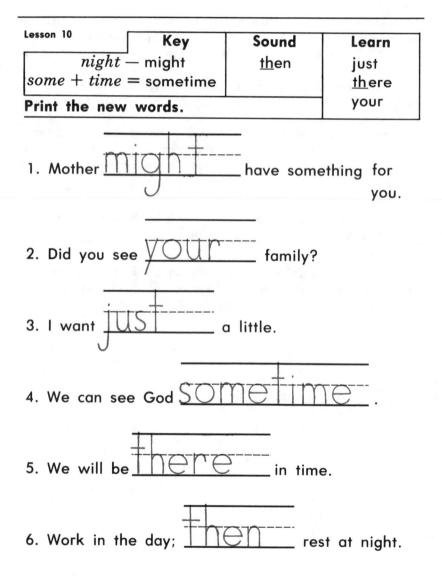

Lesson 10	Key	Sound	Learn
night — might		<u>th</u>en	just
some + time = sometime			<u>th</u>ere
Print the new words.			your

1. Mother might have something for
                                    you.

2. Did you see your family?

3. I want just a little.

4. We can see God sometime .

5. We will be there in time.

6. Work in the day; then rest at night.

24

Review words: light, what, might, first, too, so, sun, should, stars, more,
   you
Phrases: 2:10
Review phrases: our family, are happy, she helps, when we are, he called,
   right now

Reading Workbook   **Unit 2**   **Lesson 10**

Match the words to the sentences.

1. Work when it is _____.   **might**

2. Work with all your _____.   **right**

3. Do your work just _____.   **light**

Match the words that fit together.

1. sun   night   4. big——sky

2. quiet   God   5. bad   everything

3. good   daytime   6. all   Satan

Draw a red line under work children can do.

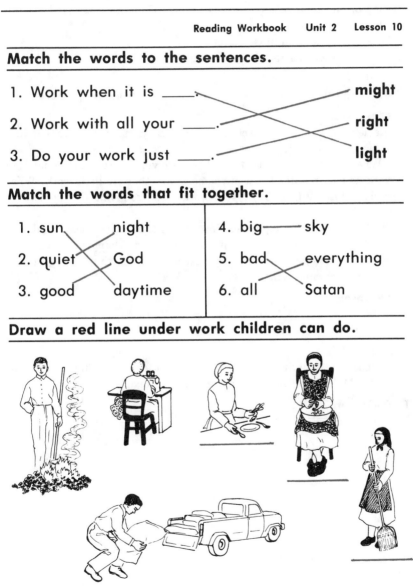

A. Vocabulary

1. Let the children say the key and sound words.
2. Help them to sound the word *just* by covering the *t* and having them sound the first three letters, then adding the /t/ sound.
3. Print these sentences as clues for *your* and *there*. *The things you have are your things.* (Underline *your* and notice the word *you* in it.) *We can not work at home when we are not there.* (Underline *there* and use the /th/ beginning as a helper.)
4. Drill the word and phrase cards.
5. Turn to the reader for *Extra Practice*.

B. Reader

Have the children study silently; then conduct oral reading class.

C. Bible lesson

Review the title of this section and the things studied so far that God likes.

"What is in this lesson that God likes? Do you like to work? What kind of work do children do? What are some things that are little work? What work do you do? When you do your work, it is like giving God something that He likes.

"When can you do big work? How do you think people learn to do big work? They learn by doing the little things first. Doing little jobs is a beginning for doing great work. What are some things that are big work?"

Review Romans 12:9c.

D. Workbook
page 24

Follow the directions.

page 25

Discuss the way the words fit together in the exercise in the middle of the page. Make sure the directions are understood.

E. Worksheet

Do as for the two previous lessons.

LESSON 11
What God Likes—When We Are Kind to Animals

Be prepared
Vocabulary flash cards
New words: 2:11
Review words: does, make, daytime, that, lights, quiet, would, have, thing,
with, homes, now, sometime, just
Phrases: 2:11
Review phrases: in his home, our family, your might, then there is, for
father, for mother, time to rest

A. Vocabulary
1. Let the children say the sound words.
2. Sketch some simple animal figures on the board and these two labels:
   some animals, one animal.
3. Print *kind* and mark the *i* with a macron. Help the children to sound it
   by first covering the last letter.
4. Print the sentence *He has some animals.* and let the children sound the
   word *has.* They should recognize it as /haz/.
5. Display the new and review words and ask which word(s)—
   a. mean "more than one." (animals, lights, homes)
   b. refer to a certain time. (daytime, sometime)
   c. begins with the /th/ sound. (that)
   d. is a number word. (one)
   e. rhymes with *how.* (now)
   f. rhymes with *crust.* (just)
   g. is something each of us has. (name)
6. Discuss the two meanings of the word *kind.*
7. Tell the children that some words take longer to say than others do. Some
   words have more speaking parts. Pronounce some of the one-syllable
   words in the list and tell the children that those words each have one part.
   A motion of the hand with each word will emphasize the one syllable. Then
   pronounce *day-time, qui-et,* and *some-time* with a distinct separation of
   syllables and two motions of the hand. Tell the children that those words
   have two parts. Then pronounce *an-i-mal* with distinct separation and three
   motions. Ask the children how many parts they heard in that word.
   Pronounce *animals* for them likewise.
8. Use the *Extra Practice* lists in the reader.

B. Reader
Conduct silent and oral reading class.
Read a word or phrase for the children to find in the story.

C. Bible lesson

"What did you read today that we can do that God likes?

"Who made the animals? God made them, and He cares about them. What does He do for the animals? What kind of homes does He give the animals? What kind of home does a bird have? What kind of home does a

---

Lesson 11

Sound	**Learn**
each	animal
name	animals
	has
	kind
	one

Print the new words.

1. We see some <u>animals</u> .

2. We see <u>one</u> big animal.

3. Each animal <u>has</u> a name.

4. Adam gave each one a <u>name</u> .

5. We want to be <u>kind</u> to them.

Print the correct word.

6. What is the name of this animal?

<u>cat</u>

fish have? a woodchuck? a monkey?

"What did Adam do for the animals?

"What can we do for the animals? Do you have animals at home? What do you do that is kind to them?"

Review Romans 12:9c. Ask the children what the verse means.

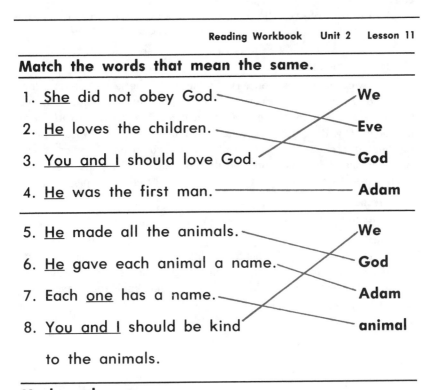

Reading Workbook   Unit 2   Lesson 11

Match the words that mean the same.

1. <u>She</u> did not obey God.　　　　　　**We**

2. <u>He</u> loves the children.　　　　　　**Eve**

3. <u>You and I</u> should love God.　　　　**God**

4. <u>He</u> was the first man.　　　　　　**Adam**

5. <u>He</u> made all the animals.　　　　**We**

6. <u>He</u> gave each animal a name.　　**God**

7. Each <u>one</u> has a name.　　　　　**Adam**

8. <u>You and I</u> should be kind　　　　**animal**

　　to the animals.

Mark each name.

Underline with <u>blue</u> each one that is he.

Circle with (orange) each one that is she.

Adam　　　Dick　　　Joe

<u>Jack</u>　　　(Eve)　　　(Nan)

(Bess)　　(Jane)　　(Kay)

<u>Bill</u>　　　(Beth)　　<u>Tom</u>

27

D. Workbook
page 26

Have the children refer to the pictures on the page to do the exercise. The number 6 is to be answered with a word the children can spell phonetically rather than with one of the new words.

page 27

Print this exercise on the board before having the children do the page.

They all have names.	Mother
She does work that I can not do.	Father
He loves his family.	The animals

"One word in each sentence is underlined. In the second column, there is a word or phrase that we could say instead of the underlined word. Read the first sentence with the word *Mother* instead of *they*. Read it with *Father* instead of *they*. Read it with *The animals*. Which is the right word or phrase for the sentence?" Let one of the children come to the board and draw a line to match the underlined word and its replacement. Complete the set.

Discuss the directions in the workbook and assign the page.

E. Worksheet

Do as in the three preceding lessons.

Extra activity

Have the children print sentences for some of the words under *Extra Practice* in the reader, and draw pictures to go with them. Encourage them to use their readers to help them spell words they know they have used in the reader.

LESSON 12

What God Likes—When We Like What God Gives

Be prepared

Vocabulary flash cards

New words: 2:12

Review words: makes, nighttime, more, now, there, each, name, animal, has, obeyed, had, they, someday

Phrases: 2:12

Review phrases: all the children, all the animals, one kind, just right, you can be, moon and stars, all of

A. Vocabulary

1. Let the children say the sound word.
2. Print *family* on the board, and while the children watch, print *families* directly under it. Match letter for letter and stop when you get to *l*. "The new word is very much like *family*. Can you guess what it is?" Add *ies*. If the children cannot tell the word, tell them it means more than one family. It is changed more than simply adding *s* to make it mean more than one.
3. Say *fam-i-lies,* emphasizing each syllable with a motion of the hand, and ask the children how many parts they hear. Pronounce some of the review words and let them tell you how many parts they hear.
4. Drill the words and phrases.

B. Reader

Have the children read the lesson silently.

"Find the word *us* in the lesson. Find a word that rhymes with *us*. Find the word *too*. Find a word that rhymes with *too*. Find the word *right*. Find a word that rhymes with *right*." Help the children to recognize the rhyming pattern in the lesson. Let them stand in pairs and take turns reading sentences.

C. Bible lesson

"Did you ever give someone a present? Did you ever give a present that somebody grumbled about? That wouldn't make you very happy, would it? We like when people are happy with the things we give. God is that way, too.

"God has given us many things. He likes when we are glad for the things He gives. He likes when we say 'Thank You' for His gifts.

"What did your lesson say we should not do? If we are glad for the things God gives, we will not fuss. We should be satisfied because He knows what is the best for us to have.

"Read the last sentence in the lesson again. What are the things God gave us?" Have the children find and list from the lesson the things God gave. Then go on and list other things if you wish. Review James 1:17a.

Review Romans 12:9c.

D. Workbook

page 28

Discuss the directions for the bottom of the page and do a few samples with the children.

page 29

Notice that each section of answers is a set of rhyming words.

Lesson 12

Sound	Learn
fuss	families

Print the new words.

fuss   families

Match the words.

animal ———— Has
each ———— Each
has ———— Fuss
his ———— Animal
fuss ———— His

families ———— Name
name ———— One
family ———— Family
one ———— Families
kind ———— Kind

Underline the words that have a short vowel sound.

a	e	i
gāve	help	children
happy	then	lïghts
māke	bëcause	gives
have	rest	kïnd
family	ëach	things
that	when	his
has	sëes	with
nāme	them	mïght

E. Worksheet

Introduce the word *thank*, and relate the picture to the lesson of being thankful and telling God "Thank You." Proceed as for previous lessons.

Extra activity

Let the children mark with macrons the long vowels in the words at the bottom of workbook page 28.

Reading Workbook   Unit 2   Lesson 12

Match the words to the sentences.

1. We like our family. They like us, _____.
   We like the animals. Yes, we _____.

   do
   you
   too

2. We like the work God gives us to _____.
   We like the sun and so should _____.

   do
   to
   you

3. We like day, and we like _____.
   God made everything just _____.

   right
   night
   might

4. Each animal to Adam _____.
   Then Adam gave each one a _____.

   same
   name
   came

5. God is very kind to _____.
   So we should not make a _____.

   fuss
   bus
   us

6. God made all the good things we _____.
   He loves each one and so should _____.

   he
   see
   we

Match the words to the pictures.

has   had | had   has | had   has

LESSON 13

What God Likes—When We Are Helpers

Be prepared
Vocabulary flash cards
   New words: 2:13

Lesson 13	Key	Learn
mother — other others	glad helpers

Print the new words.

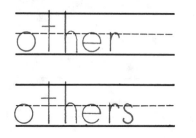

Underline the little words in the bigger words.

1. day   **day**time
2. home   **home**s
3. some   **some**day
4. love   **love**d
5. father   **father**s
6. obey   **obey**ed
7. thing   **thing**s
8. help   **help**ers
9. want   **want**s

10. animal   **animal**s
11. every   **every**thing
12. call   **call**ed
13. light   **light**s
14. mother   **mother**s
15. other   **other**s
16. night   **night**time
17. give   **give**s
18. some   **some**time

Review words: obeyed, that, would, way, called, have, thing, family, then,
your, animal, animals, kind, fuss, families
Phrases: 2:13
Review phrases: one of, they help, moon and stars, with them, his children,
because he, are happy, to work, some families

Reading Workbook   Unit 2   Lesson 13

Underline the correct answers.

1. Should you help Mother?   **yes**   no

2. Should you help Father?   **yes**   no

3. Should you help others?   **yes**   no

4. When should you help?   **now**   not now

5. Mother and Father help you ____.   **now**   not now

6. So you should help them ____.   **now**   not now

7. We are glad when we can ____.   **help**   helpers

8. We are glad we can be ____.   help   **helpers**

9. We are little ____.   help   **helpers**

Underline 2 correct answers.

10. You should help
    a. make the daytime.
    b. Father and Mother.
    c. other children.

11. You should help
    a. when you are little.
    b. when you are big.
    c. when you rest at night.

A. Vocabulary

1. Let the children say the key words.
2. Help them to sound *glad* by covering the *g* and sounding the rest of the word, then saying the /g/ sound in the beginning as they repeat the word.
3. Use the sentence *When we help, we are helpers.* as a clue to the other learn word.
4. Display the new and review words and ask which word(s)—
   a. means "did obey." (obeyed)
   b. means "did call." (called)
   c. mean the same thing except one word means "more than one." (family—families, animal—animals, other—others)
   d. means "happy." (glad)
   e. rhymes with *good.* (would)
   f. means "not now." (then)
   g. is the opposite of *mean.* (kind)
   h. means "a noisy commotion." (fuss)
   i. names people that help. (helpers)
5. "Listen for the number of parts in the words I say. We call those parts syllables. How many syllables do you hear in *other*? How many syllables do you hear in *glad*? How many syllables do you hear in *helpers? animals? families? called? obeyed?*"
6. Drill the words and phrases.

B. Reader

Review the three types of end punctuation and the comma.

Have the children read silently. In oral reading, let one child read the questions and another the answers.

Review Romans 12:9c.

C. Bible lesson

Review from the table of contents or from memory the things that God likes. "What is in our new lesson that God likes? God likes when we are helpers. It pleases Him. Who else is happy when we are helpers? The people we help are probably glad. But who else is happy? Did you ever notice how happy it makes you to do something to help others?

"Whom should you help?

"Who helps you?" Have the children find and read all three sentences that answer this question.

"How can we help God?"

D. Workbook

page 30

Print a few samples on the board to explain and practice the exercise at the bottom of the page. Caution the children to be sure their lines go under all the letters that are in the small word and only those.

page 31

Pay special attention to the directions at the bottom of the page.

E. Worksheet

Do the same as in the preceding lessons.

LESSON 14

What God Likes—When We Obey

Be prepared

1. Have construction paper ready for the worksheet booklet covers, and string, fasteners, or staples to put them together.

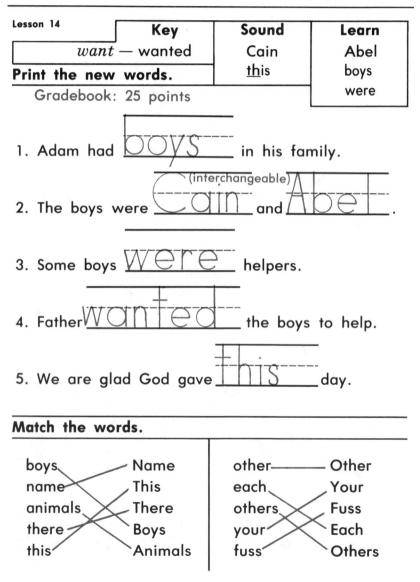

Lesson 14	Key	Sound	Learn
	want — wanted	Cain	Abel
Print the new words.		<u>th</u>is	boys
Gradebook: 25 points			were

1. Adam had <u>boys</u> in his family.

2. The boys were <u>Cain</u> (interchangeable) and <u>Abel</u>.

3. Some boys <u>were</u> helpers.

4. Father <u>wanted</u> the boys to help.

5. We are glad God gave <u>This</u> day.

Match the words.

boys — Boys
name — Name
animals — Animals
there — There
this — This

other — Other
each — Each
others — Others
your — Your
fuss — Fuss

32

2. Vocabulary flash cards
    New words: 2:14
    Review words: first, make, when, so, quiet, sees, now, sometime, animal,
        has, families, other, others, glad, helpers
    Phrases: 2:14

Underline the correct words.

1. Adam and Eve were the ____ father and mother.
    <u>first</u>   fuss   work

2. Cain and Abel were the first ____.
    <u>boys</u>   fathers   mothers

3. Cain and Abel ____ work to do.
    <u>had</u>   was   has

4. ____ was a good man.
    Cain   <u>Abel</u>

5. God ____ us to obey our fathers and mothers.
    want   <u>wants</u>

6. God can____ us to do this.
    helper   helps   <u>help</u>

Underline all the correct phrases.

God wants us to
    a. be the first family.
    b. love our fathers and mothers.
    c. love others.
    d. help our fathers and mothers.
    e. be like Cain.
    f. help others.

Review phrases: each one, just right, our homes, we should, one of, then there is, more and more, your might

A. Vocabulary

1. Let the children say the key and sound words.
2. Print *Abel* and mark the *a* with a macron. With the clue of the other name in the list, they should be able to guess the word.
3. See whether the children can figure out the two new words in this sentence: *Our fathers were boys; now they are men.*
4. Ask which of the new and review word(s)—
   a. name people. (Cain, Abel, boys, families, helpers)
   b. have the long *a* sound. (Cain, Abel, make)
   c. begins with the /th/ sound. (this)
   d. makes you think of taking turns. (first)
   e. makes you think of a family. (boys)
   f. have two syllables. (wanted, Abel, quiet, sometime, other, others, helpers)
5. Drill the word and phrase cards.
6. Use the *Extra Practice* lists in the reader.

B. Reader

Have the children study the lesson silently; then conduct oral reading class.

Read a sentence and see how quickly the children can find it in their readers.

Test them on Romans 12:9c.

C. Bible lesson

Turn to the table of contents and review the list of stories about what God likes. "What does today's lesson say God likes? Whom should we obey? [parents]

"Who were the first parents? Who were the first children? Were there other children in the family? Did Adam and Eve obey God? [The children should remember from unit 1 that Adam and Eve disobeyed at one time.] Which one of the boys obeyed? In what way should we be like Abel? What does God want us to do?" Have the children find and read the four sentences that answer the last question.

D. Workbook

page 32

Follow the directions.

page 33

Pay special attention to the directions for the bottom of the page.

E. Worksheet

Today the worksheets from lessons 8-14 may be put together to make a booklet. The picture on today's worksheet may be colored, cut out, and pasted on a piece of colored construction paper for a cover for the booklet. The words in the box may be colored and pasted on the inside cover of the booklet. Fasten the booklet with string, paper fasteners, or staples and let each child take his booklet home today.

LESSON 15
What God Does Not Like—When People Do Not Obey

Be prepared
Vocabulary flash cards
New words: 2:15

Lesson 15	Sound	Learn
	let	godly
	sad	people
	why	

Print the new words.

1. Fathers and mothers and children are

<u>people</u> .

2. When you are not happy, you are <u>sad</u> .

3. People that obey God are <u>godly</u> .

4. Will you <u>let</u> us help?

Underline the correct words.

1. children	one	**more**	7. name	one	**more**
2. all	one	**more**	8. boy	**one**	more
3. moon	**one**	more	9. helpers	one	**more**
4. stars	one	**more**	10. they	one	**more**
5. he	**one**	more	11. people	one	**more**
6. we	one	**more**	12. others	one	**more**

34

Review words: man, lights, would, thing, someday, then, animals, wanted, Cain, this, Abel, boys, were
Phrases: 2:15
Review phrases: has a name, your work, others can, we have, the sun gives, you are, one kind, with them

---

Reading Workbook   Unit 2   Lesson 15

Underline the correct answers.

1. What did God not like?
   a. God did not like what Cain did.
   b. God did not like what Abel did.
   c. God did not like Adam and Eve.

2. Why did Cain not obey God?
   a. because God could see him
   b. because he did not love God
   c. because he was sad

3. Why was Cain not happy?
   a. because he did not obey God
   b. because he made God sad
   c. because he wanted to be sad

4. What makes us sad?
   a. It makes us sad to be happy.
   b. It makes us sad to obey.
   c. It makes us sad to be bad.

5. What does God not like?
   a. God does not like when people are happy.
   b. God does not like when people are like Abel.
   c. God does not like when people do not obey.

A. Vocabulary

1. Let the children say the sound words.
2. Point out the word *god* in *godly* and let them try to sound the word. Tell them what the word is if they need help.
3. Print the sentence *Fathers and mothers and children are people.* and put a macron over the first *e* in *people*.
4. Ask the children how many syllables are in each of the new words. Drill the words and phrases.
5. Use the *Extra Practice* lists in the reader.

B. Reader

Have the children turn to the table of contents and read the title of section 3. "We read some lessons about what God likes. There are some things that God does not like, too. We will learn what some of those things are in this section." Let the children look at the titles in the section and name some of the things they find.

Then find the page of Bible verses and let the children look for any familiar words in the verse for lesson 15. Read the verse to them and explain the meaning. It tells what our attitude should be toward the things that God does not like. "Abhor that which is evil; cleave to that which is good" (Romans 12:9b). Practice the verse together, each time including the part they learned in the last section.

Turn to lesson 15 and have the children read silently; then conduct oral reading class.

C. Bible lesson

"We are glad we know what God likes. We like to do those things to please Him.

"It is also good for us to learn about what God does not like. Then we can learn to hate those things, too. 'Abhor that which is evil.'

"What is the first thing we read about that God does not like? [when people do not obey] We do not like it either when people do not obey. It makes a lot of trouble when people are disobedient.

"Who were Adam and Eve's two boys? Which son obeyed? Which one did not obey? Why did Cain not obey? How did Cain feel then? Who is sad when we are bad?" Have the children find and read the sentences that give all three answers.

D. Workbook

page 34

Print a few samples on the board to practice the type of exercise given at the bottom of the page.

page 35

Follow the directions.

E. Worksheet

Have the children find and cross out all the capital letters in the rows at the top of the sheet. The remaining letters are to be copied in the same order in the space below. Call attention to the short lines below the printing line. Tell them to place one letter above each line as they copy the letters. This will space the letters so the words are separated.

Then they are to read the message and do what it says, drawing in the space below.

The sheets for this and the next six lessons may be saved to staple together as a book or taken home daily.

The message reads: Make something sweet to eat.

LESSON 16

What God Does Not Like—When People Are Angry

Be prepared
Vocabulary flash cards
New words: 2:16

Lesson 16	**Sound**	**Learn**
	if	angry
		done
Print the new words.		liked

1. Our work is d̲o̲n̲e̲ .

2. I can do this i̲f̲ you help.

3. He l̲i̲k̲e̲d̲ the things we gave.

4. We do not want to be a̲n̲g̲r̲y̲ .

Match the words to the pictures.

little

kind

angry

godly

glad

sad

Review words: that, moon, rest, animal, has, families, other, let, sad, why,
   people, godly
Phrases: 2:16
Review phrases: the boys were, Cain and Abel, we are glad, they fuss,
   our family, right now, then there is, some families

Reading Workbook   Unit 2   Lesson 16

Underline the correct answers.

1. Was Cain angry?   <u>yes</u>   no

2. Do angry people do bad things?   <u>yes</u>   no

3. Are angry people kind to others?   yes   <u>no</u>

4. Are angry people happy?   yes   <u>no</u>

Match the words to the sentences.

1. Angry people ____ bad things. ———— **do**

2. He should have ____ it right. **did**

3. But Cain ____ not do right. **done**

---

4. Did you ____ your work? ———— **do**

5. I ____ some of it. ———— **did**

6. He should have ____ his work. ———— **done**

---

7. She has ____ a good thing. **do**

8. What the children ____ made them happy. **did**

9. We will ____ what God likes. **done**

A. Vocabulary

1. Let the children say the sound word.

2. Before you print the word *angry,* ask the children if they can guess your word. "It is an unhappy feeling that someone might have if you hurt him or broke something that was his." Print the word and a sentence for it. *Do not be angry if he is bad to you.* Let it remain on the board for the children's reference if they forget the word.

3. Let the children sound *done* according to the rules and tell them that here we have another word that does not follow the rule. Print *done = dun* on the board and help the children to understand it.

4. The word *liked* can also be very nearly sounded by the phonics that the children know. Printing *He liked the pie.* may help.

5. Ask which new or review word(s)—

    a. means "finished." (done)

    b. means "like God." (godly)

    c. names groups of people. (families)

    d. means "allow." (let)

    e. is a word you might say when pointing to something. (that)

    f. is a question word. (why)

    g. is a wrong kind of feeling. (angry)

    h. make you think of nighttime. (moon, rest)

    i. have two syllables. (angry, other, people, godly)

    j. have three syllables. (animal, families)

6. Drill the word and phrase cards.

7. Use the *Extra Practice* lists in the reader.

B. Reader

Have the children study silently and read orally.
Review Romans 12:9b.

C. Bible lesson

"Have you ever seen someone who was very angry? How does such a person act? Do you like to be around people when they are angry?

"We do not like when people are angry. God does not like it, either.

"Who was angry in our story? Why was Cain angry? Why did God not like what Cain did?

"What should Cain have done when God did not like what he did? Did Cain do right? What did he do instead? Did he have a good reason to become angry?

"Can you think of any reason it would be all right to become angry? Suppose someone kicks you on purpose. That is bad. Should you be bad then, too, just because someone else is bad? No. You should still be good. And you should not become angry. Then maybe the other person would be nice to you."

D. Workbook

page 36

Follow the directions.

page 37

Print *do, did,* and *done* on the board and say sentences with blanks for the children to choose the correct word. Have them repeat each sentence with the correct word in it.

> We should ____ good work.
> Yesterday we ____ lesson 15.
> I have ____ that before.
> I can ____ my lesson.
> He ____ his lesson already.
> When we have ____ the lesson, we will sing.

Have the children follow the directions on the page.

E. Worksheet

"Cross out the capital letters, copy the others on the lines, and do what the message says."

Message: Make a big orange seashell.

LESSON 17
What God Does Not Like—When People Are Not Sorry

Be prepared
Vocabulary flash cards
New words: 2:17

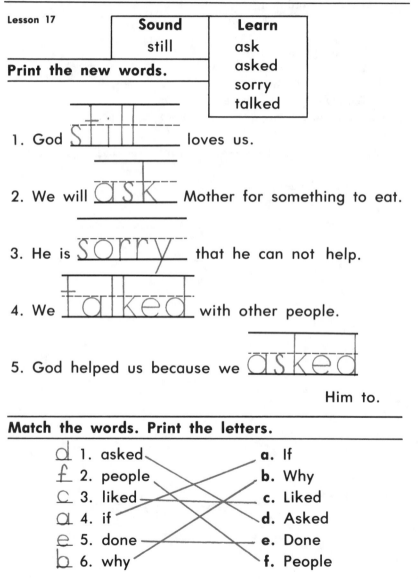

Lesson 17	**Sound**	**Learn**
	still	ask
Print the new words.		asked
		sorry
		talked

1. God ̲S̲t̲i̲l̲l̲ loves us.

2. We will ̲a̲s̲k̲ Mother for something to eat.

3. He is ̲s̲o̲r̲r̲y̲ that he can not help.

4. We ̲t̲a̲l̲k̲e̲d̲ with other people.

5. God helped us because we ̲a̲s̲k̲e̲d̲

Him to.

Match the words. Print the letters.

d 1. asked — a. If
f 2. people — b. Why
c 3. liked — c. Liked
a 4. if — d. Asked
e 5. done — e. Done
b 6. why — f. People

38

Review words: nighttime, quiet, thing, might, just, animals, wanted, Abel,
if, done, liked, people

Phrases: 2:17

Review phrases: were angry, in his home, are happy, each one, help others,
can be helpers, he called

Reading Workbook   Unit 2   Lesson 17

Match the words to the sentences.

1. Did God talk to Cain?————————————— **asked**

2. God talked to Cain.————————————→ **said**

1. God still loved Cain. **asked**

2. Did God still love Cain? **said**

1. Cain was not sorry for what he had done. **asked**

2. Was Cain sorry for what he had done? **said**

1. Should we be sorry if we do bad things?——**asked**

2. We should be sorry if we do bad things.——**said**

Match the words to the sentences.

C 1. If you help, you are a _____.   **a. lover**

d 2. If you give, you are a _____.   **b. fusser**

a 3. If you love, you are a_____.   **c. helper**

e 4. If you work, you are a _____.   **d. giver**

b 5. If you fuss, you are a _____.   **e. worker**

A. Vocabulary

1. Let the children say the sound word.
2. Use these sentences to help teach the learn words.

   Did you *ask* for the things you have?

   Yes, we *asked* for them.

   I am *sorry* that I did something bad.

   He *talked* with me. We said many things.
3. Drill the word and phrase cards.
4. Use the *Extra Practice* lists in the reader.

B. Reader

Conduct silent and oral reading class.

Review Romans 12:9b.

C. Bible lesson

Review from the table of contents the things that God does not like.

"God does not like when people are not sorry—sorry for what?

"We all make mistakes, and sometimes we do things we should not do. Maybe sometimes we forget, and we become angry with someone. Or we accidentally do something that is not nice to others. When those things happen, we should be sorry.

"Who was not sorry in the story? What should he have been sorry for? What did God ask Cain? Why did He want to help Cain?

"Does God love us when we do bad things? What should we do when we do bad things?

"What does it mean to be sorry? When we are sorry, we feel bad about what we did and never want to do it again. We should not think that it would be all right to be bad because we can be sorry after we did it. If we are really sorry, we want to never do the bad thing again."

D. Workbook

page 38

Allow the children to draw lines in the matching exercise at the bottom of the page, but then also have them print the letters in the blanks.

page 39

Print a few sentences on the board to illustrate telling and asking sentences.

   Did you see the sun?

   You can see the stars at night.

   Did you ask for something?

   You should have asked for it.

   This is how to do the work.

   Can you tell me how to do this?

Let someone read the first sentence; then ask the class whether he asked or said something. Print the words *asked* and *said* after the sentences and let someone draw a line from the end of the sentence to the correct word. Have the next sentence read, and discuss whether that sentence asked or said something. Label each sample.

Discuss the directions on the workbook page.

E. Worksheet

"Cross out the capitals, print the remaining letters, and do what the message says."

Message: Make a stack of blocks.

LESSON 18
What God Does Not Like—When People Hate Others

Be prepared
Vocabulary flash cards
  New words: 2:18

Lesson 18	Sound	Learn
	hate	killed
	kill	who

Print the new words. Gradebook: 24 points

1. Did you see W̲h̲o̲ talked to him?

2. We should h̲a̲t̲e̲ what is bad, and love
   what is good.

3. What k̲i̲l̲l̲e̲d̲ our animal?

4. Did she k̲i̲l̲l̲ the fly?

Match the words.

c 1. kill **a.** asked

b 2. talk **b.** talked

a 3. ask **c.** killed

e 4. help **d.** liked

d 5. like **e.** helped

i 6. call **f.** worked

f 7. work **g.** obeyed

h 8. love **h.** loved

g 9. obey **i.** called

j 10. punish **j.** punished

40

Review words: of, they, way, them, family, now, animal, kind, families, boys, ask, sorry, still, godly

Phrases: 2:18

Review phrases: they talked, all the people, why are, you can be, he asked, had done, this is

---

Reading Workbook   Unit 2   Lesson 18

Match the phrases.

1. Cain was angry ————— a very bad thing.

2. Then Cain did ————— with Abel.

3. He killed ————— Abel.

4. So God had ————— to punish him.

5. We do not want ————— not be angry.

6. So we should ————— to kill people.

7. God can help us not to be ————— kill people.

8. Angry people sometimes ————— angry.

Circle the correct letter.

1. Why was Cain angry with Abel?
   a. because Abel did not obey God
   b. because Cain talked to Abel
   c. because God liked what Abel did but He did not like what Cain did

2. Why did Cain kill Abel?
   a. because God did not like what he did
   b. because he did hate Abel
   c. because Abel was bad

41

A. Vocabulary

1. Let the children say the sound words.
2. Use the new word *kill* as a key for *killed.*
3. Print *Who are you? I am* ____. using the name of a child in the class, and let that child try to read the sentences. Do the same with several names.
4. Ask which of the new or review word(s)—
   a. has one of the other words in it. (killed)
   b. is the opposite of *love.* (hate)
   c. can be a question word. (who)
   d. means "quiet." (still)
   e. means "not moving." (still)
   f. means "continuing." (still)
   g. name things that people can do. (hate, kill, ask)
   h. are right ways to feel. (kind, sorry)
   i. rhymes with *do.* (who)
   j. has the /v/ sound. (of)
   k. name more than one. (families, boys, they)
   l. have two syllables. (sorry, godly)
5. Use the *Extra Practice* lists in the reader.

B. Reader

Conduct silent and oral reading class.
Review Romans 12:9b.

C. Bible lesson

"What is the opposite of love? Who loves you? Whom do you love? Isn't it wonderful to love? Love makes our lives so happy!

"What do you think hate is like? People that hate want to hurt others. They want to do bad things to them instead of helping and doing good things. Hatred is very ugly. Nobody is happy when they hate.

"Who hated someone in our lesson? Whom did he hate? Why did he hate Abel?

"What did Cain do to Abel? Then what did God do to Cain?

"What do people do when they hate?"

D. Workbook

page 40

Have the children do the matching at the bottom of the page by printing the letters only and not drawing lines.

page 41

Note the difference in the directions for the bottom of the page.

E. Worksheet

"Cross out the capitals, print the remaining letters, and do what the message says."

Message: Make a green frog in the grass.

LESSON 19

What God Does Not Like—When People Lie

Be prepared

Vocabulary flash cards

New words: 2:19

Review words: so, lights, have, more, sees, right, sometime, your, name, one, other, glad, were, asked, hate, kill, killed, who

Phrases: 2:19

Review phrases: angry people, they let, are sad, all the animals, then there is, we would, was not sorry

A. Vocabulary

1. Let the children say the key and sound words. Explain the use of the apostrophe in the word *Cain's.* An apostrophe and *s* at the end of a name shows that something belongs to that person. Use some of the children's names as more examples.

2. Print *no* on the board and have someone say the word. Then add the first and last letters to make *know* and tell the children that the word still sounds the same. The next learn word is almost like it. The children have learned to sound *ew* as the /ū/ sound and that would give nearly the correct pronunciation.

3. Print *told* and mark the *o* with a macron; then help the children to sound the word.

4. Drill the word and phrase cards.

B. Reader

Print a sentence containing a quotation on the board and point out the quotation marks. Explain that they are used to mark the beginning and the end of the words that someone said. Have someone read the words that were spoken. Have the children find some quotation marks in the lesson. Let someone read the spoken words. Ask who said them. Let someone read the other quotation in the lesson and discuss who was the speaker that time.

Have the children study the lesson silently; then conduct oral reading class.

Review Romans 12:9b.

C. Bible lesson

Turn to the table of contents again and review the things God does not like.

"Who told a lie? Did God know it was a lie? God knows everything. He knows what is true even though people tell lies. If someone told you a lie, you might believe him, but no one can ever tell a lie that will trick God.

"Why do people lie? Maybe they think they will not be punished if they lie about something they did. Maybe they think they can get something they want if they lie. But it never works out the best to tell a lie. That is just doing more and more bad things. It is better to tell the truth even when it leads to something that we do not like.

"What should we do if we lie?

"Who wants us to lie? To whom did he lie? Who was Cain's mother?"

D. Workbook

pages 42 and 43

Have the children read and follow the directions.

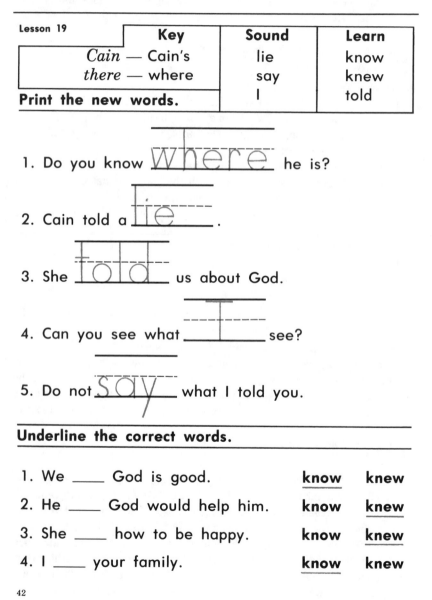

Lesson 19	**Key**	**Sound**	**Learn**
Cain — Cain's *there* — where		lie	know
		say	knew
Print the new words.		I	told

1. Do you know where he is?

2. Cain told a lie .

3. She told us about God.

4. Can you see what I see?

5. Do not say what I told you.

Underline the correct words.

1. We ____ God is good.   know   knew

2. He ____ God would help him.   know   knew

3. She ____ how to be happy.   know   knew

4. I ____ your family.   know   knew

42

E. Worksheet

Proceed as usual.

Message: Make something that can tweet. Color it blue.

Reading Workbook   Unit 2   Lesson 19

Underline the correct words.

1. God _____ Cain, "Where is Abel?"

   told   asked   said

2. "I do not _____," said Cain.

   knew   know   fuss

3. But he _____ a lie.

   told   asked   had

4. He _____ he had killed Abel.

   kind   know   knew

5. God does not want us to _____.

   like   love   lie

6. If we lie, we should be _____.

   sorry   still   called

7. We should not be _____.

   all   angry   asked

8. _____ wants us to lie.

   Abel   Satan   Cain

9. _____ does not lie.

   God   Adam   We

10. We want to _____ like God.

    been   be   see

43

LESSON 20

What God Does Not Like—When People Do Not Love God

Be prepared
Vocabulary flash cards
  New words: 2:20

Lesson 20	Sound	Learn
	will	wrong

Print the new words.

1. She said the _wrong_ thing.

2. We _will_ help the animals.

Print *right* **or** *wrong.*

1. help others _right_

2. obey God _right_

3. obey Satan _wrong_

4. be sorry _right_

5. lie _wrong_

6. be kind _right_

7. kill _wrong_

8. love others _right_

9. be glad _right_

10. be angry _wrong_

44

Review words: for, of, moon, gives, someday, homes, now, animal, has,
wanted, liked, people, ask, Cain's, told, I, know, knew
Phrases: 2:20
Review phrases: where are, should say, still was, the boys were, who did,
had done, help others, they talked, should not lie

Reading Workbook   Unit 2   Lesson 20

Underline the correct words.

1. He did not love God.   **Abel**   **Cain**

2. He was not sorry.   **Abel**   **Cain**

3. He loved God.   **Abel**   **Cain**

4. God liked what he did.   **Abel**   **Cain**

5. He told a lie.   **Abel**   **Cain**

6. He was killed.   **Abel**   **Cain**

7. God punished him.   **Abel**   **Cain**

Circle the correct letter.

1. Why did Cain do bad things?
   a. because he did not love Abel
   b. because he told a lie
   c. because he did not love God

2. What did Cain do first?
   a. He was not sorry.
   b. He did not obey God.
   c. He killed Abel.

3. What should we do when we do something wrong?
   a. We should be angry.
   b. We should be sorry.
   c. We should fuss to others.

45

A. Vocabulary

1. Let the children say the sound word.
2. Print *It is not right. It is* _____. and let the children tell you what the word should be; then print it in the blank for them to see and refer to if they need a reminder.
3. Ask which of the new or review word(s)—
   a. has the word *like* in it. (liked)
   b. has the word *give* in it. (gives)
   c. has the word *want* in it. (wanted)
   d. has the word *some* in it. (someday)
   e. mean almost the same thing, but one means "now," and the other means "in the past." (know, knew)
   f. is a word you could say instead of your name. (I)
   g. is the opposite of *right*. (wrong)
   h. make you think of talking. (told, ask)
   i. means "another time." (someday)
4. Use the *Extra Practice* list in the reader.

B. Reader

Have the class study silently and then read orally.
Review Romans 12:9b.

C. Bible lesson

"What is the opposite of hate? Love makes us happy. The very best love is loving God. We are happy when we love God. We like when the people around us love God. If the people around us do not love God, we never know what bad things they will do.

"Who did not love God in the lesson? What did he do because he did not love God? Did he do only one bad thing?

"When someone does not love God and he does bad things, he usually does more and more bad things. That is how it was with Cain. What were the bad things he did?

"What did God do to Cain?"

Contrast Cain's life with a life of love for God. Tell someone to find the sentence *We should love God.* and to keep a marker under it. Call on him to read it after you have someone read the first sentence of the lesson. Then ask for the next three sentences in the beginning and the one following *We should love God.* Continue through the lesson, pointing out the parallel development.

D. Workbook
pages 44 and 45

Discuss the directions and assign the activities.

E. Worksheet

Message: Make a black tree and a yellow leaf pile.

LESSON 21

What God Does Not Like—When People Are Bad

Be prepared

1. Vocabulary flash cards
   New words: 2:21
   Review words: rest, might, there, fuss, families, were, why, who, where, know, will, wrong
   Phrases: 2:21
   Review phrases: they knew, he killed, should not hate, this is, each one, one kind, just right, our family, quiet night
2. If you have been saving the worksheets for a booklet, be prepared to put them together today. Construction paper may be used for covers.

A. Vocabulary

1. Let the children say the sound and key words.
2. Print the word *most* on the board. Mark the *o* with a macron and help the children to sound the word.
3. Print *many* with the pronunciation *men-ē*.
4. Print *destroy* on the board and say the following sentence: "*God decided to destroy the wicked people.*" Can the children tell which word is printed on the board?
5. Discuss the meanings of the words and drill with flash cards.
6. Use the *Extra Practice* lists in the reader.

B. Reader

Review the use of the quotation marks and have the children find them in their lesson.

Proceed with silent and oral reading.

Test each student on Romans 12:9b.

C. Bible lesson

Turn to the table of contents and review the things that God does not like as well as the section on what God likes.

"Do we like when people are bad? How did God feel when He saw all the bad people? Who were the bad people? [Adam and Eve had more children. They grew up and had children, too.]

"What did God decide to do? What would be destroyed besides the bad people?

"Did God love the bad people? He loved the people, but He did not like that they were bad. When we 'abhor that which is evil,' we should not be doing wicked things. We do not want to hate any people, even if they are bad. God loves them and wants them to love Him. Then He would help them to stop doing bad things."

D. Workbook

page 46

Discuss the directions and assign the exercises.

page 47

Encourage the children to find the answers in their readers to support

Lesson 21	**Key**	**Sound**	**Learn**
would — could *moon* — soon	am	destroy many most

Print the new words.

Gradebook: 29 points

1. I like many animals.

2. I could not name all the animals.

3. We should not destroy the animal homes.

4. I am glad God loves us.

5. He is happy most of the time.

6. We will soon be done with our work.

Match the words that mean the opposite.

b 1. right   a. sad

d 2. destroy   b. wrong

c 3. love   c. hate

a 4. happy   d. make

h 5. asked   e. now

e 6. then   f. sorry

f 7. glad   g. kind

g 8. angry   h. told

their choice of answers for the top of the page.

E. Worksheets

Message: Show what you can make when you play in the snow.

Put the last seven worksheets together and let the children take the booklets home.

Circle the correct letter.

1. God gave Adam and Eve
   (a.) more children.
   b. many animals.
   c. a new home.

2. God was sorry
   a. that there were many people.
   b. that He could see the people.
   (c.) that He had made the people.

3. God said,
   a. "I will hate the animals."
   b. "I do not love the bad people."
   (c.) "I will destroy the people and the animals."

Match the words to the pictures.

some   many   most   some   many   most

some   many   most   some   many   most

47

LESSON 22
God Sees a Godly Family

Be prepared
Vocabulary flash cards
New words: 2:22

Lesson 22	Key	Sound	Learn
destroy — destroyed	an	ark
punished — punish	three	Noah
in + to = into	go	Noah's
man — man's	wife	sons

Print the new words.

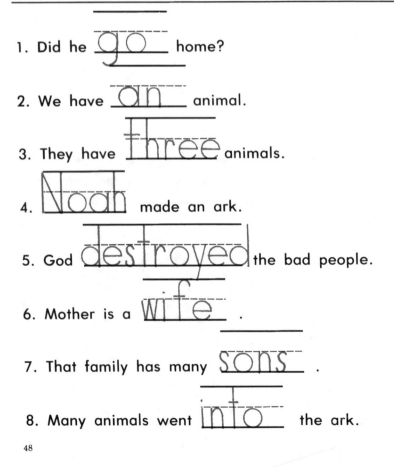

1. Did he _go_ home?

2. We have _an_ animal.

3. They have _three_ animals.

4. _Noah_ made an ark.

5. God _destroyed_ the bad people.

6. Mother is a _wife_ .

7. That family has many _sons_ .

8. Many animals went _into_ the ark.

48

Review words: nighttime, now, one, asked, sorry, still, Cain's, lie, told,
knew, could, am, soon, destroy, many, most
Phrases: 2:22
Review phrases: was wrong, did not know, where are, still was, Cain was,
all the animals, in his home, should not kill, you are

Reading Workbook   Unit 2   Lesson 22

Underline the correct words.

1. _____ of the people were bad.
      Some   **Three**   <u>**Most**</u>
2. But there was one _____ man.
      <u>**godly**</u>   **angry**   **bad**
3. He had a wife and _____ sons.
      one   **two**   <u>**three**</u>
4. This man's name was _____.
      Adam   <u>**Noah**</u>   **Abel**
5. God told him to make an _____.
      animals   **home**   <u>**ark**</u>
6. Then they _____ go into it.
      liked   <u>**could**</u>   **called**
7. They _____ not be destroyed with the bad people.
      called   <u>**would**</u>   **liked**

Underline the first word. Circle the next letter.

an (a)nimal   an (a)rk   a (b)ird   a (t)ree
an (e)gg   an (o)ak   a (t)oy   a (m)an
an (i)nch   an (e)lk   a (c)at   a (h)ome
an (o)x   an (i)cebox   a (w)all   a (l)ight
an (u)mbrella an (a)x   a (p)en   a (f)lood
   consonants   (consonants)
   (vowels)   vowels

49

A. Vocabulary

1. Let the children say the key and sound words.
2. Print *No* and tell the class that this is the beginning of a man's name. If they do not know what the name will be from the picture in the reader, tell them that this man built an ark.
3. Use *Noah* for a key to *Noah's*. Review the use of *'s* and have the children suggest some nouns to be used with *Noah's* and *man's*.
4. Print the sentence *Noah made the ark.* as a clue for *ark*.
5. Help the children to sound the word *sons*, noting the /z/ sound for the last *s*.
6. List some new and review words on the board, and a list of vowel symbols as well. Let the children draw lines to match the symbols with words that contain the sounds.

   Example: wife   ē

   Cain's   ō

   still   ī

   many   e

   told   ā

   three   i

7. Drill the words and phrases.

B. Reader

Return to the table of contents. Discuss the new section you are entering. Have the children find the first story of the section by page number.

Ask the children if they can find the quotation marks in the story and see if they remember what quotation marks are.

Have them find the apostrophes and discuss what was possessed in each case.

Proceed with silent and oral reading.

Turn to the Bible verse page and introduce "The Lord God will help me" (Isaiah 50:7a).

C. Bible lesson

"Do you see a lot of people when you go to church? Does your family sometimes visit other families that love God? It is a blessing to know many godly people. They help us to love God and obey Him.

"How lonesome it would be if you and your family were the only ones that loved God. How sad it would be to have only wicked people around you. There was a family like that in our lesson. They were the only godly people on the earth. All around them were many wicked people.

"What was the man's name? What can you tell me about Noah's family? How many godly people were there in all? [Sketch stick figures on the board to represent the family members if necessary.]

"Do you think God saw this family among all the wicked people? Yes,

He did! God sees everybody. What was God going to do to the wicked people? Would Noah be destroyed, too? What did God tell Noah to do?''

D. Workbook

page 48

Follow the directions.

page 49

Discuss the fact that sometimes we say *a* and sometimes we say *an.* In
the exercise at the bottom of the page, have the children underline *a* and
an and circle the first letter of the following word. At the bottom of each
section they are to circle the word to tell whether the letters they circled
were consonants or vowels.

E. Worksheet

Sentences begin with capital letters. Have the children cut out the capital
letters at the bottom of the sheet and find the correct place to paste each
one. After they read the sentences, they are to fill in the word at the bottom.

This worksheet may be saved with the next six to make a packet.

LESSON 23

God Tells Noah's Family What to Do

Be prepared

1. Vocabulary flash cards
   New words: 2:23

Lesson 23	Key	Sound	Learn
	now — how	safe	as

earth
tells
cover
flood
going
mountains

Print the new words.

1. God keeps us $\underline{safe}$.

2. I know $\underline{how}$ to work.

3. The $\underline{earth}$ is very big.

4. I like the big $\underline{mountains}$.

5. We are $\underline{going}$ to see the mountains.

6. You should do as many $\underline{as}$ you can.

7. Mother will $\underline{cover}$ the children at night.

8. Father $\underline{tells}$ us how to work.

9. A $\underline{flood}$ can destroy many things.

50

Review words: said, have, animal, other, boys, if, ask, told, knew, wrong, am, destroyed, into, go, man's, Noah, Noah's, sons, wife
Phrases: 2:23
Review phrases: an ark, most of them, will destroy, three of them, could be, angry people, talked to, can be helpers, who did

---

Reading Workbook   Unit 2   Lesson 23

Print *yes* or *no*.

---

1. Was God going to destroy the earth?   _yes_

2. Was God going to destroy the good people?   _no_

3. Was God going to destroy the bad people?   _yes_

4. Would the flood cover the moon?   _no_

5. Would the flood cover the mountains?   _yes_

6. Would Noah and his family be safe?   _yes_

7. Did Noah do just as God told him to do?   _yes_

8. Did that make God sad?   _no_

Circle the first letters. Print *a* or *an*.

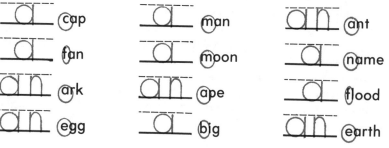

_a_ (c)ap   _a_ (m)an   _an_ (a)nt

_a_ (f)an   _a_ (m)oon   _a_ (n)ame

_an_ (a)rk   _an_ (a)pe   _a_ (f)lood

_an_ (e)gg   _a_ (b)ig   _an_ (e)arth

51

2. Print a few sentences on two sheets of paper, one with good margins and one with no margins.

A. Vocabulary
1. Hear the key and sound words.
2. Print some of the learn words on the board with their pronunciations for the children to sound and refer to.

   as = az
   tells = telz
   flood = flud

3. Print *rth* and let the children try to sound the combination. Tell them that there is not much of a vowel sound in the word, but you will show it with an *e* that has a dot over it. Print *earth* = *ėrth* and say the word for the children.
4. "We have the same sound in this word." Print *cover* = *kuv-ėr* and help them with the two syllables.
5. Use these sentences to introduce *going* and *mountains.*

   Will he go soon? He is going now.
   Very big hills are mountains.

6. Drill the words and phrases.

B. Reader
Show the children a paper with the printing crowding the very edge. Compare it with a paper that has nice margins and let the children tell you which is preferable. Tell them that they should always let such a space at the edge of their papers. "That space is called a margin. Look at the first page of your reading lesson. Put your finger in the margin at the side where we start reading. That is the left margin. Put your finger in the margin on the other side of the page. That is the right margin."

Have the children study silently and read orally.

Review Isaiah 50:7a.

C. Bible lesson
"Do you like when somebody tells you what to do? Sometimes we have work to do, and we do not know how. We need someone to tell us. Sometimes we do not know what is right or wrong. We need someone to tell us. Parents can tell us what to do. Teachers can tell us. Ministers can tell us.

"Who told Noah what to do? Everyone around Noah was wicked. Who could give him good advice? God talked to Noah. What did He tell Noah to do? For what would he use the ark? What would the Flood do?

"How did Noah know how to make the ark? Did Noah make it exactly the way God told him to? We can learn a good lesson from Noah. When someone tells us what to do, we should do exactly what they say. How do we feel when we do exactly what we are told to do?"

D. Workbook

page 50

Follow the directions.

page 51

Review the rule for using *an* before words beginning with vowels.

E. Worksheet

Let the children read and follow the directions.

LESSON 24
God Helps Noah's Family

Be prepared
1. Vocabulary flash cards
     New words: 2:24

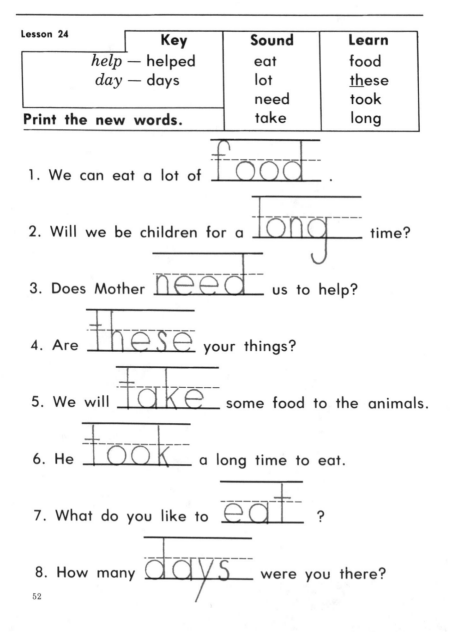

Lesson 24	Key	Sound	Learn
	help — helped	eat	food
	day — days	lot	these
		need	took
Print the new words.		take	long

1. We can eat a lot of ⎧f̲o̲o̲d̲⎫ .

2. Will we be children for a ⎧l̲o̲n̲g̲⎫ time?

3. Does Mother n̲e̲e̲d̲ us to help?

4. Are T̲h̲e̲s̲e̲ your things?

5. We will t̲a̲k̲e̲ some food to the animals.

6. He t̲o̲o̲k̲ a long time to eat.

7. What do you like to e̲a̲t̲ ?

8. How many d̲a̲y̲s̲ were you there?

Review words: lights, stars, thing, kind, families, wanted, done, where, know, destroy, as, earth, how, safe, tells, going
Phrases: 2:24
Review phrases: many were, cover the mountains, be a flood, soon there were, it has, your work, he killed, should not hate, others can

---

Reading Workbook   Unit 2   Lesson 24

Underline the correct words.

1. It took a long, long time to make the ____.   Ark   <u>ark</u>

2. The ark was very ____.   Big   <u>big</u>

3. ____ a long time Noah and his family would be in the ark.   <u>For</u>   for

4. ____ would need a lot of food to eat.   <u>They</u>   they

5. But ____ did just as God said they should do.   They   <u>they</u>

Follow the directions.

Draw a red line under words that mean one.

Draw a blue line under words that mean more than one.

1. mountains *blue*   4. people *blue*   7. <u>moon</u>   10. these *blue*
2. three *blue*   5. things *blue*   8. children *blue*   11. <u>sun</u>
3. <u>wife</u>   6. boys *blue*   9. <u>helper</u>   12. stars *blue*

53

2. The ark measured about 450 feet long by 75 feet wide and 45 feet high. Do some estimating to calculate how many buildings the size of your school or lengths of your playground would equal the ark dimensions.

A. Vocabulary
1. Hear the key and sound words.
2. Print *these* = *thēz*
3. Use sentences to introduce the other learn words.
   We eat *food.*
   Did you take the things? Yes, I *took* them.
   Will you soon be done? No, it will take a *long* time.
4. Let the children make original sentences with the new words.
5. Drill the word and phrase cards.

B. Reader
   Tell the children to point to the left margin and the right margin.
   Proceed with silent and oral reading.
   Review Isaiah 50:7a.

C. Bible lesson
   "Read the first sentence of the story again. Why do you think it took so long? How big do you think it was?" Give a comparison of the ark size to that of your school or playground.
   "What did they have to put into the ark? Why would they need so much food? What else were they to take into the ark?
   "What a lot of work they had to do! Who told them to do all that work? And who helped them to do it? God always helps us to do what He tells us to do.
   "How many animals would be going into the ark? How many can you think of?" List animal names on the board as the children say them and see how long a list they can compile. You may want to let the list remain for a day or two and add to it as the children think of more names.

D. Workbook
page 52
   Follow the directions.

page 53
   Repeat the rule that all sentences must begin with a capital letter. The exercise at the top of the page is to be done according to that rule.

E. Worksheet
   The children are to read and follow the directions.

Extra activity
   Let the children print sentences to answer some or all of the questions on page 52 of the workbook.

LESSON 25
God Calls Noah

Be prepared

Vocabulary flash cards

New words: 2:25

Review words: sometime, name, glad, Abel, why, liked, asked, sorry, kill, who, lie, say, I, knew, wrong, could, am, most, an, go, sons, wife, flood, mountains, helped, days, these, long

Phrases: 2:25

Review phrases: cover the earth, going to be, three of them, into the ark, a lot to eat, need to take, took food, he destroyed, how to make, right now

A. Vocabulary

1. Hear the key and sound words.
2. Print *been* = *bin*
3. Ask which new or review word(s)—
   a. name people. (sons, wife, Abel)
   b. name things people can do. (come, asked, kill, lie, say, go, helped)
   c. is a word we use with words that begin with vowels. (an)
   d. is the opposite of *short*. (long)
   e. is the opposite *down*. (up)
   f. make you think of *water*. (rain, flood)
   g. is the opposite of *right*. (wrong)
   h. means "happy." (glad)
   i. are big hills. (mountains)
   j. have two syllables (sometime, Abel, sorry, mountains)
4. Use the *Extra Practice* lists in the reader.

B. Reader

Review the terms *margin* and *quotation marks*. Conduct silent and oral reading. Review Isaiah 50:7a.

C. Bible lesson

"Did you ever move? Did you have a lot of things to take along? God told Noah to leave his home one day. Where did God tell Noah to go? Would he come back to his house after a while? No, he would stay in the ark a long, long time, and when he came out of the ark, he would need to make a new house.

"What was Noah supposed to take into the ark with him?

"What was going to happen soon? What would make the flood? Did you ever see it rain so much that there was water in the fields or on the road? That is a flood. Sometimes a flood gets so big that water gets into people's houses and destroys many things. How big would this flood be? What would the flood do to all the bad people?

"Why would Noah and his family be safe? God would take care of them because they obeyed Him."

D. Workbook

page 54

Print on the board or give orally some sentences for the children to

Lesson 25	Key	Sound	Learn
called — calls *some* — come		rain up	been

Print the new words.

1. Does rain come from the sky?

2. Do you come when Mother calls ?

3. When will you come to see us?

4. The stars are up in the sky.

Match the words to the sentences.

1. Where will you ____? ——————— be
2. Where have you ____? ——————— been

1. Noah had ____ a godly man. —— be
2. Will you ____ good? —————— been

1. Where has he ____? —————— be
2. Where will he ____? —————— been

54

practice the usage of *be* and *been*. If they need help other than simply deciding which one sounds right, tell them that *be* is used in sentences with *will*, and *been* is used with words that start with *h* (have, has, had).

He has ____ a good helper.

She will ____ glad to help.

Gradebook: 33 points   **Reading Workbook**   **Unit 2**   **Lesson 25**

Match the words to the sentences.

1. God told Noah to go into the ____.   rain
2. Soon God was going to make it ____.   ark

3. Then there would be a ____.   flood
4. It would cover all the ____.   mountains

5. That would destroy all the bad ____.   safe
6. But Noah and his family would be ____.   people

7. Noah was saved because he was ____.   God
8. We are safe when we obey ____.   godly

Circle the first letters. Print *a* or *an*.

a (b)oy   a (h)ome   a (l)ie

an (o)x   an (o)ther   a (f)uss

an (a)nimal   an (a)pple   an (o)range

a (h)elper   a (s)on   an (i)dol

a (t)hing   a (f)amily   an (e)el

55

I will ___ with my family.
They had ___ in the house.
We will ___ at the mountains.
We have ___ happy to see the rain.

page 55

Review the rule for using *a* or *an*.

E. Worksheet

Have the children read and follow the directions.

Extra activity

Let the children print sentences to answer the questions in the first exercise on workbook page 54.

LESSON 26
God Sends a Flood

Be prepared

1. Vocabulary flash cards

   New words: 2:26

   Review words: some, moon, one, let, ask, Cain's, many, man's, as, earth, tells, food, these, took, calls, rain

   Phrases: 2:26

   Review phrases: a long time, Noah's sons, where are, cover the mountains, will destroy, will come up, you have been, are sad, did not know

2. Cut the slit in the water on each child's worksheet.

A. Vocabulary

1. Hear the key and sound words.
2. Print some of the learn words on the board with pronunciations.

   sends = sendz

   began = bē-gan

   water = wo-tèr

   Help the children with the two syllable words and the dotted *e*.
3. Use these words and sentences for the other learn words.

   one, *two,* three

   We will not stay in. We are going *out.*
4. Display the new and review words and let the children think of clues to the words. As the children give their clues, have the rest of the class find the words.

B. Reader

Ask the children what we call the space at the edge of the page. Review the use of the apostrophe.

Proceed with silent and oral reading.

Review Isaiah 50:7a.

C. Bible lesson

Help the children to visualize the events as you discuss the story. Gesture as though the ark is at one side of the classroom. "An old man and woman go walking to the ark [across the front of the room]. Noah is six hundred years old. Then there are three more men going to the ark. Who are they? Three women go, too. Who are they? Then the animals start coming. [If you still have your list of animals, refer to it and name them.] How many animals of each kind went into the ark? Two cows and two horses; two pigs and two dogs; two bears and two rabbits; and so on. What a lot of animals came and walked into the ark! They kept coming and coming until some of every kind were in the ark. When it was time, the door of the ark went shut. Who shut it? Then what happened? It began to rain. It rained and rained, but the people and animals inside the ark were safe and dry. Soon there were puddles on the ground. Soon there was water over all the land. It kept on raining all day and night. It rained a whole week. It rained a whole month. And it rained still more. The water went up over the houses and trees. But the people and

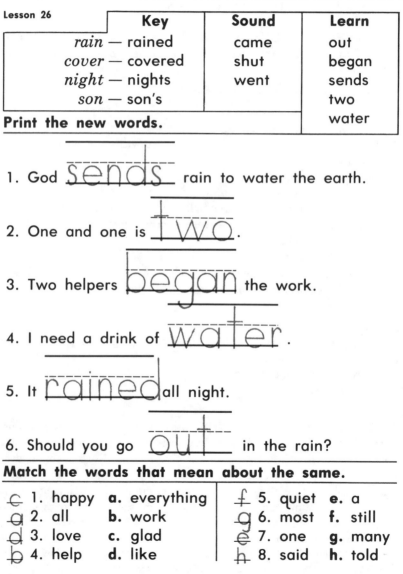

Lesson 26	**Key**	**Sound**	**Learn**
rain — rained	came	out
cover — covered	shut	began
night — nights	went	sends
son — son's		two
Print the new words.		water

1. God $\underline{\text{sends}}$ rain to water the earth.

2. One and one is $\underline{\text{two}}$.

3. Two helpers $\underline{\text{began}}$ the work.

4. I need a drink of $\underline{\text{water}}$.

5. It $\underline{\text{rained}}$ all night.

6. Should you go $\underline{\text{out}}$ in the rain?

Match the words that mean about the same.

c	1. happy	**a.** everything		f	5. quiet	**e.** a
g	2. all	**b.** work		g	6. most	**f.** still
d	3. love	**c.** glad		e	7. one	**g.** many
b	4. help	**d.** like		h	8. said	**h.** told

animals inside the ark were safe and dry. What else did the water cover? What happened to the people and animals that were not in the ark? Why did God let that happen?

"God did exactly what He said He would do. The wicked people did not believe Noah when he preached to them, but no matter what they did or

---

Reading Workbook   Unit 2   Lesson 26

Circle one or more correct letters.

1. How long did it rain?
   (a.) It rained many days and nights.
   b. It did not rain.
   c. It rained two days.

2. Who was in the ark?
   (a.) Noah was in the ark.
   b. Bad people were in the ark.
   (c.) Noah's three sons were in the ark.

3. What was covered with water?
   a. The ark was covered with water.
   (b.) The mountains were covered with water.
   (c.) The animals that were not in the ark
      were covered with water.

Underline the correct word.

1. Did Noah's family go into the ark?   **yes**   no
2. Did the animals go in one at a time? yes   **no**
3. Did the animals go in two at a time? **yes**   no
4. Did Noah shut them in the ark?   yes   **no**
5. Did God shut them in the ark?   **yes**   no
6. Were the good people safe?   **yes**   no
7. Were the bad people safe?   yes   **no**
8. Did God punish the bad people?   **yes**   no

said, God still did what He said He would do, and only the man who obeyed God was safe with his family."

D. Workbook

page 56

Follow the directions.

page 57

Make sure the children understand they are to circle all correct answers at the top of the page.

E. Worksheet

Have the children read and follow the directions.

LESSON 27
God Lets the Waters Go Down

Be prepared
Vocabulary flash cards
New words: 2:27
Review words: sees, fuss, boys, still, told, knew, am, most, how, eat, need,
long, come, been, nights, son's, rained, began, sends, two
Phrases: 2:27
Review phrases: should not lie, was wrong, be a flood, was shut out, the
water covered, they went, took food, would be safe, soon there were, could be

A. Vocabulary
1. Hear the key and sound words. You may need to help the children with
the two-syllable sound word. Tell them that the two parts should be
printed together when they print the word in the workbook.
2. Print these learn words with their pronunciations.
    opened = ō-pend
    stopped = stopt
    after = af-tėr
3. Print these sentences and numbers for the other learn words. When
something is not up, it is *down*.
    35, 36, 37, 38, 39, *forty*
4. Ask which new or review word(s)—
    a. have two *e*'s together to spell the /ē/ sound. (sees, need)
    b. breaks the rule that two *e*'s together make the /ē/ sound. (been)
    c. breaks the rule that an *e* on the end of a word gives the word a
    long vowel sound. (come)
    d. have an *s* that sounds like a *z*. (sees, boys, son's, sends, waters)
    e. make you think of your mouth. (fuss, told, eat)
    f. are number words. (forty, two)
    g. is the opposite of *bottom*. (top)
    h. is the opposite of *first*. (last)
    i. is the opposite of *shut*. (opened)
    j. is the opposite of *before*. (after)
    k. is the opposite of *girls*. (boys)
    l. is the opposite of *short*. (long)
    m. is the opposite of *up*. (down)
    n. is the opposite of *started*. (stopped)
    o. is the opposite of *stopped*. (began)
    p. have two syllables. (waters, window, after, opened, forty, began)
5. Drill the words and phrases.

B. Reader
Review the meaning of *margin*.

Proceed with silent and oral reading.
Review Isaiah 50:7a.

C. Bible lesson

"Did you ever get tired of staying inside because it was raining? How many days did it rain before the sun shone and you could go out again? How

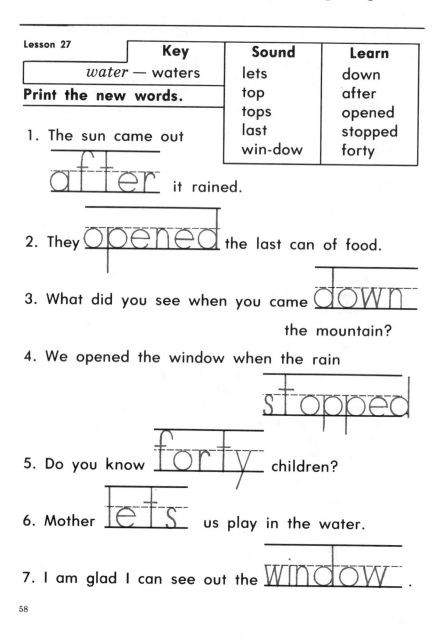

Lesson 27		Key	Sound	Learn
		water — waters	lets	down
Print the new words.			top	after
			tops	opened
			last	stopped
			win-dow	forty

1. The sun came out

   <u>after</u> it rained.

2. They <u>opened</u> the last can of food.

3. What did you see when you came <u>down</u>

   the mountain?

4. We opened the window when the rain

   <u>stopped</u>

5. Do you know <u>forty</u> children?

6. Mother <u>lets</u> us play in the water.

7. I am glad I can see out the <u>window</u>.

58

many days did it rain when Noah and his family were in the ark? They were glad to be safe from the flood, but don't you think they would have liked to be able to go outside sometime? Could they go out of the ark when the rain stopped? Why not? There was no place to go, was there? There was only water, water everywhere. What could the people see after a while? Where

---

Reading Workbook   Unit 2   Lesson 27

Underline the correct words.

1. After forty days and nights the rain ____.
   stopped   **began**   **went down**

2. The water went down a ____ at a time.
   lot   **little**   **like**

3. At last they could see the ____ of the mountains.
   flood   **food**   **tops**

4. The ark was on the ____ of the mountains.
   food   **name**   **top**

5. At last Noah ____ the window of the ark.
   shut   **covered**   **opened**

Match the words that have opposite meanings.

b 1. began   a. up

e 2. opened   b. stopped

a 3. down   c. all

c 4. some   d. wrong

d 5. right   e. shut

j 6. sad   f. take

h 7. people   g. work

i 8. first   h. animals

f 9. give   i. last

g 10. rest   j. glad

was the ark? Still they stayed in the ark. Noah and his family were in the ark more than a year while they waited for the water to go down and the earth to dry.

"Did you ever have to wait a long time for something? God has a time for everything, and we should be patient and wait for God's time."

D. Workbook
pages 58 and 59

Read and follow the directions.

E. Worksheet

"The numbers in the boxes below are to be cut out and pasted in the little squares in the pictures above to show the order of the pictures in relation to the water going down, down, down. Begin with number 1 in the picture that shows the highest water level. The pictures may be colored."

LESSON 28

God Lets Noah and His Family Come Out

Be prepared

1. Vocabulary flash cards

   New words: 2:28

   Review words: she, work, nighttime, rest, more, now, might, just, animal, has, kind, families, other, Cain, talked, killed, know, destroy, three, wife, earth, take, these, up, covered, out, water, waters, lets, top, stopped

   Phrases: 2:28

   Review phrases: began to rain, came down, opened the window, after forty days, at last, tops of the mountains, two and two, going to be, he destroyed, angry people

2. Have construction paper available to make packets for worksheets.

A. Vocabulary

1. Hear the key and sound words.
2. Print *raven* = *rā-ven*. Discuss the meaning of the words *raven* and *dove*.
3. Print *We did help one time. Now we will help again.* Can the children guess the word *again*?
4. Drill the word and phrase cards.

B. Reader

Conduct silent and oral reading class.

Test the children on Isaiah 50:7a.

C. Bible lesson

"Noah and his family were in the ark a long time. They were waiting for the time when God would tell them to come out. What did Noah open? What did he send out? What did the raven do? What else did Noah send out? What did the dove do? What did the dove do the second time Noah sent her out? What happened the third time Noah sent her out?

"When did Noah and his family go out of the ark? What else went out of the ark? Just think of all the animals walking out of the ark and going down the mountain. There were no other animals on the earth. There were no other people on the earth besides Noah and his family. How good it must have been to get out in the sunshine and the breeze and see the big sky overhead and all the hills and mountains far around.

"The big empty ark was left on the mountains. They did not need it any more."

D. Workbook

pages 60 and 61

Discuss the directions. For the exercise at the top of page 61, do a few samples together with the children.

E. Worksheet

Have the children read and follow the directions. Let them make a packet from two pieces of construction paper and paste today's picture on the front. The worksheets from lessons 22-27 may be put into the packet and taken home today.

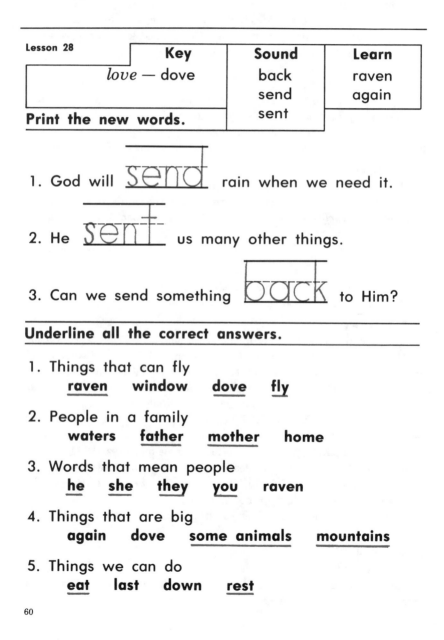

Lesson 28

Key	Sound	Learn
love — dove	back	raven
	send	again
	sent	

Print the new words.

1. God will ___send___ rain when we need it.

2. He ___sent___ us many other things.

3. Can we send something ___back___ to Him?

Underline all the correct answers.

1. Things that can fly
   <u>raven</u> window <u>dove</u> <u>fly</u>

2. People in a family
   waters <u>father</u> <u>mother</u> home

3. Words that mean people
   <u>he</u> <u>she</u> <u>they</u> <u>you</u> raven

4. Things that are big
   again dove <u>some animals</u> <u>mountains</u>

5. Things we can do
   <u>eat</u> last <u>down</u> <u>rest</u>

60

Number these sentences in the order each thing happened.

1-2

_2_ Noah made an ark.

_1_ God told Noah He would send a flood.

3-4

_3_ Noah and his family went into the ark.

_4_ It began to rain.

5-6

_6_ The rain stopped.

_5_ The bad people were destroyed.

7-8

_8_ Noah sent out a raven.

_7_ Noah opened the window.

Circle the correct letter.

1. How many times did Noah send a dove?
   a. Noah sent a dove one time.
   b. Noah sent a dove two times.
   c. **Noah sent a dove three times.**

2. How many times did the dove come back?
   a. The dove came back one time.
   b. **The dove came back two times.**
   c. The dove came back three times.

LESSON 29

God Makes a Promise

Be prepared
1. Vocabulary flash cards
   New words: 2:29

Lesson 29	**Sound**	**Learn**
	kept	promise
	rain - bow	remember

Print the new words. Gradebook: 36 points

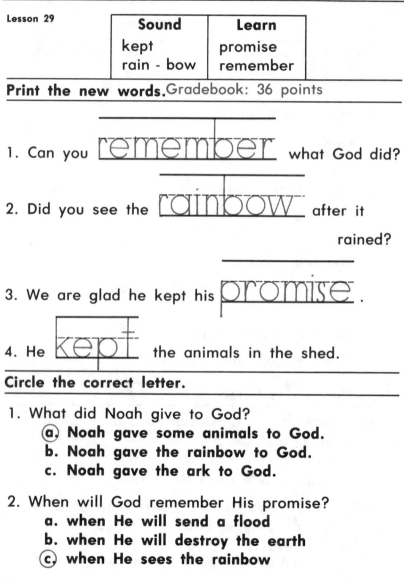

1. Can you remember what God did?

2. Did you see the rainbow after it

   rained?

3. We are glad he kept his promise .

4. He kept the animals in the shed.

Circle the correct letter.

1. What did Noah give to God?
   a. **Noah gave some animals to God.**
   b. **Noah gave the rainbow to God.**
   c. **Noah gave the ark to God.**

2. When will God remember His promise?
   a. **when He will send a flood**
   b. **when He will destroy the earth**
   c. **when He sees the rainbow**

Review words: said, lights, your, others, wanted, done, liked, asked, who, where, could, an, go, helped, food, lot, took, calls, been, began, went, down, after, opened, window, raven

Phrases: 2:29

Reading Workbook   Unit 2   Lesson 29

Underline all the correct words.   3 points for each question on this page

1. Number Words
one   food   forty   again   two

2. Words That Ask Questions
water   what   where   with   why

3. People in a Family
water   wife   children   boys   just

4. Ways We May Feel
glad   angry   have   sorry   earth

5. Good Things to Do
because   ark   help   obey   work

6. Bad Things to Do
fuss   kill   done   love   lie

7. Good Things to Be
angry   helper   fusser   worker   giver

8. When We May Do Things
give   last   soon   let   now

9. Ways Things Might Be
long   if   at   little   big

10. Names
Abel   He   Cain   Is   Noah

Review phrases: sent a dove, send it back, again and again, they knew, it rained, many were, should not hate, the water covered, into the ark, was shut out

2. Have pencil crayons available to use on the worksheets and be prepared to staple the booklets.

A. Vocabulary

1. Let the children say the sound words.
2. Print the learn words with pronunciations.

promise = prom-is

remember = rē-mem-bėr

3. Ask how many syllables are in each of the new words.
4. Let the children make original sentences with the words.
5. Drill the word and phrase cards.
6. Use the *Extra Practice* list in the reader.

B. Reader

Turn to the table of contents and read the titles for the last short section of the unit.

Turn to the Bible verse page and introduce the new verse for the section. "The Lord is good to all" (Psalm 145:9a).

Proceed with silent and oral reading.

C. Bible lesson

"How do you feel when someone has been very good to you? Do you love them? Do you feel like giving them something to show your love? How did Noah feel after the Flood? What did Noah give to God? Do you know how Noah could give animals to God when he could not see God? Look at the picture at the beginning of this section in the reader (page 76). What is Noah doing? In those days people worshiped God in a different way. The pile of stones in front of Noah is an altar. He killed an animal and put it on the altar. Then he burned it. That was the way he gave it to God.

"Did God like what Noah did? Then God made a promise to Noah. What did God promise? What did God make as a sign of His promise? Did you ever see a rainbow? Do you know who looks at it besides you when there is a rainbow in the sky? God looks at it, and He thinks about His promise to never again destroy the earth with a flood.

D. Workbook
pages 62 and 63

Have the children read and follow the directions.

You may want to tell the class that each question on page 63 has three correct answers.

E. Worksheet

There are two sheets for this lesson. The children are to color the pictures (you may want to provide pencil crayons to help them do a better job on the fine details), cut them out, and paste them on the second sheet in the order in which they took place. Then they are to cut out the titles and paste them under the correct pictures. The sections may be cut apart and stapled into a little booklet to take home.

LESSON 30

God Sees a Tower

Be prepared
Vocabulary flash cards
  New words: 2:30

Lesson 30	**Key**	**Sound**	**Learn**
many — any	same	away
do — doing	tell	tower
talked — talk	fin-ish	only
Print the new words.	from	

1. Noah and his family were the only

   people on the earth.

2. The people wanted to make a tower .

3. God did not like what they were doing .

4. God did not let them finish it.

5. He did not let the people talk the same.

6. Then they could not tell what the

   _____ others said.

7. The people went away from each other.

8. They did not work on the tower any more.

Review words: gives, name, helpers, Abel, why, sorry, say, man's, sons, as, tells, flood, days, need, come, son's, sends, waters, last, stopped, dove, kept, rainbow

Phrases: 2:30

Match the words to the pictures.

angry	again	happy		
had	came	went		
began	finish	food		
destroy	make	dove		
each	earth	eat		
three	forty	soon		
long	likes	lot		
ark	after	animals		
now	boy	day		
covered	called	could		
down	done	up		
flood	food	forty		
take	send	give		
others	opened	shut		

Review phrases: after forty days, remember his promise, the raven came, opened the window, it would cover, a long time, two and two, how to make, again and again, most of them.

A. Vocabulary

1. Let the children say the key and sound words.
2. Print these words with their pronunciations:
   only = ōn-lē
   away = a-wā
3. Sketch a flower and a tower on the board and print the word below each picture. Tell the children that the words rhyme.
4. Drill the words and phrases.

B. Reader

Review the meaning of *margin* and the use of the apostrophe.
Conduct silent and oral reading class.

Listen to the children say Psalm 145:9a. If you have time, review all the memory verses from the unit.

C. Bible lesson

"Do you have any close neighbors? Can you imagine what it would be like if there was no one living around you besides your family, and there would be no towns to which you could go and find people? Who were the only people on the earth right after the flood? Noah's sons had children, and soon there were many people on the earth. What was the same about them? Did you ever hear someone talking in a language that you could not understand? These people did not have different languages. Everyone on the earth talked the same language.

"What did the people plan to do? Did God like what they were doing? What did God do to the people? All at once people could not understand each other any more. What did they do then? Did they finish the tower?

"God can see what everybody is doing. If He wants to, He can make something happen to change people's minds and stop them from doing what they are doing."

D. Workbook
page 64

Follow the directions.

page 65

If you wish, you may read a word from each set for the children to cross out before they match the words to the pictures. Or have them choose from the three words in matching words to the pictures to make it a more challenging exercise. Words that are not used for the pictures:

again	after
had	now
food	could
make	done
each	forty
soon	give
lot	others

E. Worksheet

Have the children cut out the blocks with capital letters and paste them beside the correct small letters.

Extra activity

Let the children color the picture on page 66 of the reading workbook.

Note

At this point students should be able to independently read *The Egg and the Chick*, Book 1 of the *God Is Good Series*. See instructions to the teacher at the beginning of this little storybook.

Reading
Unit 3

GENERAL PLAN

Vocabulary flash cards are not provided for unit 3. The new words for each lesson are listed in the reader as well as in the workbook. If you wish to continue flash card drill, you may print the words on the back of the flash cards for units 1 and 2, being careful to use the cards in numbered order. You could likewise prepare phrase cards.

Always put the new words on the board for practice and discussion. This exercise can be valuable in building reading comprehension.

The reading lessons of unit 3 are poems. Develop an appreciation for poetry and rhythm as you study these lessons. Do it by reading the poems for the children to demonstrate the rhythm and by reading and discussing other poetry.

The children may read well because of the rhythm and rhyme, but miss the message unless it is studied and discussed. Discuss these lessons until they are thoroughly understood to keep the children growing in their comprehension skills.

Utilize the alphabetical order of the poems to help rivet the alphabet. Each of the children should positively be able to say the alphabet by the end of the unit.

The Bible memory work for this unit is a passage of six verses. Introduce it as a type of poem and use the verses at the rate the children can learn them. The class may enjoy saying the last phrase of each verse in unison after one child recites the beginning phrase.

The lesson plan outlines in unit 3 are reduced to four points. The Bible lesson is included in the reader discussion of part B.

Reading Lessons   Unit 3

LESSON 1
Adam

Be prepared

Have a file folder for each child to store his worksheets in as they proceed through the alphabet. After lesson 26, the pages may be fastened together

---

Lesson 1

Sound		Learn	
life	much	baby	never
me	wife's	happier	or

Print new words in the sentences.

Lord	ribs

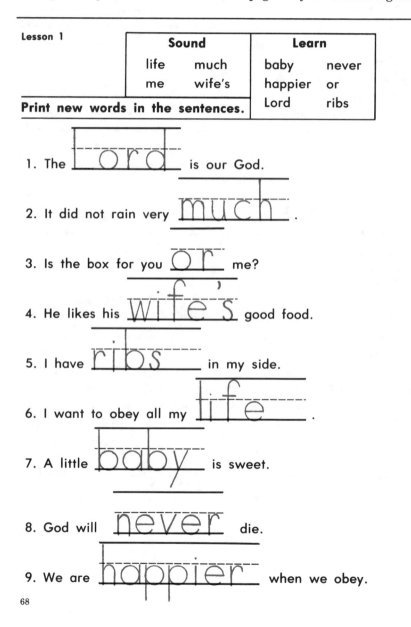

1. The **Lord** is our God.

2. It did not rain very **much** .

3. Is the box for you **or** me?

4. He likes his **wife's** good food.

5. I have **ribs** in my side.

6. I want to obey all my **life** .

7. A little **baby** is sweet.

8. God will **never** die.

9. We are **happier** when we obey.

68

in a book to take home.

A. Vocabulary

1. Listen to the children say the sound words.
2. Print this sentence on the board and let the children identify the little word *or. Are you big or little?*

Reading Workbook   Unit 3   Lesson 1

Print *yes* **or** *no.*

1. Was Adam the very first man?   yes

2. Did God make him a little baby?   no

3. Did Adam have a wife?   yes

4. Did God make Adam's wife from a rib?   yes

5. Did God want Adam to be happy?   yes

In each row, underline a word that rhymes with the first word.

1. as	has	was	gas	fuss
2. tell	will	ten	well	all
3. ribs	rids	robs	rods	bibs
4. never	every	ever	need	now
5. from	food	came	come	done
6. you	go	do	so	no

Find a word in the reader to rhyme with each word.

man can   me see   wife life

69

3. Print the word *Lord* and underline the little word *or* in it.
4. Print the other learn words with their pronunciations for the children to sound.

    baby = bā-bē
    ribs = ribz
    never = nev-ėr
    happier = hap-ē-ėr

5. List all the new words and drill them by having the class or individuals read the list and say the words as you point to them in random order.
6. Have the children tell you which word(s)—

    a. have two syllables. (baby, never)
    b. has three syllables. (happier)
    c. means "not any time." (never)
    d. names part of your body. (ribs)
    e. name a person. (baby, me, Lord)
    f. tells that something belongs to a person. (wife's)
        Let the children think of phrases using the
        word with nouns to tell what the wife has.
    g. is the opposite of *little*. (much)
    h. is the opposite of *death*. (life)
    i. is the opposite of *always*. (never)

B. Reader

1. Ask the children what looks different about the lesson in their reader. They should notice the separation of the verses and indentation of every second line. Tell them that their lesson is a poem. Have them read the poem silently a few times.
2. "Poems are a special kind of reading. When we talk, we say some words louder than others. In a poem the louder words come in a very regular pattern. That is rhythm." Read the poem to the class with exaggerated anapestic rhythm, moving your hand as in beating time.

    A is for *Ad*am,
        The *very* first *man*.
    Now *tell* me his *wife's* name
        As *soon* as you *can*.

    Have the children read the poem orally, then ask if they noticed the rhyming words. Let them find and say the pairs of rhyming words and notice where they appear in the structure of the poem.

3. Discuss the meaning of the first line. We say *A* is for *Adam* because *Adam* is a word that begins with *A*.

    "Who was Adam? Can you tell me his wife's name?

    "Was Adam ever a little boy? Why was he never little? Was your father ever a little boy? Every grown person you know was one time a little baby. They grew through all the ages that you are growing through.

If the Lord grants it, you will someday be grown-up too.

"Do you know how God made Adam? He used the dust of the earth and made the shape of man. Then God breathed into the body and Adam became alive.

"How did God make Eve? What is a rib? Where are your ribs? Why did God make Eve? How do you think it made Adam's life happier to have a wife?"

4. Turn to page 84 and introduce the new memory verse. Let the children read as much of the verse as they can. Notice the new word *Lord* and compare *forever* with *never* in structure and meaning.

Tell the children that a lord is a ruler. All rulers have a Ruler over them, and that Ruler is the Lord.

Practice saying the verse together.

C. Workbook
pages 68 and 69

The children should be able to read a good bit of the directions independently. Help them with the word *rhymes* and have them explain what they understand the directions to say.

D. Worksheet

Connect the dots to draw the large capital *A* which may be colored.

The children are to cut out the four letter blocks at the bottom of the page and paste them in the proper order to finish the sentence *A is for* ____.

The words in the boxes are to be cut out and used to finish the other sentences on the page. After their work is checked the unused words may be discarded or saved for the extra activity.

Encourage the children to be precise in their cutting and pasting. Have them print their names on the back of the sheets and store them in a special place or let the children keep folders in their desks to file the daily sheets.

Extra activity

Let the children use the discarded word slips from the worksheet and try to arrange them in a sentence, or paste them on a paper, printing any additional words they need to make a sentence.

LESSON 2
Bible

Be prepared

1. You may find it advantageous to have the vocabulary helps printed on the board ahead of class time. You may print these sentences in

Lesson 2	Sound		Learn	
	best	by	Bible	stories
	book	men	parents	women

Print new words in the phrases. Gradebook: 26 points for the whole lesson

1. by and **by**

2. the very **best** Book

3. a **book** to read (or Bible)

4. men and **women**

5. a book of **stories**

6. my **Bible** and I (or parents)

Print the new words that start with *b.*

best **book** **by** **Bible**

Print *one* **or** *more* **after each word.**

1. baby **one**

2. wife **one**

3. books **more**

4. stories **more**

5. men **more**

6. women **more**

7. Bible **one**

8. children **more**

70

preparation for teaching the new learn words:

Fathers and mothers are *parents.*

Mothers are *women.*

She can tell us good *stories.*

2. List all the new words on the board in a different order than they appear

---

Underline the correct words.

1. The Bible is the best ____.
   look   **Book**   stories

2. The Bible is ____ by many people.
   book   large   **loved**

3. Our ____ will read it.
   parents   men   women

4. It can ____ our parents what to do.
   read   **tell**   love

5. We love ____ stories.
   Bible   book   small

6. The Bible has ____ of women and men.
   stories   children   read

7. The Bible has stories of ____.
   large   again   **children**

8. We love the ____.
   read   by   **Bible**

in the reader, mixing sound and learn words.
3. Print these phrases on the board or on flash cards for drill:
   by and by
   men and women
   the very best book
   my Bible and I
   Bible stories
   baby and parents
   by the women
   a book of stories

A. Vocabulary
1. Listen to the children say the sound words.
2. Use the sentences above to introduce some of the learn words.
3. Print the word *Bible* and ask someone to spell the letters that they see. Do they recognize a song they sometimes sing?
4. Practice the phrases containing the new words.

B. Reader
1. Ask the children what we call the kind of reading they have in their lesson. The lesson is not a story. It is a poem.
   What is special about poems? Let the children find and say the rhymes. Explain rhythm again and read the poem to the class for an example.
2. Have the children read the poems for both *A* and *B* in oral reading class.
3. "*A* is for ___?
   "*B* is for ___? Do you know why the Bible is the best book? Who said the things that are in the Bible?" Compare the Bible with other books which may have faults and mistaken teachings.
   "Who loves the Bible? [The large and the small] What does that mean?
   "Why do our parents read the Bible? Do you know what some things are that the Bible tells them to do? [Love people, not kill or steal, gather to worship, tell others about God, train their children, and so on.]
   "Can you think of any Bible stories of women?
   "Can you think of any Bible stories of men?
   "Can you think of any Bible stories of children?"
4. Review the Bible memory verse.

C Workbook
pages 70 and 71
Notice that the new words are to be put into phrases rather than sentences. There may be a variation of correct responses in this exercise.

Discuss the difference between words that mean one and words that mean more than one. Say a singular word and let the children tell you how to say that word meaning more than one. Say a plural word and let them tell how to say it meaning only one. Give some words for them to tell you whether you are naming one or more.

Let the children explain the directions as they understand them.

D. Worksheet

Connect the dots and color the letter.

Cut out the letters to spell the word for which *B* stands.

Cut out the phrases and decide whether they describe the Bible or other books, then paste them in the proper place.

LESSON 3
Children

Be prepared

1. Print these learn words with their pronunciations:

   ones = wonz

Lesson 3	Key	Sound	Learn
all + so = also	poor	dear
all — small	rich	large
others — brothers		ones
		sisters

Print the new words that begin with these letters.

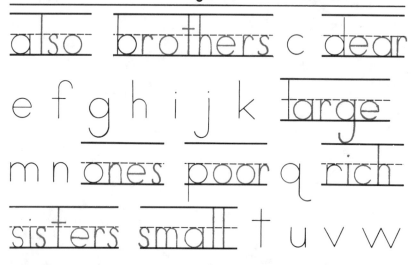

also brothers c dear

e f g h i j k large

m n ones poor q rich

sisters small t u v w

Match the words that have opposite meanings.

C 1. rich   **a.** small

a 2. large   **b.** man

e 3. brothers   **c.** poor

d 4. play   **d.** work

b 5. baby   **e.** sisters

g 6. you   **f.** men

i 7. day   **g.** me

f 8. women   **h.** wrong

j 9. happy   **i.** night

h 10. right   **j.** sad

dear = dēr (or) dir (Use the pronunciation that is right for you; do not
use both.)
sisters = sis-tėrz
2. Print the equation *big = large.*
3. List all the new words in scrambled order.

Match the phrases.

C. 1. God loves   **a.** we obey.

e 2. God made   **b.** have sisters and brothers.

b 3. Some children   **c.** all the children.

d 4. Each of the children   **d.** should want to obey.

a 5. God likes when   **e.** fathers and mothers for us.

Underline two sentences that mean the same.

1.
a. God loves the small children.
b. God loves the rich children.
c. God loves the children who have many things.

2.
a. God loves the large children.
b. God loves the women.
c. God loves the big children.

3.
a. God gave us parents.
b. God gave us sisters and brothers.
c. God gave us fathers and mothers.

4.
a. We should obey our fathers and mothers.
b. We should love our families.
c. We should do what our parents say.

73

4. Print a verse of the poem on the board to demonstrate rhythm, putting two lines together and hyphenating the word *children* to show the two syllables.

   C is for child-ren; Our God loves them all—
   The rich and the poor ones, The large and the small.

A. Vocabulary

1. Let the children say the key and sound words.
2. Have the children sound the pronunciations for the learn words. Point to the equation *big* = *large* and tell the children that the two words have the same meaning. Can they guess the new word?
3. Print all the new words on the board and ask
   which word(s)—
   a. name people in a family. (brothers, sisters)
   b. means *too*. (also)
   c. is what you call someone you love. (dear)
   d. are opposites. (rich—poor, small—large, sisters—brothers)
   e. has the /oo/ sound. (poor)
   f. has the /j/ sound. (large)
   g. have two syllables. (brothers, sister, also)
4. Page to the word lists at the back of the book and let the children practice the lists given for the first three lessons of the unit.

B. Reader

1. Let the children study the poem silently.

   Ask the children what kind of reading they have in their lesson. Let them locate the rhymes and ask them what *rhythm* is.

   Have the first verse of the poem printed on the board in two lines. Underline the stressed syllables so the children can see the stressed syllables instead of just hearing them. Let someone read the lines stressing the underlined words. Point out the pattern of two soft syllables, then one loud one. Putting a dot under each unaccented syllable may help to show this pattern.

   The word *families* in the second verse will be pronounced as a two-syllable word if the rhythm is followed strictly.
2. Let the children read the poems from *A* to *C*.
3. "*A* is for ___? *B* is for ___? *C* is for ___? What kind of children does God love? Can you think of some other kinds of children that He loves too?" (Sick, healthy, Indian, Chinese, blind, crippled, thin, stout, fast, slow, skilled, retarded—our God loves them *all*.)

   You may have in your class some children who are orphaned or who come from unfortunate home settings. They need not be pointed out, but if some thinker in the class mentions it, you may explain that sometimes God has special parents to take care of children whose first parents couldn't.

Ask the children which of them have families of sisters and brothers. "What do your fathers and mothers do for you? What should you do for them? What does God like?"

4. Review the Bible memory verse.

C. Workbook
pages 72 and 73

Make sure the children understand the exercise using the new words.

The last exercise is also a new one. You may want to do it orally with the children before you assign the lesson.

D. Worksheet

The children are again to draw the letter, cut out the blocks, and arrange them to spell the word.

Help the children to read the poem. You may want to sing it together.

Let them color the picture.

LESSON 4

Daytime

Be prepared

1. Vocabulary helps to be printed on the board

    nice = nīs

Lesson 4	Key	Sound	Learn
	right — bright	six	cloudy
	help — helping		house
	dear — near		nice
	sometime — sometimes		special
	Lord — Lord's		

Print new words in the phrases.

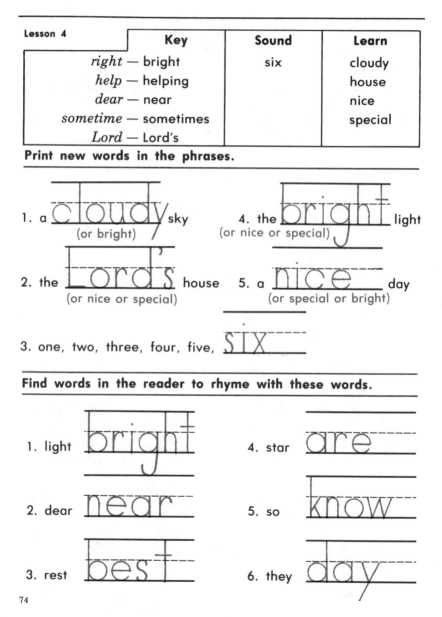

1. a <u>cloudy</u> sky
   (or bright)

2. the <u>Lord's</u> house
   (or nice or special)

3. one, two, three, four, five, <u>six</u>

4. the <u>bright</u> light
   (or nice or special)

5. a <u>nice</u> day
   (or special or bright)

Find words in the reader to rhyme with these words.

1. light <u>bright</u>

2. dear <u>near</u>

3. rest <u>best</u>

4. star <u>are</u>

5. so <u>know</u>

6. they <u>day</u>

special = spesh-ul
The *house* is big.
The sky is *cloudy*.
2. List all the new words in scrambled order.

Match the phrases.

b 1. Sometimes days

a 2. Six days

d 3. It is nice

e 4. One day

c 5. On the special day

a. are for work.

b. are cloudy.

c. we rest.

d. to have parents.

e. is special.

Circle the correct letter.

1. When is it light?
   a. It is light when we rest.
   b. It is light in the night.
   c. It is light in the daytime.

2. What do we do six days?
   a. We help our dear parents.
   b. We go to the Lord's house.
   c. Some days are bright.

3. Where do we go on the special day?
   a. We go to the Lord's house.
   b. We go to work.
   c. We go where it is cloudy.

3. Print these phrases on the board or flash cards for drill.

cloudy sky	four, five, six
nice house	helping sometimes
special day	bright light
cloudy or bright	near the house
the Lord's house	special stories

4. If you have room, print a verse of the poem on the board to show rhythm. Hyphenate the two-syllable words.

A. Vocabulary

1. Let the children say the key and sound words, and help them to get the learn words by sounding the pronunciations and studying the sentence context and picture.
2. Gain a lead on tomorrow's phonics lesson by introducing the diphthong *ou.* Help the children to recognize it in *house* and *cloudy.*
3. Ask which word(s)—
   a. rhymes with *mouse.* (house)
   b. rhymes with *mice.* (nice)
   c. rhymes with *kicks.* (six)
   d. shows that something belongs to someone. (Lord's)
   e. is a place to live. (house)
   f. means *close.* (near)
   g. is a number. (six)
   h. have the /ou/ sound. (house, cloudy)
   i. tell what something is like. (bright, cloudy, nice, special)
   Ask the children to name something that is bright, something nice, and something special.
4. Drill the phrases.

B. Reader

1. Underline the stressed syllables in a verse of the poem on the board. Have the children practice the rhythm pattern. Let them read the verse in unison, then tell them to study their lesson silently.
2. Include as many of the previous poems as suitable in oral reading class.
3. Review the letters and the words for which they stand.
   "*D* is for ___?
   "When is it light? What are days sometimes like? What are some other kinds of days like? [windy, rainy, cold, snowy]
   "How many days are for work? What kind of work do we do?
   "What are the names of those six days?" List the days of the week on the board as the children name them. Print them in order and let the list remain for the children to refer to when they do the worksheet.
   "What is the special day called? What do we do on the special day? Where is the Lord's house?"
4. Review the memory verse.

C. Workbook
pages 74 and 75

The first three words in the rhyming exercise can be found in the rhyming pattern of the poem. If the children have trouble with the others, you may give them the clue that a rhyme may be found for the first one in the first verse of the poem, the second one in the second verse, and so on. The poem does not have the words given in the workbook for numbers 4-6, but there is a word in the poem to rhyme with each one.

D. Worksheet

Follow the usual pattern of drawing the letter and arranging the word. Encourage the children to arrange the letters before they check with the book to see if they can spell the word correctly.

Let them use the list of words on the board as a guide to put the names of the days in the correct order.

Help them with the word *church* in the directions at the bottom of the sheet.

Extra activity

Have the children list the new words in alphabetical order as was done in the workbook in lesson 3. Allow them to list all the words beginning with one letter in a row without regard to any order within the row.

LESSON 5
Eve

Be prepared

1. Vocabulary helps

    her = hėr

Lesson 5	Key	Sound	Learn
	help — helper	deep	wives
		feel	her
		sleep	
		a-sleep	

Print new words for the answers. Gradebook: 21 points for the whole lesson

1. Something you can do feel

    _____ (or sleep)

2. Women wives

3. Three words that rhyme

    deep   sleep   asleep

Print *large* **or** *small* **under each picture.**

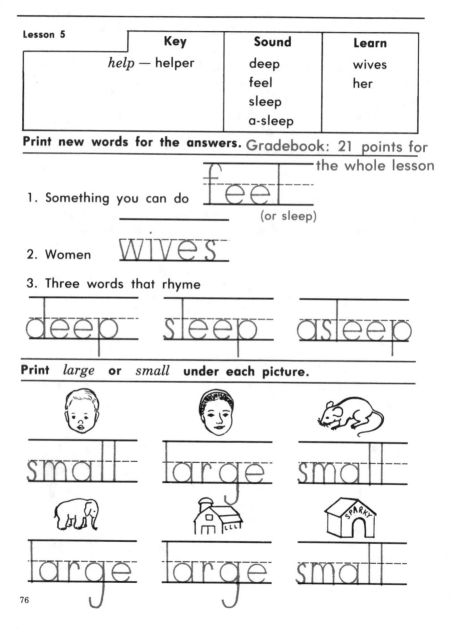

small   large   small

large   large   small

76

wives = wīvz
2. List all the new words.
3. Print a verse of the poem on the board to show rhythm, hyphenating all
   two-syllable words.

Reading Workbook   Unit 3   Lesson 5

Underline the correct words.

1. Eve was the first ____.   other   <u>mother</u>

2. She was the first ____.   <u>wife</u>   life

3. God made her from Adam
   when he was ____.   sleep   <u>asleep</u>

4. His sleep was very ____.   <u>deep</u>   keep

5. Eve was made to be a ____.   help   <u>helper</u>

6. She was to help ____.   <u>Adam</u>   Noah

7. Wives are to help the best
   that they ____.   <u>can</u>   came

Underline two sentences that mean the same.

1.
   a. Eve had a little baby.
   <u>b. Eve was never little in all of her life.</u>
   <u>c. Eve was never a baby.</u>

2.
   <u>a. Adam was asleep when God made Eve.</u>
   b. God made Eve from Adam.
   <u>c. God made Eve when Adam was asleep.</u>

3.
   <u>a. God wanted Eve to help Adam.</u>
   <u>b. Eve was to be a helper to Adam.</u>
   c. Wives are to help men.

77

A. Vocabulary

1. Let the children give the key and sound words and study the learn words.
2. Ask which word(s)—
    a. means *women that are married.* (wives)
    b. means *a woman or girl.* (her)
    c. names a person who helps. (helper)
    d. tells what you do with your hand. (feel)
    e. tells what you do at night. (sleep)
    f. describes a person who is sleeping. (asleep)
    g. can be used to describe water. (deep)

B. Reader

1. Have the students study silently first, trying to think the rhythm as they read. Then let someone come to the board and underline the syllables he thinks should be louder.
2. Have the class read orally.
3. "*E* is for ___? Who was Eve? What was her husband's name?

   "Was Eve ever little? Who else was never little?

   "How did God make Eve? Do you remember what He took from Adam to make her? Did it hurt Adam? Why not? What does it mean when you say his sleep was deep? Did you ever try to wake someone who was sleeping? Sometimes it does not take much to make someone awake, and sometimes you call and call, but they just keep on sleeping. When you do not get awake easily, we say your is sleep deep.

   "Why did God make Eve? What is God's plan for all wives? What can they do to help?"
4. Review the memory verse.

C. Workbook
pages 76 and 77

Discuss the direction for the bottom of page 76. The children are to print the word that describes the item in real life. They should not reason that since the pictures are nearly the same size, it is a large mouse and a small elephant.

D. Worksheet

Follow the usual pattern for tracing the letter and spelling the word. The phrases and sentences are to be pasted under the right heading to describe the first mother or the child's mother.

Note

At this point students should be able to independently read *The Squirrel and the Nut*, Book 2 of the *God Is Good Series*. See instructions to the teacher at the beginning of this little storybook.

LESSON 6
Father

Be prepared

1. Vocabulary helps
    shows = shōz
    live = liv
    word = wėrd
    heaven = hev-en
2. List all the new words.
3. Print a verse of the poem, hyphenating two-syllable words.

A. Vocabulary

1. Practice the new words.
2. Turn to the word lists at the back of the book and have the children practice reading the words for the lessons they have covered to this point.

B. Reader

1. Have the children study silently, then let someone mark the stressed syllables on the board.
2. Include a number of the previous poems in oral reading and do some reading in unison.
3. "*F* is for ____? What can Father do that you cannot do?

    "How does your father show you how to live? [instruct, punish, example] How does your father help you to grow? [provide food and other physical necessities, direct character in growing up]

    "Who is the Father in heaven? How does He show His children what to do? What is His Word?"
4. Review the Bible memory and introduce the second verse if the class is ready for it.

C. Workbook
pages 78 and 79

    Let the children use their readers to find the words for which the letters stand at the bottom of page 78.

D. Worksheet

    The letter and the word are to be done in the usual manner. Have the children paste the other slips under the right heading.

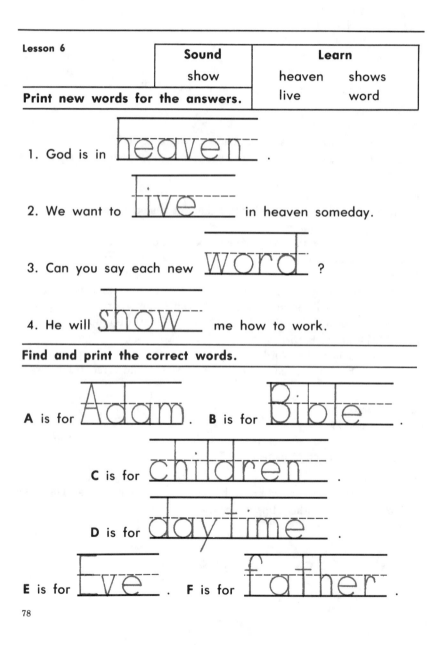

Lesson 6

Sound	Learn	
show	heaven	shows
	live	word

Print new words for the answers.

1. God is in heaven .

2. We want to live in heaven someday.

3. Can you say each new word ?

4. He will show me how to work.

Find and print the correct words.

A is for Adam . B is for Bible .

C is for children .

D is for daytime .

E is for Eve . F is for father .

78

Circle the correct letter.

1. How does a father help us?   (2 answers)
   a. He shows us how to live.
   b. He helps us to grow.
   c. He does all our work.

2. How does the Father in heaven help His children?
   a. He does all the work.
   b. He shows them what to do.
   c. He lets them do bad things.

3. Who is the Father in heaven?
   a. The Father in heaven is very kind.
   b. The Father in heaven is good.
   c. The Father in heaven is God.

Underline two sentences that mean the same.

1.
   a. Father is a very kind man.
   b. Father can do a lot of work.
   c. Father is good to me.

2.
   a. I want to someday do the things Father can do.
   b. When I am big, I want to do things Father does.
   c. I can work like Father now.

3.
   a. We help the Father in heaven.
   b. The Father in heaven helps His children.
   c. God helps His children.

LESSON 7
God

Be prepared

1. Vocabulary helps

    Print *care* with the pronunciation that is correct for your region. kār, ker, or kar

Lesson 7	Key	Sound	Learn
	take — takes	land sea a-fraid	nothing care

Print the new words that begin with these letters.

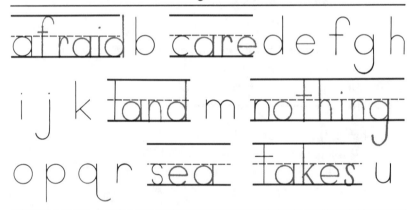

a̅f̅r̅a̅i̅d̅ b c̲a̲r̲e d e f g h

i j k l̲a̲n̲d̲ m n̲o̲t̲h̲i̲n̲g̲

o p q r s̲e̲a̲ t̲a̲k̲e̲s̲ u

Match each compound word with two words.

b 1. nothing   **a.** rain bow

c 2. sometimes   **b.** no thing

e 3. asleep   **c.** some times

a 4. rainbow   **d.** some thing

g 5. daytime   **e.** a sleep

d 6. something   **f.** any time

f 7. anytime   **g.** day time

2. List all the new words.
3. Print the following phrases on the board or cards for practice.
   takes care
   afraid of nothing
   land and sea
4. Print a verse of the poem on the board, hyphenating the two-syllable words.

Circle the letters of two sentences that mean the same.

1.
  (a.) He made all things good.
  (b.) God made everything good.
  c. Adam made all things good.

2.
  a. He made the land and the sea.
  (b.) He made you and me.
  (c.) He made us.

3.
  (a.) He takes care of the things He made.
  b. We will not be afraid.
  (c.) God takes care of everything.

Com-plete the answers.

1. How did God make everything?

   He made it from no͟t͟h͟i͟n͟g .

2. What did God make?

   He made earth and h͟e͟a͟v͟e͟n .

   He made the land and the s͟e͟a .

   He made e͟v͟e͟r͟y͟t͟h͟i͟n͟g **in them.**

3. Why will we not be afraid?

   Because God takes c͟a͟r͟e **of us.**

Read the questions and answers.

A. Vocabulary

1. Print *nothing* and *no thing* on the board. Let the children say the separated words and ask them what they have if they have no thing.
2. Practice the new words and phrases, then point out the fourth section of words on page 99 of the reader. Let the children find the new words at the head of the columns and notice the likeness of the other words in the list. Have them use the new words as keys to read the lists.

B. Reader

1. Have the children read silently, then let someone mark the accented syllables on the board.
2. You may now need to work against exaggerated sing-song accent. Tell the children that good poem reading is more than just saying some syllables louder than others. We should think of what the words are saying and read them like that is what we mean. Demonstrate by reading the verse on the board in a sing-song chant, and then repeating it with inflection of voice to make it meaningful.

   Encourage the children to think about what the words are saying as they read orally. Conduct oral reading class.
3. "*G* is for ____?

   "What did God make? What did He use to make it?

   "He made heaven and earth, and the land and the sea, and everything in them. Can you name some things in heaven? Can you name some things in the sea? How many things in the earth can you name?

   "Did God make all those things and then forget about them? No, He takes care of all the things He made, especially the people.

   "How does it make us feel when we know that God takes care of us?"
4. Review the Bible memory.

C. Workbook

pages 80 and 81

   Notice that the directions for the top of page 81 say *circle* instead of *underline*.

   Discuss the exercise at the bottom of page 81. Each number presents a question and part of the answer in sentence form. Number two has three sentences for the answer. Impress upon the children the importance of reading the sentences after they have completed them.

D. Worksheet

   The words are to be pasted under the pictures in alphabetical order. Discard the slips that are not used or let them provide extra activity for the students who have spare time. The children could paste the extra slips on a piece of paper and draw a picture for each one.

LESSON 8
Heaven

Be prepared

1. Vocabulary helps

    pretty = prit-ē

    farther = fär-thŕ

2. List all the new words on the board.

A. Vocabulary

1. Let the children say the sound and key words.
2. Study the learn words.
3. Ask the children which word(s)—
    a. tell what something looks like. (blue, pretty)
    b. name things you can do. (give, agree)
    c. shows that something belongs to someone. (God's)
    d. means more than one. (birds)
    e. tell the order of things in a row. (next, third)
    f. is the opposite of *argue*. (agree)
    g. is the opposite of *nearer*. (farther)
    h. is the opposite of *take*. (give)
    i. is the opposite of *ugly*. (pretty)
4. Let the children form some original sentences with some of the new words.

B. Reader

1. After silent reading, ask the children what the poem says.
2. "Think about the meaning as you read orally and make it sound like that is what you mean."
3. "*H* is for ____? How many heavens are there?

    "What other word do we usually use for the first heaven? What is in the first heaven? What is in the second heaven? What is the third heaven? Which heaven is the best one?"
4. Practice the memory work. Introduce the third verse, "To him that by wisdom made the heavens," but do not include it in the daily drill if the class is not ready for it.

C. Workbook
pages 82 and 83

Let the children explain the directions as they understand them. You may want to do a few samples of the exercise at the top of page 83 with the class.

D. Worksheet

Paste each sentence under the correct heading.

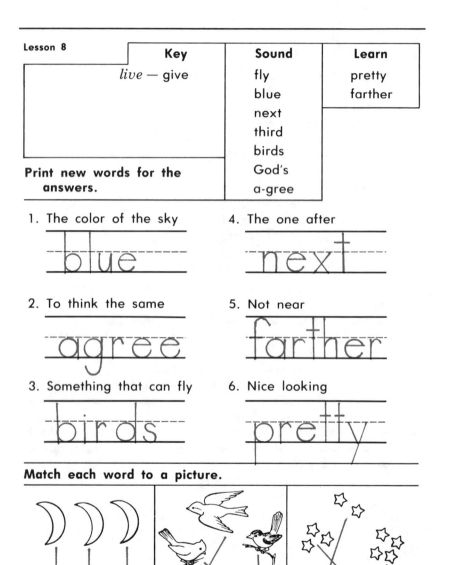

Lesson 8	Key	Sound	Learn
	live — give	fly	pretty
		blue	farther
		next	
		third	
		birds	
Print new words for the answers.		God's	
		a-gree	

1. The color of the sky

    b l u e

2. To think the same

    a g r e e

3. Something that can fly

    b i r d s

4. The one after

    n e x t

5. Not near

    f a r t h e r

6. Nice looking

    p r e t t y

Match each word to a picture.

first   next   third   farther   first   last   some   more   most

Reading Workbook   Unit 3   Lesson 8

Which words tell about the first heaven? Put a *1* **before those words.**

Which words tell about the next heaven? Put a *2* **before those words.**

Which words tell about the third heaven? Put a *3* **before those words.**

2 Where the sun is   2 Bright things give light
3 The best one   2 Where the moon is
1 Where it is blue   1 The sky
1 Where the birds fly   3 A home for you and me
3 A home God made   2 Where the stars are

Com-plete the answers.

1. What is God's name for the sky?

Heaven **is God's name for the sky.**

2. What gives us light?

The sun **,** moon **, and** stars

give us light.

3. What is the third heaven?

The third heaven is a home **that God made.**

Read the questions and answers.

LESSON 9

If

Be prepared

1. Vocabulary helps

   great = grāt

Lesson 9	Key	Sound	Learn
	up + *on* = upon	smile	great
		frown	friend
		goes	friends
Print new words for the answers.		un-to	
		de-pend	

Gradebook: 13 points, excluding the

1. What you do when you are happy
   unscrambling exercise

   smile

2. What you do when you are not happy   _frown_

3. What you call some-one you like   _friend_

4. A word that means "large"   _great_

5. We like to have many   _friends_ .

6. He _goes_ to see his friend.

Print the new words that are made with these letters.

s o g e   _goes_   n u o t   _unto_

f w n o r   _frown_   n u o p   _upon_

84

friend = frend
friends = frendz

2. Print all the new words on the board.

A. Vocabulary

1. Practice the new words.

Reading Workbook   Unit 3   Lesson 9

Circle the letter of the correct answer.

1. What should we do to have friends?
   a. We should frown at people.
   (b.) We should be a friend to every one.
   c. We should know a great word.

2. Why is *if* a great word?
   (a.) Because much will depend upon me.
   b. Because people smile and are kind.
   c. Because people frown and are cross.

3. Why is *if* a small word?
   a. Because it does not mean anything.
   b. Because much will depend upon me.
   (c.) Because it has just two letters.

Print a line from the poem for each answer.

1. What do others do if you frown?

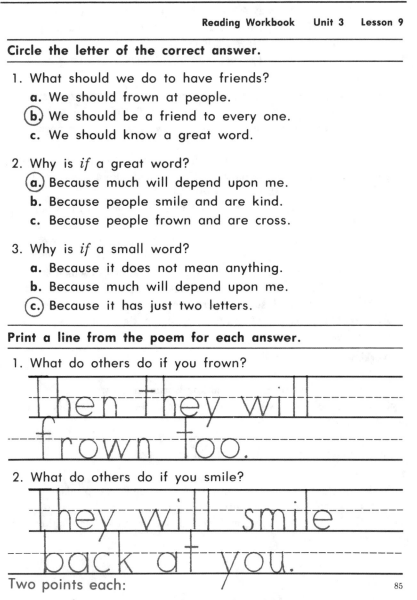

Then they will frown too.

2. What do others do if you smile?

They will smile back at you.

Two points each: 85

one for correct words, another for correct copying

2. Let the children tell you which word(s)—
   a. have two syllables. (unto, depend, upon)
   b. begin with consonant blends. (smile, frown, great, friend, friends)
   c. have long vowel sounds. (smile, goes, depend, great)
   d. rhyme. (depend—friend)
   e. are opposites. (smile—frown)
   f. makes you think of something moving. (goes)
   g. also means the way something happens. (goes—you may want to discuss the variation in meaning of the word *go*. Concerning a happening, we ask, "How did it go?")
3. Practice reading from the word lists at the back of the book again.

B. Reader
1. After silent reading, challenge the students to good expression by reading one line of the poem and letting a child fill in the next line.
2. Have the class read orally, including a few of the previous poems.
3. "*I* is for ____?

   "What does the second line of the poem mean? How can a word be great and small at the same time? Does it look like a great word or a small word? Why is it a great word?

   "*If* you want friends, what must you do? *If* you frown, what happens? *If* you smile, what happens? Things can be very, very different, depending on *if* you do one thing or another. That is why the word *if* is so important."

   Let the children suggest other *if-then* situations in which they are responsible for the way things go. (getting up when called, putting books, sweaters, and so on where they belong, getting chores and assignments finished well and on time, using kind words)
4. Review the Bible memory passage.

C. Workbook
pages 84 and 85
   The children have been unscrambling words on the worksheets. At the bottom of page 84, they will need to unscramble letters to spell some of the new words.

   For the questions at the bottom of page 85, they are to find the answer in the poem and copy the whole line in the workbook.

D. Worksheet
   Have the children cut out the phrases beginning with capital letters and paste them at the top of the seesaw in any order. Then they are to match them with the phrases ending with periods to make complete and correct sentences.

LESSON 10
Just

Be prepared

1. Vocabulary helps
   chance = chans
   please = plēz
   fair = fār, fer, (or) far
2. Print all the new words.
3. Print these phrases on the board or on cards for drill.
   a fair chance
   always smile
   please your friends
   try to please
   fair play
   a great chance

A. Vocabulary

1. Practice the new words.
2. Ask the children which word(s)—
   a. have a long vowel sound. (always, try, play, please, fair—if you use the /ā/ pronunciation)
   b. have *y* used as a vowel. (always, try, play)
   c. begin with a consonant blend. (try, play, please)
   d. begins with a consonant digraph. (chance)
   e. means "all the time." (always)
   f. means "to make someone happy." (please)
   g. is a word you should say when you ask for something. (please)
   h. tells how we should be when we play. (fair)
3. Drill the words and phrases.

B. Reader

1. After silent reading, let individuals read lines between the ones you read, working for good expression. Give commendation for sincere efforts, though they may not have the most eloquent results.
2. Let the children read the whole poem and some previous poems orally.
3. "*J* is for ____? What does *just* mean? Being just is being fair, and treating everyone exactly the way they should be treated.
   "Who is always just? To whom is God fair?
   "Would it be fair if the bad people were never punished?
   "God is always just and fair. We should try to be just too. How can we be just in our work? [Do assignments well and without looking at another's work for answers, do one's full share of home chores.]
   "How can we be just in our play? [Discuss situations on the playground that apply.]

"Who will be pleased when we are fair?"
4. Review the Bible memory.

C. Workbook

pages 86 and 87

Page 86 begins with a familiar activity but the directions are printed

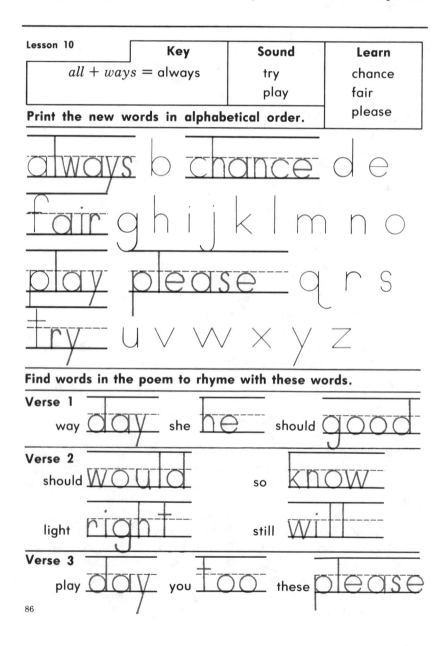

Lesson 10	Key	Sound	Learn
	all + *ways* = always	try play	chance fair please

Print the new words in alphabetical order.

always b chance d e
fair g h i j k l m n o
play please q r s
try u v w x y z

Find words in the poem to rhyme with these words.

Verse 1

way day   she he   should good

Verse 2

should would   so know

light right   still will

Verse 3

play day   you too   these please

in a new way. Try to get the children to understand what the directions say, but make sure they understand that the exercise is done just like the previous ones.

The first word in each section of the exercise at the bottom of page 86 is part of the rhyming pattern for that verse. The other words are not

---

Print *yes* **or** *no.*

Is it just?

1. To help play only when others play the games you like to play. **no**

2. To let everyone help play even if he can not play very well. **yes**

3. To give back something nice if you spoil something for someone. **yes**

4. To sell or give something that is not very nice but others do not know it. **no**

5. To pay for something you get. **yes**

6. To say "thank you" when someone does something nice for you. **yes**

7. To do your work fast even if it isn't well done so you can play. **no**

8. For God to punish bad people when it is time. **yes**

9. To cheat if no one knows or sees it. **no**

10. To help people who need help. **yes**

used in the poem, but a rhyming word for each one can be found somewhere in the verse.

D. Worksheet

The children are to finish each verse of the poem on the worksheet with a word that rhymes with the end of the second line.

Note

At this point students should be able to independently read *God Makes Seeds That Grow*, Book 3 of the *God Is Good Series*. See instructions to the teacher at the beginning of this little storybook.

LESSON 11
Kind

Be prepared

1. Vocabulary helps
   Jesus = jēzus
   oh = ō
   younger = yung-gėr
2. Print all the new words.
3. Phrases
   old and sick
   kindness of Jesus
   even a blind person
   younger person
   oh, yes

A. Vocabulary

1. Practice the new words.
2. Tell which word(s)—
   a. has the little word *kind* in it. (kindness)
   b. has the little word *young* in it. (younger)
   c. is a name. (Jesus)
   d. is a word you might say when you are excited. (oh)
   e. can be used to describe people. (blind, old, sick, younger)
   f. have long vowel sounds. (blind, old, even, kindness, oh)
   g. makes you think of eyes. (blind)
   h. makes you think of pills. (sick)
3. Drill the phrases.
4. Let the children make original sentences with some of the words.

B. Reader

1. Conduct silent and oral reading class. Let the children take turns reading by verses or by lines.
2. "*K* is for ____? What does it mean to be kind?

   "To whom should we be kind? What could we do that would be kind to old people? How can we be kind to younger people? How can we be kind to rich people? How can we be kind to sick people? How can we be kind to blind people?

   "What should we do if somebody is mean to us? How could we show kindness to such a person? [Smile, share toys; 'A soft answer turneth away wrath.'] Who was kind to those who were not kind to Him?"
3. Teach and practice the third verse of the Bible memory passage.

C. Workbook
pages 88 and 89

Have the children follow the directions.

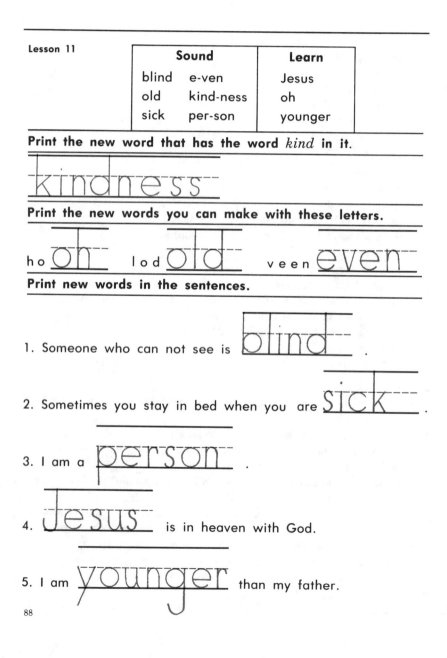

Lesson 11

Sound		Learn
blind	e-ven	Jesus
old	kind-ness	oh
sick	per-son	younger

Print the new word that has the word *kind* in it.

kindness

Print the new words you can make with these letters.

h o oh   l o d old   v e e n even

Print new words in the sentences.

1. Someone who can not see is blind .

2. Sometimes you stay in bed when you are sick .

3. I am a person .

4. Jesus is in heaven with God.

5. I am younger than my father.

D. Worksheet
Have the children match the answers to the questions.
After the sheet is done, it may be used for reading practice by having the boys read the questions and the girls read the answers or vice versa.

Reading Workbook   Unit 3   Lesson 11

Match the words that have opposite meanings.

C 1. kind   **a.** young   i 7. blind   **g.** glad

a 2. old   **b.** well   k 8. good   **h.** white

e 3. large   **c.** mean   j 9. little   **i.** see

d 4. rich   **d.** poor   g 10. sad   **j.** big

b 5. sick   **e.** small   L 11. right   **k.** bad

f 6. quiet   **f.** loud   h 12. black   **l.** wrong

Print the correct word for each picture.

old
young
blind

young   old   blind

sick
large
small

large   small   sick

89

LESSON 12
Light

Be prepared

1. Vocabulary helps

    four = fôr (or) fōr

Lesson 12	Key	Sound	Learn
	word — words	dark spoke	four wonderful
Print new words for the answers.		which plan	

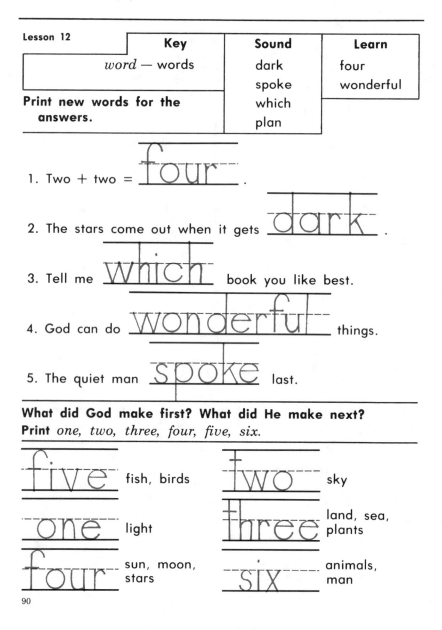

1. Two + two = four .

2. The stars come out when it gets dark .

3. Tell me which book you like best.

4. God can do wonderful things.

5. The quiet man spoke last.

What did God make first? What did He make next?
Print *one, two, three, four, five, six.*

---

five fish, birds

one light

four sun, moon, stars

two sky

three land, sea, plants

six animals, man

90

wonderful = won-der-ful

2. Print all the new words.
3. Phrases

spoke words   dark and light
wonderful plan   four friends
which words

Reading Workbook   **Unit 3**   **Lesson 12**

Match the phrases.

d 1. L is for   **a.** the first day.

a 2. Light was made   **b.** the Word of God.

b 3. It was made by   **c.** wonderful way.

c 4. It was made in a   **d.** light.

Com-plete the answers.

1. When did God make light?

God made light the _first_ **day.**

2. What words did God say?

God said, " _Let there_

be light ."

3. What did God call the light?

God called the light _day_ .

4. What did God call the dark?

God called _the dark night_ .

A. Vocabulary

1. Practice the new words.
2. Which word(s)—
    a. have modified vowels? (dark, wonderful, four, words)
    b. begin with consonant blends? (spoke, plan)
    c. begins with a consonant digraph? (which)
    d. has three syllables? (wonderful)
    e. means "an idea of how to do something"? (plan)
    f. means "very good"? (wonderful)
    g. makes you think of reading? (words)
    h. makes you think of arithmetic? (four)
    i. makes you think of night? (dark)
    j. makes you think of a mouth? (spoke)
3. Drill the phrases.
4. Let the children make original sentences with some of the words.

B. Reader

1. Have the children read silently, then read it like they mean it.
2. "*L* is for ____? When was light made? How was light made? What was so wonderful about the way God made the light? Can we make things the way God did?

    "What did God call the dark? What did He call the light? God's plan is still being followed today. The dark and light take turns and we have daytime and night again and again.

    "Do you know what God made the second day?" Review the days of creation by repeating the poem studied at the beginning of the year (found in unit 1).
3. Review the Bible memory passage.

C. Workbook

pages 90 and 91

Read the questions on page 91 (bottom) with the children and let them give oral answers. They should realize that the answers will be sentences and they need to print more than one word for some of them.

D. Worksheet

Have the children read the verse at the top of the page and review the meaning of the word *just.*

The path represents the way just people live. It leads to heaven and it is a shining way that other people can see and follow. Life is like a wilderness for people who are not just.

The children are to paste the words on the path which fit to the life of a just person, and paste the others in the wilderness.

LESSON 13
Mountains

Be prepared
1. Vocabulary helps
   high = hī
2. Print all the new words.
3. Phrases
   high peaks
   reach high
   stop on time

A. Vocabulary
1. Practice the new words.
2. Drill the phrases.
3. Let the children make original sentences with some of the words.
4. Let the children read from the word lists at the back of the books.

B. Reader
1. Conduct silent and oral reading class.
2. "*M* is for ___? What are mountains like? What are the peaks of the mountains? How high are they? Did you ever stand on a mountain?

   "What happened to the mountains in the great flood? Think of standing up on a big mountain. Imagine all the water there would have to be to cover everything up to the mountain and over it! Where did the water come from that covered the mountains?

   "How long did it rain? Does forty days seem like a long time?" (If you are covering the reading book at the rate of a lesson a day, a unit of thirty lessons would last six weeks. Six weeks including weekends is 42 days. The rainfall of the flood would have lasted very nearly as long as it takes the class to complete one unit in their books, raining all the time day and night, not just during the minutes that the children are working at their lessons.)
3. Review the Bible memory passage.

C. Workbook
pages 92 and 93
   You may want to have the children print each letter of the alphabet on a piece of paper as they consider it, to help them keep organized as they put the new words in alphabetical order.

D. Worksheet
   Follow the directions.

Extra activities

1. Give the children sheets of paper blocked off as a calendar month, and help them to copy the numbers for the present month. During the flood, it rained about ten days longer than a month.

Lesson 13	Key	Sound	Learn
mountains — mountain		stop	high
Print new words for the answers.		peaks	
		reach	

1. Which word means a very high hill?   mountain

2. Which word means "tops"?   peaks

3. Which word rhymes with *top*?   stop

4. Which word means "up far"?   high

5. What do you do to get something that is high?   reach

Underline the little word in the bigger word.

1. wonder	wonderful		6. sleep	asleep
2. mountain	mountaintop		7. kind	unkind
3. cloud	cloudy		8. depend	depending
4. help	helper		9. parent	parents
5. kind	kindness		10. young	younger

92

2. Have the children print the new words in alphabetical order on a piece of paper.

Underline the words that mean about the same as the words that are underlined.

M is for <u>mountains</u>   plains   <u>hills</u>

    So <u>big</u> and so high;   <u>large</u>   long

The <u>peaks</u> of the mountains   <u>tops</u>   sky

    Reach up to the <u>sky</u>.   sun   <u>heaven</u>

But in <u>the great</u> flood   plan   <u>big</u>

    <u>Every</u> high mountain top   Which   <u>Each</u>

Was under the <u>sea</u>   <u>water</u>   wonderful

    <u>When</u> God made the rain stop. <u>As</u>   What

It rained <u>forty</u> days   four   <u>many</u>

    And the water was <u>high</u>.   <u>up</u>   fair

It covered <u>all things</u>   something   <u>everything</u>

    But the <u>ark</u> and the sky.   <u>boat</u>   box

LESSON 14
Noah

Be prepared

1. Vocabulary helps
    planned = pland

Lesson 14	Key	Sound	Learn
in + side = inside	boat float stay	planned

In each row, underline the word that rhymes with the first word. Gradebook: 25 points for the whole lesson

1. read	earth	dear	<u>need</u>
2. book	food	<u>took</u>	moon
3. there	rain	<u>fair</u>	then
4. bird	kind	first	<u>word</u>
5. any	<u>many</u>	away	always
6. blue	both	safe	<u>knew</u>
7. friend	lie	<u>send</u>	said
8. stay	<u>they</u>	lie	many
9. show	<u>go</u>	you	how
10. inside	away	<u>ride</u>	planned
11. high	light	time	<u>by</u>
12. blind	window	plan	<u>kind</u>
13. boat	<u>float</u>	try	dark
14. planned	peaks	blind	<u>and</u>
15. all	kill	<u>small</u>	will
16. other	<u>mother</u>	farther	father
17. which	when	<u>rich</u>	sick

2. Print all the new words.
3. Phrases
    float on the water
    planned to stay
    inside the boat
    stay inside

Reading Workbook   Unit 3   Lesson 14

Circle the letters of two sentences that mean the same.

1.
  a. The Lord talked to Noah.
  (b) Noah was a kind, godly man.
  (c) Noah did not do bad things.

2.
  (a) The Lord told Noah His plan.
  b. God was going to send a flood.
  (c) God told Noah what He was going to do.

3.
  a. They had never had a flood.
  (b) God planned to send a flood to destroy bad people.
  (c) God was going to destroy the bad people with a flood.

4.
  (a) Noah would be safe in the ark.
  (b) Noah would not be destroyed in his boat.
  c. The bad people would be destroyed.

Complete the answers. Two points each

1. What kind of man was Noah?   **Noah was a**

kind, godly man.

2. Where would Noah be safe?   **Noah would be safe**

inside his big boat.

95

A. Vocabulary

1. Practice the new words.
2. Which word(s)—
    a. rhyme with each other? (boat—float)
    b. has the long vowel spelling of rule 1? (inside)
    c. have the long vowel spelling of rule 2? (boat, float, stay)
    d. has the letter *y* as a vowel? (stay)
    e. has the little word *plan* in it? (planned)
    f. begin with consonant blends? (float, stay, planned)
    g. tells what one of the other words should do? (float)
3. Can you think of a word that—
    a. is the opposite of *inside*? (outside)
    b. is the opposite of *stay*? (go)
    c. is the opposite of *float*? (sink)
4. Drill the phrases.

B. Reader

1. Have the class study silently, then encourage expressive reading.
2. Review the letters from *A* to *N* and the word used for each letter.
    "What kind of man was Noah?
    "Who told Noah some plans? What was God planning to do? How was He going to do it? Do you think having a flood would be strange to them? Why?
    "Why do you think God told Noah about these plans? What would happen to Noah in the flood? What would happen to the bad people?"
    Help the children to visualize the picture of only sea and sky, and one lonely boat, with nothing else in the whole wide world.
3. Review the Bible memory passage.

C. Workbook

pages 94 and 95

    The children will again need to print more than one word to complete the sentence answers at the bottom of page 95.

D. Worksheet

    The sentences are to be pasted on the sheet in the order in which each thing happened. It may help the children to get started if they compare their sentences with the poem in the reader. Not all the thoughts in the sentences are included in the poem though.

LESSON 15
Others

Be prepared

1. Vocabulary helps
     place = plās
     door = dôr (or) dōr
     entered = en-tèrd
2. Print all the new words.
3. Phrases
     find any place
     working until dark
     entered by the door
     until I find it
     entered the place
     any door
4. Provide paper for the vocabulary exercise on the bottom of page 96 in the reading workbook.

A. Vocabulary

1. Practice the new words.
2. Which word(s)—
     a. have two syllables? (working, until, entered)
     b. is the opposite of *playing*? (working)
     c. is the opposite of *lose*? (find)
     d. names part of a house? (door)
     e. means "went in"? (entered)
     f. rhymes with *face*? (place)
     g. makes you think of waiting? (until)
     h. makes you think of hunting? (find)
3. Drill the phrases.
4. Let the children make original sentences for some of the words.

B. Reader

1. Conduct silent and oral reading class.
2. "*O* is for ___?

   "What was Noah doing? What did other people do? What did Noah do then? Suppose your father told you to work in the garden. Perhaps while you were working some people would come along and make fun of what you were doing. Would you feel like keeping on with your work?

   "Noah didn't stop. He was doing what God wanted him to do and he kept working. Do you think he was glad that he kept on? Why?

   "Who went into the ark? What else went in? Who did not go into the ark? Why did they not go in? Why could they not get in later? Do you know who shut the door? What happened to the people who were not in the ark?''

3. Review the Bible memory passage.

C. Workbook

pages 96 and 97

Have the children follow the directions.

Lesson 15	**Key**	**Sound**	**Learn**
work — working	find	place
	un-til	door
Print new words in the blanks.		entered

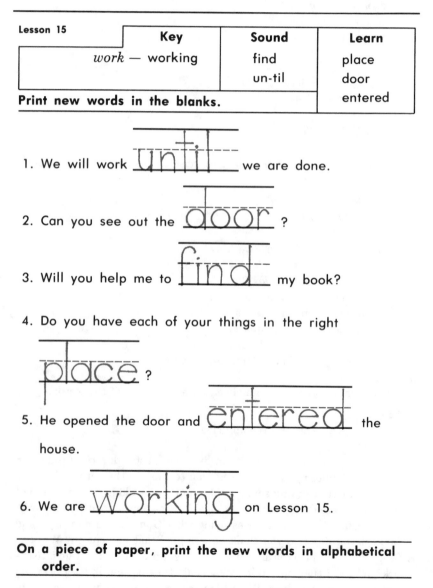

1. We will work ___until___ we are done.

2. Can you see out the ___door___ ?

3. Will you help me to ___find___ my book?

4. Do you have each of your things in the right

___place___ ?

5. He opened the door and ___entered___ the

house.

6. We are ___working___ on Lesson 15.

On a piece of paper, print the new words in alphabetical order.

D. Worksheet

The children are to paste the phrases under the correct headings.

Note

At this point students should be able to independently read *God Made the Animals*, Book 4 of the *God Is Good Series*. See instructions to the teacher at the beginning of this little storybook.

Reading Workbook   Unit 3   Lesson 15

Print *yes* **or** *no.*

---

1. Did people make fun of Noah? yes

2. Did Noah keep working? yes

3. Did Noah stop working because they made fun? no

4. Noah and his family went into the ark. Did other people go in? no

5. Could others have gone in? yes

6. Did others obey? no

7. Could they go in after the door was shut? no

8. Did the flood destroy Noah and his family? no

9. Did the flood destroy the others? yes

10. Could they find a safe place to go? no

LESSON 16
Promise

Be prepared

1. Vocabulary helps
   surely = shoor-lē   since = sins

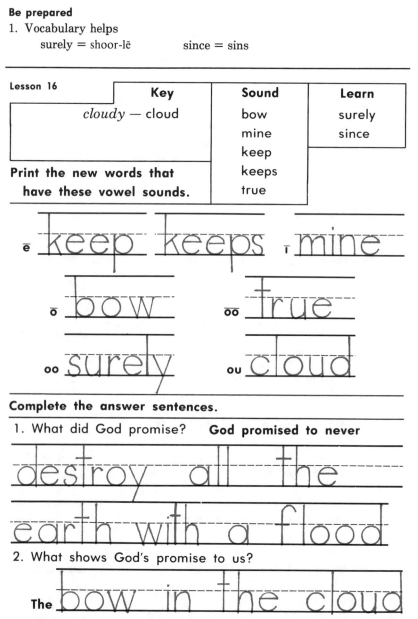

Lesson 16	Key	Sound	Learn
	cloudy — cloud	bow	surely
		mine	since
		keep	
Print the new words that		keeps	
have these vowel sounds.		true	

ē keep keeps   ī mine

ō bow   ōō true

ōō surely   ou cloud

Complete the answer sentences.

1. What did God promise?   **God promised to never**

destroy all the

earth with a flood

2. What shows God's promise to us?

The bow in the cloud

shows God's promise to us.   (or rainbow)

2. Print all the new words.
3. Phrases
     a bow in the cloud
     surely true   since it is true
     mine to keep   keeps working

Reading Workbook   Unit 3   Lesson 16

Print the correct words in the sentences.

We	**God**	**flood**	**sky**
seven	**rainbow**	**promise**	

1. The rainbow helps us remember God's
   promise.

2. God will never again send such a great flood.

3. After a rain we can see the rainbow.

4. It is up in the sky.

5. God keeps His promise every time.

6. We should try to keep our promises, too.

7. There are seven colors in the rainbow.

99

A. Vocabulary

1. Practice the new words.
2. Which word(s)—
   a. is the opposite of *maybe*? (surely)
   b. is the opposite of *give*? (keep)
   c. means "right and correct"? (true)
   d. names water in the sky? (cloud)
   e. begin with consonant blends? (cloud, true)
   f. begins with the /sh/ sound? (surely)
   g. have the /ē/ sound? (keep, keeps)
   h. has the /o͞o/ sound? (true)
   i. has the /oo/ sound? (surely)
   j. has the /ō/ sound? (bow)
   k. has the /ou/ sound? (cloud)
3. Drill the phrases.
4. Let the children make original sentences for some of the words.

B. Reader

1. After silent reading, have the children read it like they mean it!
2. "*P* is for ____? Who promised something in our lesson? What is a promise? What did God promise?

   "How does God remind us of His promise? He thinks of the promise, too, when there is a rainbow in the sky. God said He will look at the rainbow when He makes one, and remember His promise.

   "Did you ever promise to do something, and then you could not do it after all? Does that ever happen to God? God's promise is always true. He always does what He says.

   "Should we keep our promises? What does it mean to keep a promise?"
3. Teach and practice the fourth Bible memory passage.

C. Workbook
pages 98 and 99
Have the children follow the directions.

D. Worksheet
Have the children follow the directions.

LESSON 17
Quiet

Be prepared

1. Vocabulary helps
   warm = wȯrm
   cozy = kō-zē
2. Print all the new words.
3. Phrases
   warm cozy beds
   pray in the morn
   warm and loving
   looking for morn
   put to bed
   get warm

A. Vocabulary

1. Practice the new words.
2. Which word(s)—
   a. names pieces of furniture? (beds)
   b. means "the beginning of the day"? (morn)
   c. could describe a good bed? (cozy, warm)
   d. make you think of things you can do? (pray, loving, looking)
   e. has a *y* with the /ē/ sound? (cozy)
   f. has a *u* with the /oo/ sound? (put)
   g. has an *o* with the /u/ sound? (loving)
   h. have the /ôr/ (or /ōr/) sound? (morn, warm)
3. Let the children make original sentences with some of the new words.
4. Drill the phrases.

B. Reader

1. Conduct silent and oral reading class.
2. Review the alphabet from *A* to *Q* and the word used for each letter.
   "When is it quiet? What do we do at night? What is good to pray at the end of the day? [Thank God for His gifts of the day, ask His protection, tell Him we love Him.]
   "What kind of beds does the poem describe? What kind of bed do you have?
   "What does *morn* mean?
   "Who keeps us safe while we sleep? Does God ever sleep? What kind of care does God give us?"
3. Review the Bible memory passage.

C. Workbook
pages 100 and 101

Discuss the directions for each part to be sure the children understand what to do.

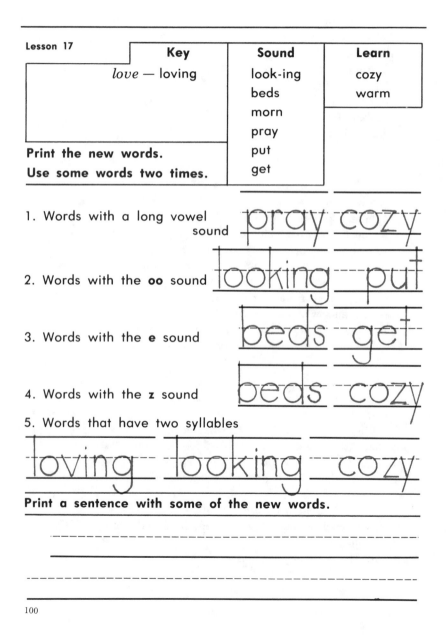

Lesson 17	Key	Sound	Learn
	love — loving	look-ing	cozy
		beds	warm
		morn	
		pray	
Print the new words.		put	
Use some words two times.		get	

1. Words with a long vowel sound   pray cozy

2. Words with the **oo** sound   looking put

3. Words with the **e** sound   beds get

4. Words with the **z** sound   beds cozy

5. Words that have two syllables

loving looking cozy

Print a sentence with some of the new words.

_____

_____

D. Worksheet

Let the children read the prayer, and then go over the letters with colored pencils.

Reading Workbook   Unit 3   Lesson 17

Circle two words to describe each underlined word.

1. We like to sleep at <u>night</u>.
   bright (quiet) bad (dark)

2. We sleep in our <u>beds</u>.
   (cozy) (warm) kind happy

3. Our <u>God</u> takes care of us.
   dark (kind) (loving) old

Match the words to show if each sentence tells or asks.
Put . or ? at the end of each sentence.

1. Do you pray at night ? — asks
   We like to pray at night . — tells

2. Are we safe at night ? — asks
   We are safe at night . — tells

3. Nighttime is a quiet time . — tells
   Is it a good time to sleep ? — asks

4. Do you sleep all night ? — asks
   We sleep until the next morn . — tells

LESSON 18
Remember

Be prepared
1. Print the new words on the board.

Lesson 18	Key	Sound
	ask — asking	gifts
	you + *are* = you're	thank
		rule
		brings

Print the new words in alphabetical order.

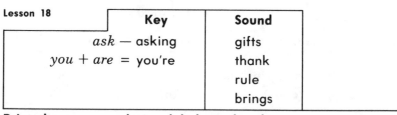

Print *yes* **for each thing we should remember.**
Print *no* **for each thing we should not remember.**

1. To thank the Lord every day

2. The bad things others do to us

3. To do what is right

4. To be kind and fair

5. All the things we do not like

6. Bad words others might say

102

2. Phrases
   brings gifts
   asking the rule
   thank you
   what you're asking

Circle the letters of two sentences that mean the same.

1.
(a.) Thank the dear Lord for His gifts.
b. Pray to God every day.
(c.) Say "Thank You" to God for what He gives us.

2.
(a.) Remember the "please" when asking for things.
(b.) Remember to say "please" when you want something.
c. Remember when people say "please" to you.

3.
(a.) Remember the "thank you" for what your "please" brings.
b. Remember when people say "thank you."
(c.) Remember to say "thank you" when you get what you asked for.

Circle the letter of each thing you like others to do to you.	Circle the letter of each thing you should do to others.
a. When others hit you	a. Hit others
(b.) When others let you go first	(b.) Let others go first
(c.) When others let you play with their toys	(c.) Let others play with your toys
d. When others frown at you	d. Frown at others
(e.) When others smile at you	(e.) Smile at others
f. When others take your things	f. Take things from others
(g.) When others say kind words to you	(g.) Say kind words to others

103

A. Vocabulary

1. Practice the new words.
2. Print the words *your* and *you're* on the board. "We say these two words just the same, but they do not mean quite the same thing. This word [point to *your*] is the word we say when we talk about something that belongs to you: your desk, your shoes, your head, your book, your father. This word [point to *you're*] means *you are*. You are in first grade. You are a boy (or girl). You are studying reading words." Squeeze a small *a* in the contraction with colored chalk and trace *re*.
3. Drill the phrases.
4. Practice reading the word lists in the back of the reader.

B. Reader

1. Conduct silent and oral reading class.
2. "*R* is for ____? What should we remember to do? How often should we remember to do it? For what should we thank God? What are some gifts that He has given us today?

   "What rule should we remember?" Reword the rule in its usual form—do unto others as you would have them do unto you. Discuss the meaning of the rule and the term "golden rule."

   "Should we treat others the way they treat us, or the way we want them to treat us?

   "What polite words should we remember to say? What are some other polite words we should remember to use?" (I'm sorry. Excuse me.)
3. Review the Bible memory passage.

C. Workbook

pages 102 and 103

   Discuss the exercise on the bottom of page 103. Notice the correlation between the two columns. "If I like others to do it, I should do it to them."

D. Worksheet

   The sentences list things that are good to remember. The first letters pasted in the words will spell the word *remember* going down the page.

LESSON 19
Singing

Be prepared
1. Print all the new words.
2. Phrases

    singing praise
    whenever we sing
    morning praise
    hear us sing

A. Vocabulary
1. Practice the new words.
2. Which word means "good things that we say about someone"? Let the children give definitions for the other words.
3. Drill the phrases.

B. Reader
1. Have the children study the lesson silently. Are they still improving in oral expression?
2. "*S* is for ___? When do we sing? What are some of the other times we sing?

    "Who hears us when we sing? What is praise? Can you think of some songs that bring praise to God?"

    Little Children, Praise the Lord
    Thank You
    Who Made the Pretty Lilies
    Little Children, Can You Tell
    We Thank the Lord
    The Birds Upon the Tree-Tops
    Yesterday, Today, Forever

    "When do we feel like singing? Do you feel like singing when you are sad? What happens if you sing anyway?"
3. Practice the Bible memory passage.

C. Workbook
pages 104 and 105

Let the children tell you what they understand from the directions and sample on the bottom of page 105.

D. Worksheet

Cut out and paste the shapes on the matching outlines. The children need not understand the relationship of the shapes to the notes of the scale. You may want to spend a little time singing the scale with the class.

Gradebook: 20 points for the whole lesson

Lesson 19	Key	Sound	
	dear — hear	bring	when-ev-er
	morn — morning	sing	praise
	we + *are* = we're	sing-ing	

Print new words for the answers.

1. What is the first part of the day?   morning

2. What do we do when someone talks to us?   hear

3. What do we do when we are happy?   sing

4. Which word means "any time"?   whenever

5. What do we do when we come with something?   bring

Print all the new words that have *ing.*

morning   sing

bring   singing

Match the phrases to make sentences.

b 1. We love
c 2. We sing in
a 3. The Lord loves
d 4. We sing to
f 5. We sing when
e 6. Singing helps

a. to hear us sing.
b. to sing.
c. the morning.
d. praise God.
e. to make us glad.
f. we are happy.

Put together the two words in each rolling pin.

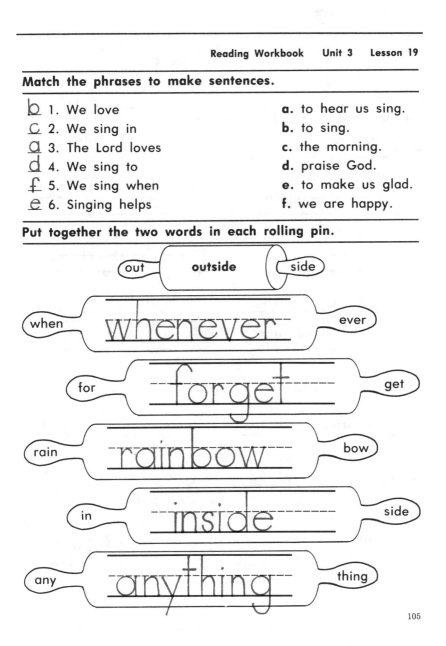

out   **outside**   side

when   whenever   ever

for   forget   get

rain   rainbow   bow

in   inside   side

any   anything   thing

105

LESSON 20
Truthful

Be prepared

1. Vocabulary helps

truth = trŏŏth   truthful = trŏŏth-ful

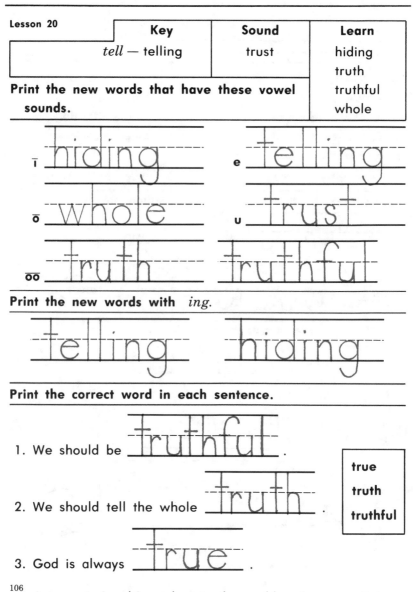

Lesson 20	Key	Sound	Learn
	tell — telling	trust	hiding
			truth
Print the new words that have these vowel			truthful
sounds.			whole

ī   hiding   e   telling

ō   whole   u   trust

ōō   truth   truthful

Print the new words with *ing.*

telling   hiding

Print the correct word in each sentence.

1. We should be truthful .

2. We should tell the whole truth .

true
truth
truthful

3. God is always true .

106
Answers to *1* and *3* may be interchangeable unless you tell the
children to get the answers from the poem.

whole = hōl   hiding = hīd-ing

2. Print all the new words.
3. Phrases

telling the truth   hiding some truth
trust in God   always truthful
the whole day

Reading Workbook   **Unit 3**   **Lesson 20**

Print *yes* **or** *no.*

---

1. Should we be truthful?   *yes*

2. Should we tell the whole truth?   *yes*

3. Should we hide some truth?   *no*

4. Is God always true?   *yes*

5. Can God lie?   *no*

6. Can we trust God?   *yes*

Complete the answers.

---

1. When should we be truthful?   **We should be truthful**

when *telling to others*

what we hear or see.

2. How could we lie?   **We could lie by hiding**

some truth .

A. Vocabulary

1. Practice the new words.
2. Which word(s)—
    a. rhymes with *must*? (trust)
    b. rhymes with *roll*? (whole)
    c. rhymes with *riding*? (hiding)
    d. means "all of something"? (whole)
    e. make you think of things you can do? (trust, telling, hiding)
    f. have two syllables? (telling, hiding)
        What words do you have if you say them without the second syllable?
    g. does not begin with the sound of its first letter? (whole)
3. Drill the phrases.
4. Let the children make original sentences with some of the words.

B. Reader

1. Conduct silent and oral reading class.
2. "*T* is for ____? What does truthful mean? When should we be truthful? What is something that you have heard or seen this morning that you could tell about?

    "What does the *whole truth* mean? [Discuss how a question could be answered evasively to give a wrong impression without stating a direct falsehood. Discuss also the difference between telling the whole truth when being questioned on a matter, and tattling all the details one sees or hears.]

    "What is a lie? Can a person lie when he is not saying anything? [Yes, by hiding some truth that he should tell.]

    "Who is always true? Who can never lie? We can trust God because He will never say anything that will not be the way He says."
3. Review the Bible memory passage.

C. Workbook
pages 106 and 107

You may want to direct the children to find their answers in the reader. The exercise on the bottom of page 106 presents one fact from each verse of the poem.

The questions at the bottom of page 107 may present a challenge. Read the questions in class and let the children read from the poem the part that answers each question. Can they reword the thought using the part of the answer sentence given in the workbook?

D. Worksheet

Have the children read the verse on the Bible. The ribbon is to be colored and pasted on the Bible.

Note

At this point students should be able to independently read *God Made Me*, Book 5 of the *God Is Good Series*.

LESSON 21
Under and Understand

Be prepared

1. Print the new words on the board.
2. Phrases

>teachers understand
>under the bed
>all day today
>you understand
>for today

A. Vocabulary

1. Practice the new words.
2. Which word(s)—

>a. is in one of the other new words? (under)
>b. names a time? (today)
>c. names some people? (teachers)
>d. means "below"? (under)
>e. means "to know"? (understand)
>f. have two syllables? (today, under, teachers)
>g. has three syllables? (understand)

3. Drill the phrases.
4. Let the children read from the word lists at the back of the book.

B. Reader

1. Have the children study silently, then encourage them to read with good expression and volume so others can understand what they read.
2. "*U* is for ____? What does *under* mean? Use the word in a sentence. What does *understand* mean? What should we understand?

>"What is God's Word? Can you understand much of it? Who understands it for you and tells you what you should do?

>"Should we refuse to do something if we do not understand all about it? What helps us to understand things that we do not know now?

>"What is something that we can understand now?"

3. Teach and practice the fifth verse of the Bible memory passage.

C. Workbook

pages 108 and 109

Tell the children to do a few examples in the exercise at the bottom of page 108 so you can see if they understand the directions.

D. Worksheet

Have the children underline the correct answer for each question.

Extra activity

In the exercise at the bottom of page 108 in the reading workbook, have the children print a 1 beside each long vowel word that follows rule 1, a 2 beside each word that follows rule 2, and a 3 beside the rule 3 word.

Lesson 21	**Key**	**Sound**
to + day = to day	un-der
Print new words in the sentences.	un-der-stand
	teach-ers

1. We sat <u>under</u> the tree.

2. Did you see the sun <u>today</u> ?

3. Our <u>teachers</u> help us to understand many things.

4. Do you <u>understand</u> how to do your work?

Circle the first vowel in each word.
If the vowel is long, put a macron over it.

tēachers	vĕry	ĕntered	nĕxt
hīde	whōle	jŭst	nō
yŏunger	gĭfts	ōld	ăsking
dărk	sĭnging	cōld	rūle
bōw	kēep	mīne	fīnd
plāce	ŭntil	ĭnside	lŏoking

Circle the letters of two sentences that mean the same.

1.
- **a.** U is for under and understand, too. *(circled)*
- **b.** U is for under, and U is for understand. *(circled)*
- c. Understand that U is for under.

2.
- **a.** Understand the Bible. *(circled)*
- b. Do what the Bible says.
- **c.** God's Word understand. *(circled)*

3.
- a. Always say what you do.
- **b.** Always do what the Bible says. *(circled)*
- **c.** What it says always do. *(circled)*

4.
- **a.** We understand more when we do what we know. *(circled)*
- **b.** If we obey, we will understand more. *(circled)*
- c. We understand more than we know.

5.
- a. God can understand us.
- **b.** God can show us more of His will. *(circled)*
- **c.** God can more of His will to us show. *(circled)*

Complete the answer.

What can we understand now? **We understand that we**

should obey our fathers and mothers and teachers.

109

LESSON 22
Very

Be prepared

1. Vocabulary helps

    often = ôf-en   heard = hèrd

Gradebook: 13 points for this page

Lesson 22	Sound	Learn
	ti-ny	often
	strong	heard

Print the new words in alphabetical order.

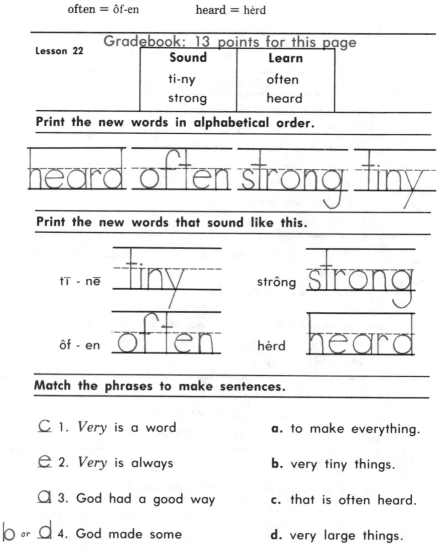

heard often strong tiny

Print the new words that sound like this.

tī - nē   tiny   strông   strong

ôf - en   often   hèrd   heard

Match the phrases to make sentences.

_c_ 1. *Very* is a word   **a.** to make everything.

_e_ 2. *Very* is always   **b.** very tiny things.

_a_ 3. God had a good way   **c.** that is often heard.

_b_ or _d_ 4. God made some   **d.** very large things.

_d_ or _b_ 5. God made some   **e.** a strong word.

2. Print all the new words.
3. Phrases
   often heard
   big and strong
   tiny things

Reading Workbook   Unit 3   Lesson 22

Color black every space with a vowel sound.
Color blue every space with a consonant sound.

God made some things *very large.*
God made some things *very tiny.*

This is something  very large .

111

4. The General Sherman Tree in Sequoia National Park in California is more than 272 feet tall and about 36 feet wide. Translate that into terms of your schoolhouse or a large tree on the grounds. Farm children may be impressed by the comparison of a tree to several silos stacked on top of one another.

A. Vocabulary
1. Practice the new words.
2. Which word(s)—
    a. means "very little"? (tiny)
    b. has a consonant that you do not hear? (often)
    c. describes someone that can do a lot of work? (strong)
    d. have two syllables? (tiny, often)
    e. rhymes with *wrong*? (strong)
    f. rhymes with *bird*? (heard)
    g. makes you think of your ears? (heard)
    h. makes you think of a baby? (tiny)
    i. makes you think of a big man? (strong)
3. Drill the phrases.
4. Let the children make original sentences with the new words.

B. Reader
1. Conduct silent and oral reading class.
2. Review the letters of the alphabet and the words used for the poems.

"What word do we hear many times? How many times is it used in the poem? What does the phrase *strong word* mean? It is a word we say for things that are important or more than usual. We should not use strong words to make things seem greater than they are. If you are hungry or thirsty, or a little cool or warm, we should not try to make it sound much worse than it really is.

"What was God's way to make the things that we see? [He spoke the word and all things came into being.] What are some very tiny things that God made? Do you know of anything that is too tiny to see? Did you ever hear of germs? Germs are tiny living things that live in our bodies. They are so small you cannot see them without a microscope which is a special machine to make thing look much, much bigger than they are. Scientists have discovered many kinds of such tiny living things. Some of them help things to grow in the soil. Some of them help to make the food we eat.

"What are some things that God made very large? *Very* is a strong word. How large a thing can you think of? The largest tree people have seen is . . . [Give your comparison in terms the children can relate to, although they still probably won't fully comprehend.]

"God made some things much bigger than that. He made the great big earth. And He made the sun which is more than 100 times bigger than the whole world.''

3. Practice the Bible memory passage.

C. Workbook

pages 110 and 111

The coloring puzzle should reveal a whale and the sentence below should be finished with *very large*.

D. Worksheet

The words in the boxes below are descriptive words to fit the words and pictures above. The children are to paste the correct description below each word or picture.

LESSON 23
Work

Be prepared

1. Vocabulary helps
   don't = dōnt

Lesson 23	Key	Sound	Learn
be + gun = begun *father* — father's *mother* — mother's		dig	don't
		Print new words for the answers.	

1. Which word means "started"?   begun

2. Which word means "do not"?   don't

3. Which word names something you can do?   dig

Print new words in the sentences.

4. If father has a hat, it is ___father's___ hat.

5. If mother has a coat, it is ___mother's___ coat.

Make new words by adding 's to a word in the sentence.

6. When God says some words, they are ___God's___ words.

7. When Cain had a brother, it was ___Cain's___ brother.

8. When Noah made an ark, it was ___Noah's___ ark.

112

2. Print all the new words.
3. Phrases

work was begun   don't understand
father's work   dig under
mother's child

Reading Workbook   Unit 3   Lesson 23

Who should do the work? Print the correct word.

		father	
		mother	
		brother	
		sister	

1. mother — make a dress
2. brother — feed the animals
3. father — make a house
4. sister — do the dishes
5. mother — make the food
6. sister father brother mother — pull weeds
7. sister brother — pick up the toys
8. mother — take care of the baby
9. father — fix the car
10. mother sister — water the plants
11. father mother — teach the children
12. father — paint the house

113

A. Vocabulary

1. Practice the new words.
2. Which word(s)—
    a. means "do not"? (don't)
    b. means "started"? (begun)
    c. tells that something belongs to father? (father's)
    d. tells that something belongs to mother? (mother's)
    e. means "to make a hole or to get something out of the ground"? (dig)
    f. has the long *e* sound? (begun)
    g. has the long *o* sound? (don't)
    h. have two syllables? (begun, father's, mother's)
    i. makes you think of a shovel? (dig)
3. Drill the phrases.
4. Let the children make original sentences with some of the new words.

B. Reader

1. Have the children study silently and read orally. Comment on the quality of expression in oral reading.
2. "*W* is for ____? Who gives you work to do? [parents, and teachers, too]

    "Is there some work that is just for you to do regularly at home? What jobs do you do?

    "What are some jobs that look interesting to you but they are for your parents or older brothers or sisters? How can doing our work help them? Perhaps your job may be to pick up toys. Mother can clean much better if your things are not in the way. Perhaps your job is to pull weeds. Someone else will have it much nicer to pick the peas or beans if you did a good job.

    "How should we do our work? [Discuss how different it can make a job seem to get at it with zeal instead of dawdling and complaining.]

    "How long should we keep working?" (Discuss the satisfaction of a job completed. Apply this to schoolwork if there is a tendency for some students to lag behind and be unfinished.)
3. Practice the Bible memory passage.

C. Workbook

pages 112 and 113

A number of items on page 113 could have various correct responses. The children will probably realize that and may wonder which name they should choose. Tell them that different ones may be right for some items, and they may choose the one they want, but they should be sure to use each of the names at least once. You may want to have them use just the first letter of the names and indicate all the possibilities for those with multiple answers.

D. Worksheet

The children are to select the sentences that tell how good workers do their work, and paste them on the lines on the sign.

Extra activity

Draw and color a picture for one of the items on page 113 of the reading workbook.

LESSON 24
Six

Be prepared

1. Vocabulary helps

exactly = eg-zakt-lē

Lesson 24	Sound	Learn
	beasts	exactly
	shade	

Print the words below in the correct place.

	one	more than one
child	child	feet
feet		
both	cloud	both
wives		
them	her	wives
cloud		
beasts	gift	them
her		
gift	he	beasts
he		
Bible	Bible	people
people		
friends	house	friends
house		

answers interchangeable within columns

2. Print all the new words.
3. Phrases
      exactly right
      in the shade
      strong beasts

Reading Workbook   Unit 3   Lesson 24

Complete the answers.

1. In how many days did God make everything?

God made everything in <u>six</u> **days.**

2. What do the trees make for us?

The trees make <u>shade</u> .

3. How did God make all the things? **Everything was made by** <u>God's Words</u> .

4. What do we give to God? **We give God**

<u>The praise</u> .

5. What did God make? **God made the**

<u>light</u> , <u>sky</u> , <u>trees</u> , <u>sun</u> ,

<u>moon</u> , <u>stars</u> , <u>fish</u> ,

<u>birds</u> , <u>man</u> , and <u>beasts</u>

A. Vocabulary

1. Print the learn word in syllables to help the children say it *ex-act-ly*.
2. Practice the new words and phrases.
3. Which word(s)—
   a. means "animals"? (beasts)
   b. means "a cool place out of the sunshine"? (shade)
   c. names something alive? (beasts)
   d. means "just right"? (exactly)
   e. names more than one? (beasts)
   f. have a long *e* sound? (beasts, exactly)
   g. has a long *a* sound? (shade)
   h. makes you think of trees? (shade)
   i. makes you think of working carefully? (exactly)
4. Let the children practice reading the word lists at the back of the book.

B. Reader

1. Conduct silent and oral reading class.
2. "*X* is in ___? How is the first line of this poem different from all the others? Why do you think it is that way?

   "What does the poem tell us about the number six?

   "Find and name all the things that the poem says God made. How many more things can you name that God made? How did He make them?

   "What do we give to God? Why do we praise Him?"
3. Teach and practice the sixth verse of the Bible memory passage.

C. Workbook

pages 114 and 115

Have the children put an *x* beside each word as they choose it for one of the columns on page 114, so they will get all the words used and not repeat any.

Discuss question number 5 on page 115. Help the children to understand the form of the answer as provision for them to print a list of all the things God made that the poem names.

D. Worksheet

The words are to be cut out and pasted over the numbers to show the order in which each thing was created. The things are listed in order the poem. If anyone has trouble remembering the order, let them refer to the reader for help.

Have the children draw and color pictures for the words in each box.

LESSON 25
Years

Be prepared
1. Vocabulary helps
   lives = līvz
2. Print all the new words.
3. Phrases
   few years
   number of years
   given a few
   filled with love
   all our lives

A. Vocabulary
1. Practice the new words.
2. Which word(s)—
   a. has the long *u* sound? (few)
   b. has the short *u* sound? (number)
   c. means "not many"? (few)
   d. makes you think of counting? (number)
   e. makes you think of birthdays? (years)
   f. makes you think of a big meal? (filled)
   g. belongs with the words *give* and *gave*? (given)
   h. have two syllables? (given, number)
   i. is the opposite of *empty*? (filled)
   j. is the opposite of *taken*? (given)
3. Drill the phrases.
4. Let the children make original sentences with some of the new words.

B. Reader
1. Have the children study silently.
2. Review the term *margin* by asking the children to point to the left margin and the right margin. Ask them what they notice about the left margin. Do all the lines begin at the same place? The second line begins in farther than the first one. The second line is indented. The fourth line is indented, too. Ask someone to read a line that is indented from the second verse.
   Tell the children that the lines are indented because they are in a poem. Poems are often written in that pattern.
   Proceed with expressive oral reading.
3. "*Y* is for ___? Of what are years made? Do you know how many days it takes to make one year? [Tell the children that seven days makes one week, about thirty days makes one month, and let them guess how many days are in a year. Tell them that there are 365.]
   "Does a year seem like a long, long time? The longer a person lives,

the faster time seems to go. So a year may seem like a long time to you, but someone older may say that a year is not very long.

"What does the poem say about our number of years? Why do we say life is only a few years? Some people live to be ninety or one hundred years old, but that still is not very long if you think about eternity. The

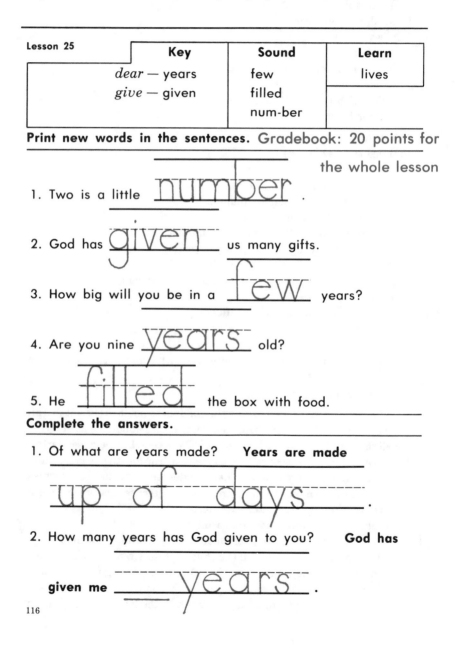

Lesson 25

Key	Sound	Learn
dear — years	few	lives
give — given	filled	
	num-ber	

Print new words in the sentences. Gradebook: 20 points for the whole lesson

1. Two is a little number .

2. God has given us many gifts.

3. How big will you be in a few years?

4. Are you nine years old?

5. He filled the box with food.

Complete the answers.

1. Of what are years made?   **Years are made**

up of days .

2. How many years has God given to you?   **God has**

given me years .

Bible says that the days of a man are few.

"Can you tell me how many years God has given to you? What is the usual way of asking that question?"

4. Review the Bible memory passage.

Reading Workbook   Unit **3**   Lesson **25**

Underline the correct words.

1. A is for ___. animals <u>Adam</u> ark

2. B is for ___. <u>Bible</u> birds boat

3. C is for ___. cross Cain <u>children</u>

4. D is for ___. <u>day</u> dove dark

5. E is for ___. everything <u>Eve</u> earth

6. F is for ___. food flood <u>father</u>

7. G is for ___. <u>God</u> gifts good

8. H is for ___. happy <u>heaven</u> helpers

9. I is for ___. in it <u>if</u>

10. J is for ___. Jesus <u>just</u> jar

11. K is for ___. <u>kind</u> keep kill

12. L is for ___. love <u>light</u> little

13. M is for ___. moon <u>mountains</u> month

C. Workbook
pages 116 and 117

Encourage the children to do page 117 without using the reader. Let them use the reader to check and change any after they are done.

D. Worksheet

The calendar names of the months are to be placed according to the numbers on the slips. More capable students with extra time may copy the names of the months and memorize them.

Note

At this point students should be able to independently read *God Made Us*, Book 6 of the *God Is Good Series*.

LESSON 26
Zebra

Be prepared

1. Vocabulary helps
    alive = ä-lĭv
    penned = pend
    safely = sāf-lē
    striped = strīpt
    zebra = zē-brä
2. Print all the new words.
3. Phrases
    runs wild
    black coat
    white striped
    penned in the zoo
    safely alive
    zebra lands
4. Be prepared to compile the alphabet books from the collected worksheets. The remaining worksheet projects may be taken home daily.

A. Vocabulary

1. Practice the new words.
2. Drill the phrases.
3. Which word—
    a. has the /o͞o/ sound? (zoo)
    b. names something to wear? (coat)
4. Let the children think of clues to ask the rest of the class or make sentences using a new word for others to identify the word that was used.

B. Reader

1. After the children have studied silently, ask them to read some lines that are indented.
    Ask the children what kind of letters they see at the beginning of each line, indented or not. One of the rules for poems is to have a capital letter at the beginning of each line even if the line before does not end with a period or question mark.
2. Conduct oral reading class.
3. "Z is for ____? Have you ever seen a zebra? What did it look like? Where did you see it? Where else may zebras be found?
    "Does a zebra wear a coat? What kind of a coat are we talking about?
    "How was a zebra kept alive one time? What happened to most of the other zebras? How long were they in the big boat? What do we usually call that boat?"
4. Practice the Bible memory passage.

C. Workbook
pages 118 and 119

Have the children again test their memory by doing page 119 without using the reader.

Lesson 26

Sound		Learn	
lands	black	alive	striped
runs	white	penned	zebra
coat	wild	safely	
zoo			

Print new words for the answers.

1. Which words have two syllables?

alive   safely   zebra

2. Which words are colors?

black   white

3. Which word can mean both black
and white?   striped

4. Which other words tell what an animal can be like?

wild   alive

5. Which word names an animal?   zebra

6. Which word names something the
zebra does?   runs

D. Worksheet
It is self-explanatory.

	Reading Workbook	Unit 3	Lesson 26

Underline the correct words.

1. N is for ___.	now	<u>Noah</u>	night
2. O is for ___.	<u>others</u>	opened	old
3. P is for ___.	people	plan	<u>promise</u>
4. Q is for ___.	quilt	queen	<u>quiet</u>
5. R is for ___.	rainbow	<u>remember</u>	rich
6. S is for ___.	stars	sin	<u>singing</u>
7. T is for ___.	time	teachers	<u>truthful</u>
8. U is for ___.	up	<u>understand</u>	us
9. V is for ___.	vine	vest	<u>very</u>
10. W is for ___.	water	<u>work</u>	window
11. X is in ___.	fox	mix	<u>six</u>
12. Y is for ___.	you	<u>years</u>	yes
13. Z is for ___.	<u>zebra</u>	zoo	zip

LESSON 27
One

Be prepared

1. Vocabulary helps
   idols = ī-dulz

Lesson 27	Key	Sound	Learn
	care — cares	mouths	idols
	one — none	step	though
	talk — walk	yet	world
	whenever — whatever	liv-ing	
		feet	

Print new words that have these sounds.

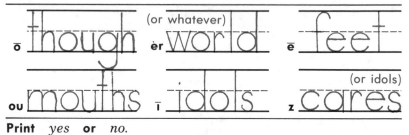

ō though   (or whatever)

ėr world

ē feet

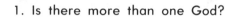

ou mouths

ī idols   (or idols)

z cares

Print *yes* **or** *no.*

1. Is there more than one God?   no

2. Is God alive?   yes

3. Do idols have mouths?   yes

4. Can idols talk?   no

5. Can idols walk?   no

6. Can God do what He wants?   yes

7. Does God care for us?   yes

120

though = thō
world = wėrld
2. Print all the new words.
3. Phrases
    feet to walk

Reading Workbook   Unit 3   Lesson 27

Print the correct word under each picture.

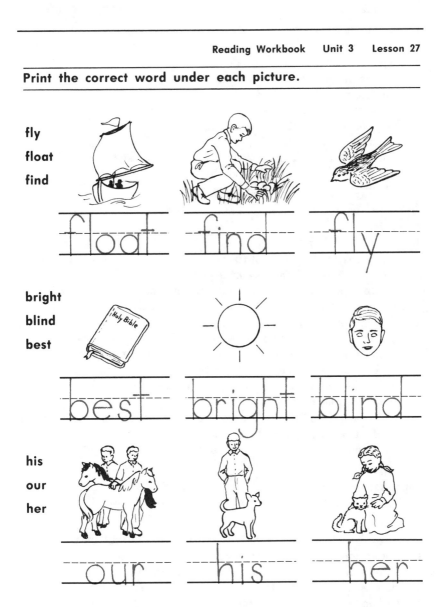

fly
float
find

float   find   fly

bright
blind
best

best   bright   blind

his
our
her

our   his   her

121

though he cares
none whatever
living yet
living in the world
mouths to feed
walk one step

A. Vocabulary

1. Practice the new words.
2. Which word(s)—
    a. name parts of the body? (mouths, feet)
    b. means "not any"? (none)
    c. tell what you can do with your feet? (walk, step)
    d. means "the earth"? (world)
    e. means "takes care"? (cares)
    f. names something wicked people worship instead of God? (idols)
    g. name more than one? (mouths, idols)
    h. is the opposite of *dead*? (living)
3. Drill the phrases.

B. Reader

1. Have the children study the lesson silently.

    Ask the children to point to the right and left margins, and to count how many indented lines are in the poem.

    "Your poem has a title. The title is the name of the poem. It is at the top of the page in bold print. What is the title of the poem?"
2. Conduct oral reading class.
3. "*One* is for ____? What kind of God do we have? Can you think of other words to tell what He is like? [holy, wise, powerful, loving, caring]

    "Find all the words in the poem that begin with capital letters even though they are not at the beginning of a line. Do you know why they have capital letters?

    "What are idols like? What can idols do? What can our God do? What has He done in the past? What does He do now?"
4. Teach and practice the last verse of the memory passage.

C. Workbook

pages 120 and 121

Follow the directions.

D. Worksheet

Have the children color lightly the word boxes and cut them out. Find the word beginning with *a* and paste the ends together to form a circle with the word on the outside. Find the *b* word and paste it in a circle linked through *a*. Link the *c* word through the *b* circle, etc. until the chain goes from *a* to *z*.

The work at the bottom of the sheet is extra work. The children are to use the numbers 1-10 in the blanks to finish each sentence.

Extra activity

Let the children print sentences for some of the pictures on page 121 of the reading workbook, using the word given for each picture in the lesson.

LESSON 28
Two

Be prepared

1. Print the new words on the board.

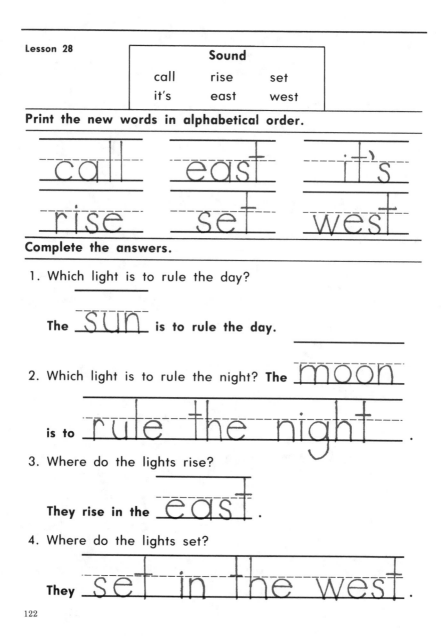

Lesson 28			
	Sound		
	call	rise	set
	it's	east	west

Print the new words in alphabetical order.

call   east   it's

rise   set   west

Complete the answers.

1. Which light is to rule the day?

The _sun_ is to rule the day.

2. Which light is to rule the night? **The** moon

is to rule the night .

3. Where do the lights rise?

They rise in the east .

4. Where do the lights set?

They set in the west .

122

2. Phrases

      rise in the east   east or west

      set in the west   call to rise

3. Print the sample for the workbook exercise found under part C of this lesson plan.

Reading Workbook   Unit 3   Lesson 28

Follow the directions.

1. Put a cross over the boat.
2. Put two lines under the Bible.
3. Put a cross on the picture next to the baby.
4. Draw a line under the bed.
5. Draw three lines over the baby.

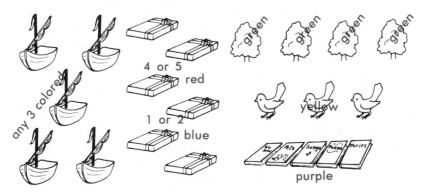

1. Color most of the books purple.
2. Color all the trees green.
3. Color the next to the last bird yellow.
4. Color only three boats.
5. Color more gifts red than blue.

A. Vocabulary

1. Practice the new words and phrases.
2. Which word(s)—
   a. rhymes with *fall*? (call)
   b. rhymes with *eyes*? (rise)
   c. has the /ô/ sound? (call)
   d. has the /z/ sound? (rise)
   e. is made from the words *it* and *is*? (it's)
   f. have the same ending? (east, west)
   g. make you think of morning? (rise, east)
   h. make you think of evening? (set, west)
3. Think of a word that rhymes with *set*. Think of a rhyme for *east*, for *west*.
4. In what direction does the sun come up? Can you point to the east? Which direction is west?
5. Let the children make original sentences with the new words.

B. Reader

1. Have the children study the lesson silently.
   "Point to the title of your lesson. Point to a margin. Point to a line that is indented."
2. "Let's read the lesson with good expression."
3. "*Two* is for ____? What does one light do? What does rule mean? [Tell others what to do.] Can you think of any way that the sun rules the day? [In general, we arise when the sun gives us light and retire when the departing sun brings darkness. This is even more definite in the animal world. Do you ever plan the activities of the day with consideration to when it will be the warmest or brightest?]
   "When does the moon rule? Where do the sun and the moon both rise? Where do they set? What is a sunset? At what time of the day can you see a sunset? What time of the day is a sunrise?"
4. Review the Bible memory passage.

C. Workbook

pages 122 and 123

Sketch these figures on the board and print the following sentences to acquaint the children with following such directions. Let different children do the different items. Explain that *over* means *above*, and the cross is to be an *x*.

1. Draw one line under the tree.
2. Draw two lines under the leaf.
3. Make a cross in the box.

4. Put a line over the house.
5. Draw a line from the leaf to the tree.
6. Put a cross over the next to last picture.

D. Worksheet

The children are to color the two great lights and paste the correct phrases under each picture.

LESSON 29
Three

Be prepared

1. Vocabulary helps
    Christ = krīst

Lesson 29 Gradebook: 17 points for the whole lesson		
Key	**Sound**	**Learn**
live — lived	till	Christ
	son	here
		spirit
Print the new words that sound like this.		trinity

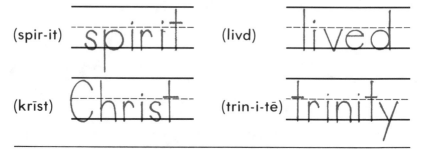

(spir-it) spirit   (livd) lived

(krīst) Christ   (trin-i-tē) trinity

Circle the letter of the correct answer.

1. God is three in one. Who are the three?
    a. Christ and Jesus and Son
    b. Father and Son and Spirit
    c. God and Trinity and Father

2. Why did God send His Son?
    a. Because He loved the world
    b. Because He lived on this earth
    c. Because they agree

3. When did God send the Spirit?
    a. To live in His children
    b. To help them each day
    c. When Christ went away

here = hēr (or) hir
spirit = spir-it
trinity = trin-i-tē

2. Print all the new words.

Follow the directions.

A̲ ✗ f I̅ ē r d Q̲ ū L̲ ✗ g

1. Put a line under every capital letter.

2. Put a line over each vowel.

3. Make a cross after the first letter.

4. Draw a line from the third letter to the last letter.

5. Make a cross over the next to the last letter.

---

z O̲O̲   ~~east~~   keep   ~~or~~ ✗ bright

1. Put a cross on the words that begin with a vowel.

2. Put a line over the very small word.

3. Finish the word that goes with this picture and begins *z*.

4. Put a cross between the very small word and the last word.

5. Draw a line from the first word to the third word.

3. Phrases
   lived here
   Christ the Son
   Spirit of God
   Trinity of God
   till Christ came
4. Print the class exercise in part C if you plan to use it.

A. Vocabulary

1. Practice the new words.
2. Which word(s)—
   a. name Jesus? (Son, Christ)
   b. names a place? (here)
   c. has three syllables? (trinity) That word means "three."
   d. means "did live"? (lived)
   e. can mean any boy when it does not have a capital letter? (son)
   f. are names for God? (Son, Christ, Spirit, Trinity)
   g. makes you think of waiting? (till)
   h. has the long *i* sound? (Christ)
3. Drill the phrases.

B. Reader

1. After silent reading ask the children what we call the space at the edge of the page, the name of the lesson, and the lines that start in farther than the others.
2. Conduct oral reading class.
3. "*Three* is for ____? What does trinity mean? What did we study in the poem for *one*? Our God is one God, and yet He is three at the same time. Who are the three who are part of our one God?

   "Find all the words in the poem that have capital letters even though they are not at the beginning of a line. Why do they have capital letters?

   "Which one of the three sent the others to the world? Why did God send the Son? Do you know what the name of the Son is? How long did the Son live on the earth? Do you know what some of His work was while He lived on the earth?

   "When did God send the Spirit? What does the Spirit do on the earth?" (Perhaps you can tell the children of a time when you recognized definite direction or help of the Spirit.)
4. Practice the Bible memory passage.

C. Workbook
pages 124 and 125

   You may again want to give the class some practice in following directions.

F   u   the   B   d   D   him   O   we   i

1. Draw a line under each word.
2. Put a cross between two letters that are the same.
3. Make a line over each capital letter.
4. Put a cross after the word with a long vowel.
5. Draw a line from the first letter to the first word.

D. Worksheet

"What is the new word that means *three*? How many 3's do you see on the worksheet?"

Discuss the trinity diagram, the three sides and corners of triangles, and the triangle-shaped things of nature.

The large triangles are to be cut out and pasted together on two sides, forming a pocket. Show the children how to first fold the tabs with the words on the outside, then apply the paste over the words. The triangles with pictures are to be colored and stored in the pocket.

LESSON 30
Four

Be prepared

1. Vocabulary helps
   direction = di-rek-shun

Lesson 30	Sound	Learn
	north	direction
	south	directions
	hun-dreds	guessed

Print new words for the answers.

1. Which word means very many?

2. If you said an answer when you did not know, what did you do?

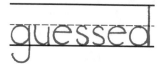

3. Which words are directions?

Match the phrases to make sentences.

C 1. North, south, east, and west   **a.** the same.

d 2. Many people   **b.** for all the people.

f 3. God loves all the   **c.** are four directions.

e 4. God made   **d.** live in every direction.

b 5. God cares   **e.** all the people.

a 6. God loves everyone   **f.** people on the earth.

directions = di-rek-shunz
guessed = gest
2. Print all the new words.
3. Phrases
   all directions

Underline all the correct words.

Sample: things on land	<u>horse</u> moon sea <u>serpent</u>
1. colors	<u>blue</u> back which <u>purple</u>
2. animals	zoo <u>zebra</u> home <u>horse</u>
3. birds	<u>dove</u> west done <u>raven</u>
4. people	<u>children</u> <u>men</u> mean plan
5. good	sin <u>love</u> Satan <u>kindness</u>
6. things to eat	flood <u>food</u> <u>fish</u> float
7. things we can do	fly <u>grow</u> <u>sleep</u> read
8. things we should not do	<u>lie</u> work <u>kill</u> <u>fuss</u>
9. directions	<u>north</u> <u>east</u> easy <u>south</u>
10. the Trinity	<u>Father</u> <u>Son</u> <u>Spirit</u> His
11. words to tell where	<u>here</u> always even <u>under</u>
12. things that can grow	<u>baby</u> stars <u>beasts</u> sun

> hundreds in the north
> north or south
> which direction

4. Locate maps or a globe to discuss directions as suggested in part B of the lesson plan.

A. Vocabulary

1. Practice the new words and phrases.
2. Which word(s)—
   - a. are opposite directions? (north—south)
   - b. makes you think of riddles? (guessed)
   - c. means "very many"? (hundreds)
   - d. has the /ou/ sound? (south)
   - e. has a modified vowel? (north)
3. Which direction makes you think of cold lands? Which direction makes you think of warm lands? (Looking at the diagram in the reader may help to answer these questions.)
4. You may want to discuss the difference between directions as instructions, and directions as ways to face or point.

B. Reader

1. Conduct silent and oral reading.
2. "*Four* is for ____? What are the four directions? Can you point to each direction? [Some helps would be to label the classroom walls or have the children face the north.]

   "What would you find if you traveled in any of these directions? Who made all the people that you might find? Who cares for all those people?"

   Locate on a map the point at which you are. Depending on the scale of the map you may be able to show the direction and location of relatives, other congregations, or mission points. Also point from the classroom in the direction of the place you have located on the map.
3. Grade individuals on Bible memory recitation.

C. Workbook

pages 126 and 127

Make sure the children understand that more than one word may be underlined for each answer on page 127.

D. Worksheet

Each phrase below is to be cut out and pasted in the proper place on the lines under the homes.

Note

At this point students should be able to independently read *We Should Be Thankful*, Book 7 of the *God Is Good Series*.